CREATING MEANING IN YOUNG ADULTHOOD

Creating Meaning in Young Adulthood explores the ways in which young adults are creating meanings in life through their relationships with the world. Chapters synthesize research in the fields of child psychology, counseling, multicultural education, and existential-humanistic psychology to offer readers a contemporary understanding of the greater challenges for growth and development that youth currently face. Using ample case studies, the book also sets forth a resilience-based approach for helping readers facilitate the healing, growth, and enlightenment of young adults.

Christopher J. Kazanjian, PhD, is an associate professor of educational psychology at El Paso Community College and author of *Empowering Children: A Multicultural Humanistic Approach*. He is currently the program director of the after-school program Kidz n' Coaches-El Paso.

"*Creating Meaning in Young Adulthood* presents an innovative approach for understanding the potential of working towards self-actualizing relationships for young adults in existential crises. Young adults are our future, and this book offers a guide for ways to live consciously and to tend to our most sacred and spiritual relationships. Christopher Kazanjian adapts the humanistic philosophy of Carl Rogers to a modern world of complex challenges."

Terri Goslin-Jones, PhD, *REACE faculty in psychology/creativity studies at Saybrook University*

"*Creating Meaning in Young Adulthood* provides a timely discussion of ways that COVID-19 has disrupted the lives of young people around the world and the resources that young people have used to bolster well-being in the face of these challenges. Meaningful insights into ways that social relationships, nature, animals, volunteerism, and even solitude can bolster well-being are provided through a synthesis of scientific research and in-depth case studies with young people."

Jennifer E. Lansford, PhD, *research professor at the Center for Child and Family Policy at Duke University*

"Dr. Kazanjian shows how empathy and care are central to a multicultural humanistic approach. Furthermore, Kazanjian's inclusion of humanist philosophy highlights the value of relationships across the age spectrum. His multicultural humanistic approach enlightens the constant state 'becoming young adults' endure during the early 21st-century/COVID-19 era. This is a timely book that educators should engage with as they build relationships with young adults."

David Rutledge, PhD, *associate professor in the School of Teacher Preparation, Administration, and Leadership at New Mexico State University*

"What is most important in life? Relationships. Building positive, nurturing, and growth-promoting relationships is what has helped human beings to thrive. How do we teach young adults this life-changing skill? Dr. Kazanjian's book is the perfect companion. It is a practical guide to obtaining clarity and being able to truly connect with young people and help them realize their unique potential in our challenging global community."

Mayra Cordero, *founder and sustainable happiness coach of TheHappyRs*

CREATING MEANING IN YOUNG ADULTHOOD

The Self-Actualizing Power of Relationships

Christopher J. Kazanjian

NEW YORK AND LONDON

Cover image: © Getty Images

First published 2023
by Routledge
605 Third Avenue, New York, NY 10158

and by Routledge
4 Park Square, Milton Park, Abingdon, Oxon OX14 4RN

Routledge is an imprint of the Taylor & Francis Group, an informa business

© 2023 Christopher J. Kazanjian

The right of Christopher J. Kazanjian to be identified as author of this work has been asserted in accordance with sections 77 and 78 of the Copyright, Designs and Patents Act 1988.

All rights reserved. No part of this book may be reprinted or reproduced or utilized in any form or by any electronic, mechanical, or other means, now known or hereafter invented, including photocopying and recording, or in any information storage or retrieval system, without permission in writing from the publishers.

Trademark notice: Product or corporate names may be trademarks or registered trademarks, and are used only for identification and explanation without intent to infringe.

Library of Congress Cataloging-in-Publication Data
Names: Kazanjian, Christopher J., author.
Title: Creating meaning in young adulthood : the self-actualizing power of relationships / Christopher J. Kazanjian.
Description: New York, NY : Routledge, 2023. | Includes bibliographical references and index. |
Identifiers: LCCN 2022000849 (print) | LCCN 2022000850 (ebook) |
ISBN 9781032170169 (paperback) | ISBN 9781032170176 (hardback) |
ISBN 9781003251651 (ebook)
Subjects: LCSH: Self-actualization (Psychology) in adolescence. |
Interpersonal relations in adolescence. | Youth development.
Classification: LCC BF724.3.S25 K39 2023 (print) | LCC BF724.3.S25 (ebook) | DDC 155.2--dc23/eng/20220309
LC record available at https://lccn.loc.gov/2022000849
LC ebook record available at https://lccn.loc.gov/2022000850

ISBN: 978-1-032-17017-6 (hbk)
ISBN: 978-1-032-17016-9 (pbk)
ISBN: 978-1-003-25165-1 (ebk)

DOI: 10.4324/9781003251651

Typeset in Bembo
by Taylor & Francis Books

For Cupcake and Frosty, always.

CONTENTS

Acknowledgments   *x*

Introduction   1

PART I   **9**

1 Young Adulthood in the End of Times   11

   In the Shadows of Normalcy 11
   The Things Children Carry into Young Adulthood 14
   　　The Ghost and Its Shell 21
   Possibilities in No-Thing-Ness 22

2 Multicultural Humanistic Psychology   28

   A Global Framework 28
   Multicultural Beginnings in Humanistic Psychology 31
   The Potential of Humanity: Growth-Promoting Relationships 31
   Third Force—Third Dimension 33
   Developing a Multicultural Humanistic Psychology 35
   　　Culturally Relative Self-Actualization 37
   Processes of Young Adulthood in Multicultural Humanistic
   　Psychology 39

viii Contents

3 Existential Terror and the Necessary Distractions 46

Being the Center of the Universe 46
Managing the Terror of Death 47
Knowing the Night 49
    Expanding an Inclusive Existential Philosophy 50
Discovering Relationships with the World 53
The Loneliness of Death 56
Existential Loneliness: Solitude and Broken Life 58
    The Icy Chill of Death 59
Loneliness Anxiety: Streaming in the Darkness 61
    Loneliness Anxiety's Effects on Well-Being 63
    To Be or Not to Be 64
Loneliness in a Cyber-Youth 67

4 Constellations within the Darkness: Growth-Promoting
  Relationships 76

Rhythms and Rituals of Being Together 77
The Space between the Stars 81
The Pursuit of Meaning 83
Growth-Promoting Brain Development 85
Socio-Emotional Intelligences for Relationship Building 87
The Tides of Emotions 89
Living Life in Widening Rings 93

5 The Bold Companionship of Defeat 99

"My Deathless Courage" 102
Mindful Defeat 106
Learning from Defeat in Relationships 110
Knowing Relationships within the Darkness 113
Empirical Explorations of Mindfulness 113

6 Healing, Growth, and Enlightenment 120

Exploring Spirituality 125
Spiritual Disturbances 127
Spirituality for a Personal Existentialism 130

Contents ix

PART II   133

7 Creating Meaning with the Natural World   135

Being an Outsider 135
   Shinrin-yoku: The Restorative Powers of the Forest 137
   In Awe of It All 140
Hyun: For Those I Will Never Meet 143
Tala: Finding My Nature 145
Companions that Lead Us through the Darkness 148
   Therapeutic Animal Encounters 153
   Humans' BFFs (Best Friends Forever) 154
Hyun: Two Encounters 157
Tala: The Companionship of Twinkie 160

8 Precious Silence of Solitude   164

The Mindful Self 166
Monserrat: On My Own 168
Tala: Compassion for Thyself 169

9 Volunteer Group Activity   173

Expressing Altruism through Volunteer Programs 176
Monserrat: Open Eyes, Open Heart 182
Tala: Helping Others, Faith Restored 184

10 The Nature of Growth-Promoting Relationships   187

Social Support and Relationship Challenges 188
Tala: Climbing Mountains of Emotions, Together 192
Monserrat: Celebrating Kovacs 193

Conclusion   195

Index   *197*

ACKNOWLEDGMENTS

Of all my greatest teachers and most influential philosophers that have taught me the utmost profound existential, multicultural, and humanistic lessons are Cupcake and Frosty. They have bestowed within me a joyful and loving process of transcendental enlightenment which reveals an ocean of possibilities to create meaningful ways of Being, *ad infinitum*.

I am sincerely appreciative of the boundless love and support of my wife Sandra. She, without hesitation, courageously ventured into existential discussions and adventures, especially for our after-school program, Kidz n' Coaches-El Paso. Sandra is an extraordinary multicultural educator that helped develop the theoretical foundations of this book (multicultural humanistic psychology) into a praxis that empowers emerging children and young adults.

I only knew my grandfather Morgan L. Jones for a short period. In his life, he worked as a county coroner, mortician, and funeral home director. Morgan was courageous for devoting his life work to compassionately help people accept the reality of death by honoring loved ones that passed. I am thankful to my mother Patricia for discussing her existential experiences as a young adult living above my grandfather's funeral home. Exploring feelings, ideas, and cultural paradigms, she helped me understand how it was to grow up having to know death in a unique and familiar way. I would also like to thank my father John for always supporting my projects and providing opportunities to explore existentialism and multicultural humanistic psychology. My sincere gratitude also goes to my brother, author John Kazanjian, for his guidance in helping me develop effective writing skills and for our conversations on existentialism.

With the guidance and mentorship of Mr. James D. Smrtic, I learned about humanistic psychology and his after-school program Kidz n' Coaches. This program has encouraged young adults at Mohawk Valley Community College to actualize the potentials of a multicultural community for over 38 years. He welcomed me into the program to learn its methodology while also coaching me to develop Kidz n' Coaches-El Paso. Mr. Smrtic has shown me what multicultural humanistic psychology can do for the well-being and growth of young adults—through the power of growth-promoting relationships. I would also like to thank Mr. Richard Kelly and Dr. Dina Radeljas for supporting this book and helping me understand their experiences as the current program directors of Kidz n' Coaches.

Dr. Daniel Rubin offered unique multicultural insights that have helped develop the theoretical perspectives of this book. I am thankful for his support and friendship. I would also like to express my gratitude to publisher Anna Moore, whose sincere and encouraging guidance allowed this book to be shared with the world. She has made publishing with Routledge such a wonderful experience. A special thanks to Ms. Amber Rhodes and Ms. Cynthia Casas for their continued encouragement over the years in my projects that have sought to understand and help others, animals, and the environment. *Creating Meaning in Young Adulthood* was also inspired by my students who, in my eyes, will always be champions.

There are countless meaningful relationships and encounters that have inspired the multicultural, existential, and humanistic psychological ideas of this book. Even though I have not mentioned them, know that I am sincerely grateful.

INTRODUCTION

The COVID-19 pandemic has awakened the world to the realities of mortality, the absurdity of meaning, isolation as a unique being, and the freedom to determine choice. As the pandemic intensified with higher rates of infection and death, mandatory quarantines were enacted. Concerns led to anxieties, which may have turned into trauma. The traumatic events caused by the pandemic significantly disturbed cultural paradigms; how people made sense of their lives and created meanings. COVID-19 caused young adults to experience a paradigm shift as the dreams of a future that were created prior to the pandemic became largely irrelevant because the social, economic, and academic spheres of society altered drastically. The personal challenges that young adults endured during lockdowns, such as exposure to home violence, the sufferings or deaths of loved ones, and intense loneliness from isolation, compromised their sense of safety, certainty, and meaning. *Creating Meaning in Young Adulthood* explores the self-actualizing power of creating meanings within growth-promoting relationships during and after existential trauma and crisis.

Existential trauma is an emotional response to a disturbing experience in which a person has suffered the immediate threat of death, loss of a loved one, destruction of a cultural paradigm or meaning-making system, intense isolation, or severe limitations of freedom. This suffering disrupts systems of well-being, development, and vitality. Existential crisis is a dread to face the givens of existence, where questioning life's meanings, choices, purpose, and value generates despair and feelings of estrangement. This book explores the existential traumas and crises that young adults faced during the pandemic through themes of mortality, freedom, isolation, defeat, loss, and meaninglessness (Yalom, 1980). These themes are not limited to the pandemic but were brought forth with intensity. There are many other existential traumas within history, current situations, and perhaps ones

DOI: 10.4324/9781003251651-1

2 Introduction

to exist in the future. *Creating Meaning in Young Adulthood* focuses on the COVID-19 pandemic because it was a shared experience for young adults worldwide. The existential and multicultural humanistic psychological themes are applicable and relevant to all existential traumas.

It must be noted that when exploring the experiences of young adults, one must realize that not all young adulthood is the same. A 13-year-old's abilities and perceptions are along a different spectrum than that of a 22-year-old's—but they remain in the same category as youth. Young adults cannot be ranked by intelligence according to their age or stage of brain development. The 13-year-old is not a being of lesser intellectual value than the 22-year-old. Each age designates a continuum of intelligence, where developmental capacities and abilities are appropriate for their life-stage circumstances. A 13-year-old's brain and body are developed to designate a particular life-stage and cannot be reduced when compared to developmentally matured persons. Human beings are holistically intelligent at every age. As Moshman (2011) argued:

> Adolescents are rational agents interacting with each other and with their environments and constructing their own futures. They cannot do this without their brains, but they are constructing their brains, not simply being driven by them. Adolescents may indeed develop, but their development is not caused by their brains. Adolescents may become more rational, but there is no universal or biological state of maturity waiting to be reached.
>
> *(p. 173)*

To explore phenomena, we must acknowledge that there is no hierarchy of intelligence or final stage of maturity, but rather a horizontal plain of diverse forms of abilities and intelligences.

As for terminology, the term *young adult* will be used in this book to designate youth between the ages of 13 to 24 years. The research literature on this age bracket ascribes various terms for specific sub-brackets that include adolescents, tweens, teenagers, and emerging adults. There are also different age ranges for each category depending on the researcher's theoretical model. For example, the term young adult has unique categorizations for age ranges in the fields of medicine, young adult literature, pop culture, governmental agencies, and empirical research. Many are based upon psychologist Erik Erikson's (1902–1994) developmental category that understood young adulthood as 18 to 39 years of age. However, libraries and booksellers market young adult literature to people ages 12 to 18. Many developmental categories are even found to have overlapping age brackets.

Most of the sub-brackets or categories of youth were created as early as the start of the twentieth century. For instance, in 1904, psychologist G. Stanley Hall (1846–1924) wrote about a new phenomenon that was blossoming in the Western world called adolescence (Moshman, 2011). Prior to the nineteenth century, models of developmental psychology designated only two key phases: childhood and adulthood. Childhood typically ended around the age of 13, where the person was expected to fully take on adult responsibilities as they were meaningful to cultural and societal norms, values, and expectations. The category of adolescence is a relatively new developmental phase that reflects historical, social, cultural, and institutional transformations. The creation of this category has brought with it new opportunities in youth for self-exploration, play, and discovery.

A common theme amongst the sub-categories of young adulthood is the formation of identity. Erikson's developmental paradigm for the years (12 to 18) of adolescence suggested that identity formation is a critical milestone for long-term psychological well-being (e.g., self-esteem) (Chen, 2019; Pond, 2018). He described the psychosocial stage of adolescence as a moratorium, where there is time and ability to explore and form identity. This allows adolescents to assert themselves and make decisions that support their development as unique selves.

After the turn of the millennium, the developmental category of emerging adulthood was introduced to designate youth between 18 and 25 years of age (Arnett, 2000; Bochaver et al., 2018). This period has unique challenges for identity formation, where many young adults are still dependent upon guardians for finances and housing while responsible for reaching out to the community to fulfill social roles, such as jobs or volunteering efforts that are part of a greater life vision. Within emerging adulthood, there is a burgeoning motivation to explore experiences in freedom, self-development, complex romantic partnerships, greater social responsibilities, and to figure out insecurities and instabilities. These experiences create a sense that the person exists in a liminal space between adolescence and adulthood. Emerging adulthood places young people into adult themes and responsibilities, while exploring sexuality, race, and ethnicity as ways to solidify an evolving identity (Martinez et al., 2020).

Therefore, as this book explores existential concerns for people aged 13 to 24 years, it will use the term young adulthood as a broad window to understand a diversity of categories (i.e., adolescents, teenagers, and emerging adults) and developmental experiences (e.g., changes in the body, brain, cognitive ability, identity formation, and motivation). The abundance of shared themes within these categories warrants the usage of the term young adult.

However, there are scholars and practitioners in the study/service of young adults (i.e., within the many sub-categories) that continue to perpetuate ageism (Moshman, 2011). They condescendingly perceive young adults as pre-adults, where the premise is that they are sub-adults—not fully functioning or able. Some possess reductionist views of young adults' motivations as solely driven by emotions and hormones that cause irrational decisions and behaviors because their brains are not fully developed. To ageists, young adults are entirely impressionable. Moshman (2011) explained that reductions and determinisms argue that,

The current state of a developing or developed organism as caused by genes, culture, or some other specific factor, thus either denying the developmental

4 Introduction

process or attributing development to the direct causal effect of that factor. Forces beyond our control change our brains, a determinist would argue, and thus change us. We become whatever our brains become when they get changed.

(p. 173)

Western culture largely views young adulthood as an unpleasant and dangerous stage of development. However, this ageist perspective is misperceived because young adults exhibit the same higher-order thinking skills, emotional intelligences, dialectical and moral reasoning, and identity formations that adults do, even though they are on different parts of the spectrum.

Creating Meaning in Young Adulthood explores the process of creating of meanings in relationships for people aged 13 to 24 years to offer new perspectives on existential and multicultural humanistic psychological philosophies. Throughout young adulthood the person develops greater abilities to explore a world outside of the self, where the existential concerns of death, meaninglessness, isolation, and freedom have inclusive awareness and depth. There is a gradual sense of transcendence over self-needs, where one can see beyond their own needs through empathic perspective-taking and innovate ways to meet the needs of others. A young adult finds significance by realizing that the spectrum of their emotional experience fits within universal human experiences, such as needs, challenges, conflicts, morality, defeats, and desires (DeRobertis & Bland, 2020). These are observed as the human condition.

An important consideration that has significant consequences on developmental well-being and growth is race. The current realities of racial minorities are filled with challenges of inequity, oppression, discrimination, and violence. The well-being and holistic development for young adults of color suffer from having to live with constant vigilance, fear, limited healthcare and psychological services, less stimulating academic curriculum, and stigmas in which self-worth deteriorates. Young adults will no longer tolerate the violence and injustices against racial minorities. According to the Organisation for Economic Co-operation and Development (OECD) (2020),

Young people are concerned about racism and widespread disinformation associated with the COVID-19 pandemic to persist in the long-term. Some of the initiatives led by young people tackle these challenges by disseminating information and providing support to the most vulnerable and marginalized groups, including minorities, indigenous communities and migrants.

(p. 13)

The United Nations Office of the High Commissioner for Human Rights (2021) reported that even during the pandemic (early 2020), "Young people massively showed their support to the movement at the Black Lives Matter marches, which drew millions of demonstrators worldwide. On the streets, groundswells of youth – mostly teens and twenty-somethings – came together to protest against racial injustice" (para. 1). Social media exposures of killings and violence committed against racial minorities by authorities and extremists/terrorists have been able to incite indignation throughout the world and mobilize communities of young adults to take civic action.

Throughout *Creating Meaning in Young Adulthood*, we will explore contemporary research and foundational theories to broaden our sense of what health means in young adulthood. However, the term health is culturally relative. For that reason, this book seeks to fathom a model of health outside of respective cultural paradigms, because definitions are always incomplete, circumstantial, and relative. Instead, we will employ a term that encompasses a broad spectrum of flourishing, while minimizing cultural bias.

The term *well-being* will be used and is operationally defined as an extensive continuum of complex and dynamic processes within an organism where the fulfillment of needs and satisfactions of life are sought to promote vitality and the realization of potentials. Well-being is contextually and subjectively influenced by environmental stimuli, availability of psychosocial resources, as well as physical and psychological differences/needs unique to the organism (Martinez et al., 2020). Research studies often use the term subjective well-being (SWB) to refer to the person's unique perceptual assessment of overall life satisfaction and the state of vitality within given contexts (Hariharan & Kapoor, 2020; Lawton et al., 2021; Wicker & Downward, 2020). Well-being is associated with having high-quality relationships, absence of psychological or physical disturbances, habits that promote emotional equanimity, and longevity.

Throughout Part I of *Creating Meaning in Young Adulthood*, we explore topics of adverse childhood experiences, multicultural humanistic psychology, existential terror, growth-promoting relationships, failures/defeats in relating, and healing for enlightenment. Part II of the book utilizes a multicultural humanistic psychological lens in order to understand the processes of meaning creation for the existential concerns of three young adults during the pandemic. Specifically, the case studies explore the existentialism of individuals creating meanings amongst growth-promoting relationships with nature and animals, solitude, volunteerism, and encounters. The three young adults in the case studies were between the ages of 18–24 years and were given pseudonyms (Hyun, Tala, and Monserrat) to assure anonymity. All participant identifiers in this book have been masked to protect the privacy of the participants.

The interview data was collected toward the later phases of the pandemic (mid-2021), when social restrictions were being lifted and vaccines distributed. The data revealed that growth-promoting relationships helped young adults create meaning for existential concerns. These meanings promoted well-being, healing, and enlightenment. Each case study explores how these individuals achieved deeper existential awareness through their relationships. To prevent publication bias, the case studies are purely exploratory and seek to make no formal conclusions.

6 Introduction

The presentation of the case studies is unique because the interview data was synthesized into thematic brackets where invariant qualities were extrapolated. These qualities became the basis for stories that explore underlying existential themes. Story-telling is an essential human activity, as it teaches "us cultural wisdom, the process of traveling with the hero is an experiential journey that serves to build our brains, regulate our emotions, and rehearse our skills" (Cozolino, 2014, p. 392). The syntheses of meaning units and invariant qualities represents how each participant became self-aware of their existential concerns (i.e., through emotions, body sensations, meanings, and thoughts). *Creating Meaning in Young Adulthood* explores how the most significant meanings in young adults' lives are created amongst their relationships with people, animals, solitude, and nature, all of which become constellations in an existential sky.

References

Arnett, J. J. (2000). Emerging adulthood: A theory of development from the late teens through the twenties. *American Psychologist*, 55(5), 469–480.

Bochaver, A. A., Zhilinskaya, A. V., & Khlomov, K. D. (2018). The future prospects of modern adolescents in the life course perspective. *Russian Social Science Review*, 59(6), 508–518. https://doi.org/10.1080/10611428.2018.1547060.

Chen, K.-H. (2019). Self-identity and self-esteem during different stages of adolescence: The function of identity importance and identity firmness. *Chinese Journal of Guidance & Counseling*, 55, 27–58. https://doi.org/10.3966/172851862019050055002.

Cozolino, L. (2014). *The neuroscience of human relationships: Attachment and the developing social brain* (2nd ed.). W.W. Norton & Company.

Hariharan, K., & Kapoor, R. (2020). Impact of practicing spirituality on psychological well-being. *Indian Journal of Positive Psychology*, 11(3), 252–257.

Lawton, R. N., Gramatki, I., Watt, W., & Fujiwara, D. (2021). Does volunteering make us happier, or are happier people more likely to volunteer? Addressing the problem of reverse causality when estimating the wellbeing impacts of volunteering. *Journal of Happiness Studies*, 22(2), 599–624. https://doi.org/10.1007/s10902-020-00242-8.

Martinez, C. T., McGath, N. N., & Williams, K. C. (2020). Pursuit of goals in the search for happiness: A mixed-method multidimensional study of well-being. *Psi Chi Journal of Psychological Research*, 25, 245–259. https://doi.org/10.24839/2325-7342. JN25.3.245.

Moshman, D. (2011). Adolescents are young adults, not immature brains. *Applied Developmental Science*, 15 (4), 171–174. https://doi.org/10.1080/10888691.2011.618098.

Office of the High Commissioner for Human Rights. (2021, March 16). Youth are standing up against racism. OHCHR. https://www.ohchr.org/EN/NewsEvents/Pages/anti-racism-day-2021.aspx.

Organisation for Economic Co-operation and Development. (2020, June 11). Youth and COVID-19: Response, recovery and resilience. OECD. https://www.oecd.org/coronavirus/policy-responses/youth-and-covid-19-response-recovery-and-resilience-c40e61c6/.

Pond, J. (2018). Treading water: Considering adolescent characters in moratorium. *Children's Literature in Education*, 49(2), 87–100. https://doi.org/10.1007/s10583-017-9312-z.

DeRobertis, E. M., & Bland, A. M. (2020). From personal threat to cross-cultural learning: An eidetic investigation. *Journal of Phenomenological Psychology*, 51, 1–15. doi:10.1163/15691624-12341368.

Wicker, P., & Downward, P. (2020). The causal effect of voluntary roles in sport on subjective well-being in European countries. *Journal of Sport Management*, 34(4), 303–315. https://doi.org/10.1123/jsm.2019-0159.

Yalom, I. D. (1980). *Existential psychotherapy*. Basic Books.

PART I

1

YOUNG ADULTHOOD IN THE END OF TIMES

In the Shadows of Normalcy

The return to social normalcy cannot stifle the existential embers burning in each person living in a pandemic or even in a post-pandemic world. The novel SARS-CoV-2/COVID-19 virus altered global societies in function and restructured the psychosocial atmosphere in the years to follow. Those in the U.S. that survived the pandemic witnessed their family, social, and professional lives radically altered to comply with the Center for Disease Control (CDC) guidelines and state government policy. Physical and mental well-being for people across the country took on new meanings as the darkness of existential reminders crept into their daily lives. The existential concerns of mortality, meaninglessness, isolation, and freedom have become reignited from the extreme environments and threats of death.

Particularly, mortality designates our observable sense of corporeal finiteness in this life, where death is an impending transition or interval for all beings. Meaninglessness is an existential concern based in the realization that meanings in life are not absolutes but were/are created in our universe. In addition, isolation is an existential loneliness, which Moustakas (1961) outlined as "an intrinsic and organic reality of human life in which there is both pain and triumphant creation emerging out of long periods of desolation. In existential loneliness man is fully aware of himself as an isolated and solitary individual" (p. 24). Lastly, existential freedom allows us to become determinants of the meanings in our lives, where we have free will to choose how to live and what events will mean within our contexts. These existential concerns were most notably studied by Yalom (1980) as the basis for human preoccupations, dissonances, disturbances, well-being, and vitality. COVID-19 has intensified existential concerns for most to become a trauma of depthless and terrifying darkness. For young adults, growth and

DOI: 10.4324/9781003251651-3

developmental challenges were exacerbated by the intense psychosocial effects and restrictions. Their normative existential curiosities and explorations were accelerated at disorienting speeds and depths.

Although the age categorization for what constitutes as young adulthood varies per organization, study, or discipline, this book will focus on 13 to 24 years of age, respectively. Young adulthood contains the new processes of socio-emotional intelligences, identity formation, holistic development, and new responsibilities. Yet, this unique and critical phase of human growth is often overlooked.

The percentage of young adults in the world's population is rising, and they have become integral to the success and function of all nations. Kumar et al. (2020) described how young adults

> represent the potential influencers of future economic growth and development and this period between 10 to 19 years of life is the ground for investment and provides a window of opportunity for laying a strong foundation to a brighter and healthier future.
>
> *(p. 5485)*

Supporting a nation's success and well-being means taking precautionary steps to reduce high-risk behaviors of citizens and promote healthy habits. For example, the worldwide leading cause of mortality for young adults continues to be road accidents (Mirkovic et al., 2020). Other risky behaviors include suicide, unprotected sex, violence, and substance experimentation or abuse. Unhealthy habits can result in malnutrition, health problems, STDs or STIs, mental disturbances, as well as death. The long-term well-being of young adults is influenced by their habit formations and availability of psychosocial resources.

Young adults are typically a disregarded population (Sun et al., 2021). During the pandemic, they were at greater risk for "increased school drop-outs; increase gender gaps in education; stress and other mental health disorders; smartphone dependence or addiction; early age of initiating smoking, alcohol, or drugs; interrupted learning depriving opportunities for growth and development; parents unprepared for distance and home schooling" (Kumar et al., 2020, p. 5485). The onset of most mental disturbances begins in young adulthood and have sequelae of effects and consequences to well-being, such as lower academic success/graduation rates, substance abuse, and somatic disorders.

Furthermore, young adults may wonder what happened to their youth cultures, routines, and sense of stability, as the "new world order of mass quarantine to prevent the spread of COVID-19, reveal[ed] the arbitrariness and privilege of this discrete separation between the mentally disordered and the 'normal'" (Calder et al., 2020, p. 641). The psychosocial atmosphere had been altered by constant reminders of mortality. For example, the daily death toll reports and news media images of body bags being stored in mobile morgues caused nothing less than death anxiety. Cultural norms were promptly created in order to help people stay alive and be free of infection, even though these behaviors were once considered clinically abnormal. Excessive hand washing, social distancing, hoarding cleaning and paper products, long periods of isolation, and hypervigilance became the new normal (Fegert et al., 2020). These practices offered power and control over the risk of death and the abysmal sense of uncertainty. Young adults may have wondered if these behaviors were considered abnormal before the pandemic and normal during it, then what society determines as normal, health/illness, or sanity must be culturally relative and contextually dependent. Szasz (1970) argued that clinical definitions of normal and abnormal are relative and have occluded our understandings of mental phenomena:

> The finding of mental illness is made by establishing a deviance in behavior from certain psychosocial, ethical, or legal norms. The judgment may be made, as in medicine, by the patient, the physician (psychiatrist), or others. Remedial action, finally, tends to be sought in a therapeutic—or covertly medical—framework. This creates a situation in which it is claimed that psychosocial ethical, and legal deviations can be corrected by medical action. Since medical interventions are designed to remedy only medical problems, it is logically absurd to expect that they will help solve problems whose very existence have been defined and established on non-medical grounds.
>
> (p. 17)

If what constituted as abnormal becomes normal in different contexts, then young adults begin to see the absurdity of many exclusive cultural norms, definitions, and customs. The danger of certainty about mental disturbance phenomena is that, "one culture can reshape how a population in another culture categorizes a given set of symptoms, replace their explanatory model, and redraw the line demarcating normal behaviors and internal states from those considered pathological" (Watters, 2010, p. 197). Although cultural norms shift over time with new knowledge, global integration, and transmigration, COVID-19 has accelerated a critical evaluation of cultural norms by causing existential trauma. For many young adults, the pandemic revealed the absurdity of predetermined values and conclusions, leaving many with a sense of meaninglessness or despair.

Breaking news, smartphone alerts, and social media feeds constantly reminded young adults to stay home or offered death tolls for the day, week, or month. Johns Hopkins University's Coronavirus Resource Center (2021) reported that in almost one year, COVID-19 claimed roughly 2.7 million people worldwide. The violence caused by the virus cannot be solely left to quantification, as its trauma has caused many other forms of death and suffering, while having long-term, intergenerational consequences. During the pandemic, the emotional and physical trauma regardless of geographical locale increased in rate and severity; most notably in the abuse and violence toward children and young adults (Blosnich et al., 2020). These effects are pronounced for minority and marginalized populations of youth. For

14 Part I

example, youth that were classified as refugees or internally displaced persons were faced with greater economic hardships, psychological and social challenges, and at an increased risk of being infected by COVID-19 (Fegert et al., 2020). Restricted travel and detention centers reduced the quality of life for immigrant and refugee populations while limited safety precautions increased the likelihood of contracting COVID-19. The virus spread at alarming speeds and societies around the world entered states of emergency, where the care of immigrant and refugee populations were no longer a priority.

Fear and hypervigilance have damaged the physical and emotional well-being of global societies. The fear of others influences young adults to develop habits of distrust and cynicism, while also causing chaos and rigid mental schemas that decrease openness to experience for forming new diverse relationships (Francica, 2020). Nevertheless, some young adults may feel that the psychological sense of community has broken down and may never be regained. Conversely, a perceptual shift can enlighten them to a stronger human community that formed during the pandemic; one that worked together to stay home, be vigilant for loved ones, and do their part to follow CDC guidelines to end the suffering for all. The story of cynicism and loss of faith in humanity during the pandemic may be as absurd as determining what is normal—a different perspective reveals another reality.

The Things Children Carry into Young Adulthood

Mandatory quarantines and curfews worsened the degree of trauma for youth with increased exposure to adverse childhood experiences (ACEs), especially for underserved populations (Houtepen et al., 2020; Purkey et al., 2020). ACEs are categories of experience that designate: sexual abuse, emotional abuse, physical abuse, emotional neglect, domestic violence, separation from guardians, substance abuse, incarceration, and having a person with a mental disturbance in the household. The mandatory quarantines increased the opportunities for these events to take place or worsen ones already present. Families where parents have lost their jobs due to the economic consequences of the pandemic experienced increased socioeconomic pressures and challenges. Increased levels of socioeconomic pressures and stress is correlated to higher incidences of emotional disturbance, domestic abuse, and neglect of children (Herrington et al., 2021; Pinchoff et al., 2020). Research has shown that children that experience ACEs have a high probability of suffering from long-term somatization disorders and emotional disturbances (Maunder et al., 2020). Longitudinally, empirical studies have revealed that these children have greater chances of experiencing lower subjective well-being, cognitive impairments, challenges with regulating emotions, accelerated aging, and shortening their lives by up to 20 years (Colich et al., 2020; Kalia & Knauft, 2020; Lorenc et al., 2020; Park et al., 2020; Yağci et al., 2020).

For most young adults, the pandemic increased the risk and severity of mental disturbances, especially for anxiety and depression (Folayan et al., 2020). The incidence rates for depression tripled in U.S. throughout 2019 and 2020 (Çoban & Tan, 2020). Young adults that have limited social support systems and nonexistent growth-promoting coping methods are at a greater risk for developing destructive habits of thought and behavior, which reduce their quality of life (Read et al., 2020; Yağci et al., 2020). Emotional disturbances disrupt the normative processes for identity formation that is independent from the family unit. Managing social spheres, navigating romantic encounters, and detangling inner-core values from externally given ones are challenges where emotional disturbances can intensify (Reinhardt et al., 2020).

A young adult's depression may have begun during childhood and gone unnoticed—which begets the question that if the pandemic's quarantines increased the rates of ACEs, how does existential trauma factor into the intensity of long-term depressive (dysthymia) symptomology in young adulthood? Incidence rates of depression have been shown to increase throughout young adulthood; "during adolescence the prevalence increases from a lifetime prevalence of 8.4% in the age group of 13–14 years to 15.4% in the age group of 17–18 years" (Eigenhuis et al., 2021, p. 2).

Furthermore, Tsehay et al. (2020) studied the relationship between ACEs and depression in Ethiopia. The researchers found that females had a higher incidence rate of depression than males, and 9.3% of both genders reported having experienced more than three ACEs. Studies have found that abuse or child neglect were strong predictors of developing bipolar disorder (BD) later in life, especially during young adulthood. Moreover, an analysis of clinical data from the National Institute of Mental Health Genetics Initiative for Bipolar Disorder sampled 2,675 people diagnosed with BD and data on ACEs. The data showed that 63.1% of BD patients reported at least one ACE (Park et al., 2020). Females with BD reported more incidence of ACEs and higher suicidality than did the males. Clinical outcomes such as psychotic episodes, suicidality, substance abuse, and poor life function were consistently found to be associated with BD patients that had ACEs (i.e. primarily physical injury or disability, death in the family, chronic illness, and negative life changes) (Park et al., 2020).

Additionally, Antiporta et al. (2021) found that the pandemic's lockdowns had grave consequences for the mental well-being of people in Peru, as their "findings reveal an overall prevalence of depressive symptoms five times higher than the one reported previously at a national level in 2018 (34.9% vs. 6.4%, respectively)" (p. 8). Treatment young adults that experienced emotional disturbances during the pandemic was limited, as Eigenhuis et al. (2021) discovered that only 15% to 36% of youth will receive adequate treatment for depression. The remaining two-thirds will experience the sequelae of mental disturbance. Those that received treatment had a long delay between the onset of symptoms and the first contact with a mental health professional—this delay has developmental consequences for young adults.

However, there were also populations of youth that benefitted from the lockdowns of quarantines; many of which experienced pre-pandemic anxiety or victimization at school. Those that found safety in online learning from home adapted to the virtual lifestyle. The return to face-to-face modalities of school may cause these young adults to experience higher levels of depression or anxiety—which lead to physical malaise. Although classifications, such as ACEs, allow us to investigate, collect data, and understand the lives of children and the previous experiences of young adults, they have limitations that do not explore the complexity of mental and physical phenomena, nor the intersectionality of society, economics, cultures, and meanings (Lorenc et al., 2020). With these psychosocial and physical challenges compounded by the pandemic, trauma became deeply seeded within many young adults. Compartmentalization of disturbances or categorization of experiences do not fully understand the subjective person living in unique contexts.

Being confined to an abusive or toxic living environment and/or exposure to cyber-victimization during the pandemic has deleterious effects for mental and physical well-being. Even though young adults may be resilient, resourceful, and find ways to cope with the crises—many develop maladaptive strategies that lead to destructive long-term habits (Folayan et al., 2020). These habits may be motivated by escapism, where they wish to remove themselves from current emotions/circumstances by means of social media usage, substance abuse, sexual promiscuity, violence, or risky behaviors. Young adults that abuse substances for escapism, such as alcohol or narcotics, are an often-overlooked population. Bhatia et al. (2021) observed that youth with substance abuse habits were at higher risks for being affected by COVID-19; either from the virus's extreme effects on health or negative consequences for home environments and social relationships.

In addition, many young adults emerged from the pandemic with post-traumatic stress disorder (PTSD), which entails hypervigilance, anxiety, or depression caused by triggers, problems with cognition and sleep, as well as aggressiveness (Çalişkan et al., 2020). Although they will one day discard the face masks, the trauma that came with COVID-19 will be carried for years, if not a lifetime in implicit memories. These implicit memories are deeply interwoven throughout the biological and psychological systems, so that many cannot recognize or identify the triggers or symptomology—instead, they establish overly routinized, structured, and limited lives to protect against novel triggers (Cozolino, 2020).

The reality of one's own mortality was prevalent during the pandemic—especially during the period when refrigerated trucks were converted into mobile morgues to accommodate the overflow of deceased at hospitals. Young adulthoods' previous curiosities of mortality may have turned into an all-out fear of death. This fear generated a hyper-vigilance for new or existing threats to life.

The cultural coping mechanisms that young adults utilized to deal with existential angst, such as recreation and sports, socialization with peers, gatherings, religious ceremonies, spiritual gatherings, movies, concerts, school, extracurricular

Young Adulthood in the End of Times 17

activities, cultural activities, or local hang-outs became restricted. Instead, the cultural spheres became limited to immediate family members and online interactions (Fegert et al., 2020). The social and cultural factors that protected/promoted mental well-being were largely removed during the pandemic, as Herrington et al. (2021) outlined:

> Access to usual outlets and coping mechanisms like after-school activities, playgrounds, and time with friends and extended family has been dramatically restricted. School closures have removed a source of material support, such as free and reduced-price meals for children from low-income families, as well as of psychosocial support. School closures have also reduced the likelihood that abuse and neglect are recognized and intervened upon, as children now rarely encounter adults outside the home.
>
> *(p. 2)*

Young adults had limited spaces and opportunities to access services or support for help. For examples, phone or internet usage were extremely difficult for some because of crowded households, limited privacy, and no space to hold confidential conversations.

The year and a half of intense social restrictions also resulted in limited opportunities for time-sensitive growth spurts within social situations/challenges (Cozolino, 2020). van de Groep et al. (2020) studied a population of Dutch young adults (10–20 years of age) to understand how COVID-19's lockdown and social distancing guidelines affected their levels of empathy (or perspective taking concern), moods, and prosocial behaviors. The researchers found that participants reported lower levels of empathy in the first phase of social lockdown compared to surveys that were taken prior to the pandemic. Opportunities for social interaction (i.e., empathy) and prosocial actions declined, thus the researchers understood that their sense of self-isolation redirected the focus to be emotionally tuned to the self instead of others.

In addition to the socio-emotional consequences, constant hypervigilance caused challenges to biological and neural development. Unremitting fear and stress causes neural malformations in the brain, particularly with the hippocampus, amygdala, prefrontal cortices, and the interdependent connections therein (Tsehay et al., 2020). Fear that generates high levels of anxiety for long periods of time engages the sympathetic nervous system, in which survival mode is employed and new circumstances (that hold potential threats) are avoided. In addition, high levels of prolonged stress have been found to cause premature aging in young adults. A study done by Colich et al. (2020) revealed that a new "metric of cellular aging is an epigenetic clock that considers genome-wide DNAm patterns (both increased and decreased methylation of select CpG sites) to quantify biological age independent from chronological age" (p. 4). High levels of negative stress cause cells to advance in chronological age, which is why there

18 Part I

is a positive relationship for cellular aging and mortality. Warner et al., (2020) found that accelerated aging is due to chronic stress's effects on telomeres, which are,

> repetitive DNA sequences at the ends of chromosomes that prevent physical deterioration of the chromosome during cell division. Telomeres shorten with each cellular replication, are an important regulator of cellular senescence and apoptosis, and are considered an important biological clock, measuring aging at a cellular level.
>
> *(p. 2)*

Habitual exposure to or being the recipient of violence or victimization during young adulthood shortens relative leukocyte telomere length and leads to accelerated biological aging. How individuals cope with and interpret negative stressors are important. If young adults interpret the situation negatively and are under physical or psychological threat, biological age advances. Elements of resilience, social support, and mindful coping methods are preventatives for negative stress and cellular aging.

Developmental progress in young adulthood may become hastened if long-term stressors or threats are present. Research has shown that females faced with early life adversity or ACEs in the manner of sexual abuse most often experience precocious puberty (Sapolsky, 2017). Furthermore, a strong correlation exists between socio-economic status (SES) and young adults' exposure/experiences to interpersonal traumas, such as sexual violence (Colich et al., 2020; Williams et al., 2020). SES is an indicator for adversity that is associated with advanced cellular aging but findings have not found strong direct correlations between SES and precocious puberty. Although research data reveal important findings, there are issues with developing prepackaged one-size-fits-all approaches to young adults because there are countless variations and circumstances that cause advanced biological age.

Well-being is not determined by a single factor; rather, the flourishing of an organism is determined by an accumulation of experiences, resources, and contexts which cultivate the actualization of inner potentials of the being. Promoting well-being for young adults means accessibility to psychosocial support and safety in the face of adversity and hardship (Mead, 2020). During the developmental years, each life experience has potential to influence the maturation of the person (Kalia & Knauft, 2020). These can range from exposure to infections, viruses, toxins and pollutants, physical injury or surgeries, and psychological experiences that can evoke depression, anxiety, or loneliness. Traumatic experiences have greater effects, as neglect or abuse can fundamentally alter the dopamine system or the course of neural circuit development. Particularly affected is the prefrontal cortex (PFC), which facilitates strategic planning, as well as cognitive and emotional regulation for goal-directed behaviors throughout adulthood (Sapolsky, 2017).

Environmental factors interact with biological, psychological, immunological, and other systems to engage epigenetic potentials. According to Mead (2020), "Epigenetics refers to the process by which life experiences influence the attaching and detaching of molecules to the surfaces of genes and alter how they function without changing genes themselves" (pp. 300–301). Trauma at this level has historical implications; as Cozolino (2020) pondered, "how might experiences like slavery, the Holocaust, the Armenian genocide, and the Russian Revolution be showing up today in the symptoms of our otherwise safe, successful, and healthy clients who find their way to our office?" (p. 225). In addition, trauma and victimization alter physiological function, such as neurochemistry, immune systems, and glucocorticoids, in order to avoid or survive threatening situations (Cozolino, 2020). Young adults' socio-emotional support systems, including family, friends, culture, and social institutions are important factors for coping. These support systems aid in the development and establishment of emotional regulation, physical well-being, and growth-promoting relationships that are protective factors against gene damage (Tsehay et al., 2020).

Regardless of the influence that the circumstance has on the person, the young adult has the freedom of choice for how to survive, adapt, and seek out conditions in which to actualize inner potentials. Although young adults learn to endure long-term hostile situations, their effects decrease abilities to adapt to new circumstances or form new associations. The existential trauma caused directly or indirectly by the COVID-19 pandemic forced young adults to create adaptive or maladaptive coping methods within their complex circumstances.

The economic repercussions of the pandemic have revealed global systems of inequality, fragility, and privilege (Fegert et al., 2020). The CDC reported that COVID-19 affected minority populations and underrepresented racial/ethnic groups at disproportional rates (Dhongde, 2020). In the U.S., the largest populations affected by infection cases, hospitalizations, and deaths were Hispanics followed by Blacks. These minorities were found to live in certain hotspots around the country, which were correlated to economic deprivation. Moreover, Pinchoff et al., (2020) reported that,

> The worsening COVID-19 pandemic in India is causing prolonged social and economic disruptions that are yielding unintended consequences including economic and food insecurity, and challenges in accessing healthcare. Challenges in accessing essential health services may lead to increases in other adverse health outcomes, from vaccine preventable diseases to poor birth outcomes and malnutrition.
>
> *(p. 2)*

Females in India experienced greater social challenges from pandemic than compared to males. They experienced high levels of stress from taking care of their family's healthcare needs as well as self-care needs amidst the economic insecurities of 2020.

Females faced challenges in accessibility to healthcare services for nutrition, pediatrician services for their children, or gynecologist visits. Pinchoff et al. (2020) also reported that females in India were less likely to be fully informed about COVID-19 symptoms because they received less or inaccurate information. Moreover, the females in the study reported greater incidence of depressive symptomology.

Those that were classified as essential workers retained employment but at the cost of a higher risk of exposure to COVID-19 and its variants (Luiggi-Hernández & Rivera-Amador, 2020). In this case, physical distancing was not an option. More difficulty for families came when children and young adults were required to engage in remote learning and guardians that were essential workers could not supervise or assist their children. Privileged populations were able to work from home or hire caretakers to supervise their child while at work. Sapolsky (2017) found that, generally, youth from higher socio-economic status (SES) levels have a greater chance to actualize cognitive potentials because of the many options and opportunities to receive guidance, learn, and be stress-free. The higher the SES, the greater chances for academic success (mastery of content, skill acquisition, degree completion) in secondary and higher education. Whereas the children in lower SES levels have shown to have higher levels of stress, which results in decreases for executive functioning abilities, emotional regulation, and problem-solving abilities (Williams et al., 2020). Young adults that attended college or who were working during the pandemic experienced greater stressors as they had to figure out ways to pay for tuition and/or become a significant source of income for their families (where members could not work due to health risks or job unavailability).

SES is a central component for understanding what young adults have been through and how it has influenced their current existential meanings. Reports from the Organisation for Economic Co-operation and Development (2020) stated that:

> Economic and health impacts of the COVID-19 pandemic have been asymmetric across age groups. Current evidence suggests that young people are less at-risk in terms of developing severe physical health symptoms linked to COVID-19 than older age cohorts. However, the disruption in their access to education and employment opportunities as a result of economic downturn is likely to put the young generation on a much more volatile trajectory in finding and maintaining quality jobs and income.
>
> *(p. 4)*

Economic challenges for households were shown to have exacerbated the mental distress and disturbances for all members. According to Panchal et al., (2021), "During the pandemic, adults in households with job loss or lower incomes report higher rates of symptoms of mental illness than those without job or income loss (53% vs. 32%)" (para. 4). Mental disturbances were also found to be more prevalent for people of color. Young adults during the pandemic, experienced a number of pandemic-related consequences, such as closures of universities and loss of income, that may contribute to poor mental health. During the pandemic, a larger than average share of young adults (ages 18–24) report symptoms of anxiety and/or depressive disorder (56%). Compared to all adults, young adults are more likely to report substance use (25% vs. 13%) and suicidal thoughts (26% vs. 11%). Prior to the pandemic, young adults were already at high risk of poor mental health and substance use disorder, though many did not receive treatment.

(Panchal et al., 2021, para. 3)

The pandemic's negative effects on the psychological and physical well-being of young adults of color, females, and those of lower SES have revealed injustices and inequalities that have social, institutional, and cultural foundations.

The Ghost and Its Shell

The consequences of existential trauma have profound effects on the developing bodies of young adults. Particularly, persistent high levels of norepinephrine during intense stressors fuels anxiety and fright levels, which causes higher cortisol levels to decrease the size of the hippocampus. This neurobiological change results in learning and memory impairment. Immune systems are also compromised during high levels of stress, in which protein synthesis for T-cells are halted in order to support current survival functions and metabolism. This ultimately leads to the inabilities to fight infection and illness. In addition, intense stressors cause the release of endorphins, which are hormones that reduce the feelings of pain. Higher endorphin levels have the ability to create distorted visions of reality; which can cause emotional disturbance, such as depersonalization or low affect. Higher endorphins also cause serotonin levels to be lower, causing higher risks for depression, restlessness, physical harm, and suicide ideation.

For example, Pretorius (2021) reported that the pandemic increased the rates of anxiety, depression, suicide ideation and attempts for 174 university healthcare students (18 to 24 years of age) in countries such as India, Britain, and Saudi Arabia. The researcher called for preventative measures to be proactively taken by universities to offer young adults easily accessible educational and clinical resources to cope with existential trauma and emotional disturbance.

When young adults have excessive amounts of long-term stress or have been through traumatic events, their bodies experience higher glucocorticoid levels, challenges with emotional regulation, and problems with critical thinking for problem solving (Fegert et al., 2020; Sapolsky, 2017; Tsehay et al., 2020). Many young adults learned to survive the trauma of COVID-19, but to return to normalcy may prove challenging. Once the person becomes hypervigilant, new learning and neurodevelopment are left by the wayside (Mead, 2020). The hypothalamus–pituitary–adrenal (HPA) axis provides facilitation of the stress response protocols to transform perception of externally dangerous stimuli into high arousal states of the body in order to fashion appropriate neurophysiological responses to survive (Cozolino, 2014). When the threat has been resolved, the body should return to its unique homeostatic state of well-being. However, if unresolved, chronic stress or threat forces the HPA axis to form habits of activation, ultimately dissolving long-term neurobiological health of the hippocampus and the normative function of the HPA axis. This information is relevant to young adults' academic success, as the positive challenges found in secondary and higher education that promote neuroplasticity, immune system function, and cell health, are sacrificed for immediate all-out survival mode.

Possibilities in No-Thing-Ness

Existential concerns are ubiquitous, where people are confronted with the reality of death, absurdity of meaning, responsibility and freedom to create a life story, and intense solitude as a unique being (Yalom, 1980). Death can be a motivator to live fully or it can become an anxiety that limits possibility. Those who do not live by inner values and explore personal desires/directions will realize that their time to live how they wish diminishes daily. Yalom (2012) wrote: "I had come to believe that the fear of death is always greatest in those who feel that they have not lived their life fully. A good working formula is: the more unlived life, or unrealized potential, the greater one's death anxiety" (p. 133). Existential concerns can become anxieties when potential is unrealized. There can be anxieties for loneliness, meaninglessness, freedom of choice, and death. Existential anxiety causes the individual to develop rigid patterns of living and thinking in order to gain control over concerns.

Within states of existential anxiety, emotional disturbances have greater opportunities to cultivate or exacerbate. Studies in neuroscience have sought to understand phenomena such as anxiety and depression—but these are just pieces of understanding *what* is happening, not necessarily exploring an existentialism *that* they happen. A person does not need neuroscience in order to validate a feeling, emotion, or state of Being (Sapolsky, 2017).

Neuroscience has recorded important findings for understanding developmental patterns in the brains of young adults. The neuroplasticity that is imperative for learning new skills, knowledge, and creativity cannot develop in states of anxiety (Cozolino, 2014). Brains need to have challenges just beyond current abilities alongside factors, such as safety and love in order to stimulate the interconnection of regions. Interconnected brains have greater resources and creative possibilities for novel solutions, emotional regulations, and cognitive functioning. However, in death anxiety neuroplastic processes are given up so that energy can be devoted to all-out survival of the current moment.

When secondary and post-secondary educational institutions in the U.S. were seeking to overcome the challenges of the pandemic, most teachers, professors,

Young Adulthood in the End of Times   23

and students were required to create and learn in online/remote classrooms. The realization of *what* was changing in the world was set beside a realization of *how* the world was changing. There was a recognition that the learning environments, skills and curricular content to master, career development, and pedagogies from school of days passed would no longer have the value or relevance in a post-pandemic world (Calder et al., 2020). Relevant questions became: How do students learn in the wake of the existential trauma left by COVID-19? How do I create pedagogies and lessons where students can learn curricular material and make sense of a world that has experienced intense fear, death, and anxiety? How can I prepare students through virtual learning environments to engage the uncertainties of the future?

Educational professionals acknowledged that the experience of the pandemic had holistic and pedagogical effects on youth. For instance, existential trauma can result in anxieties that generate emotional distress, such as panic attacks with the presence of a trigger. The student had learned through implicit and explicit memory processes to encode stimuli during a previous threat to be detected in new circumstances. There may be classroom situations where certain educational videos are shown without a trigger warning, classroom discussions veer toward a certain topic, the lighting, temperature, sound, smell, or any sensory input unique to that person's implicit memory systems have the ability to trigger the sympathetic nervous system to begin releasing glucocorticoids. Holistic processes shift to a survival mode through fight, flight, or freeze with the aid of the HPA axis. The endocrine and immune systems are altered in order to devote energy and resources to making sure the body can either defeat or escape the threat. When the HPA axis has prolonged activation, the body cannot return to homeostasis, which it leads to holistic damages, especially to cell health and regions of the brain, such as the hippocampus. The amygdala has ultra-fast processing abilities that encode memories to create a reference guide for surviving future threats.

Educational professionals know that in a post-pandemic classroom, there may be higher levels of anxiety and more sensitivity to triggers. Young adults may have difficulty resuming the norms of pre-pandemic processes of schooling. We cannot misperceive the young adult as being entirely invulnerable or resilient because the fact that they are young. Nor can one assume that young adults are unable to grasp their own experiences due to their age, where the old adage "you will understand when you are older" usually results in gross misunderstandings. Cozolino (2020) stated, "There certainly appears to be considerable evidence to support the claim reflected in our societal resistance to accepting the incidence, scope, and magnitude of early trauma" (p. 221). There is no "getting over" existential trauma; only coming to peace and understanding. One must choose to either continue to deny existential realities or venture into the darkness to create meanings therein. The challenges for mental well-being after existential trauma (e.g., COVID-19 pandemic) are prevalent for young adults. However, there will be new challenges in the coming years. Accordingly, it is necessary for young

24 Part I

adults to learn the processes necessary to adapt to a rapidly changing world. One such adaptive process is developing socio-emotional intelligences to help form and succeed in new diverse relationships—these provide necessary support systems to explore existential concerns across paradigms (Folayan et al., 2020).

There is an innate tendency for young adults to be prosocial in times of global need and necessity. Franzen and Wöhner (2021) found in an online survey of 510 young adults in Switzerland's University of Bern that participants were eagerly compliant with the coronavirus safety guidelines in the first phase of lockdown. The researchers were surprised that the majority of young adults forwent social gatherings or situations that increased risk of exposure, because they were motivated to contribute to the safety and well-being of the greater community. Previous studies found young adults' concern for public good were relatively low in favor of a self-concern; where attitudes of public or environmental concern were not aligned with the actual behaviors to contribute. One limitation of the study was that the surveyed time period was short (six weeks) and compliance may have been high because the restrictions were not as strict as other European countries. Greater time in lockdown may have shown a change in prosocial attitudes and behaviors.

In the complexity of existential trauma, a consilience is needed amongst disciplines and departments. Developing a multicultural humanistic psychology as a theoretical foundation will offer greater perspectives from which to understand the self-actualizing power of relationships during times of existential trauma. Multicultural humanistic psychology is a modern framework that seeks to help young adults understand and embrace the realities of existential givens together. Existentialism is a source of renewal, strength, and enlightenment. Young adults must come to know that the pandemic has not left them living in the end of times, but placed them in the existential nothing-ness, where there are infinite possibilities as to what human beings can decide to become.

References

Antiporta, D. A., Cutipé, Y. L., Mendoza, M., Celentano, D. D., Stuart, E. A., & Bruni, A. (2021). Depressive symptoms among Peruvian adult residents amidst a National Lockdown during the COVID-19 pandemic. *BMC Psychiatry*, 21(1), 1–12. https://doi.org/10.1186/s12888-021-03107-3.

Bhatia, G., Chatterjee, B., & Dhawan, A. (2021). Adolescents, drugs, and COVID-19: Special challenges during the pandemic. *Indian Journal of Psychological Medicine*, 43(2), 95–99. https://doi.org/10.1177/0253717621988998.

Blosnich, J. R., Henderson, E. R., Coulter, R. W. S., Goldbach, J. T., & Meyer, I. H. (2020). Sexual orientation change efforts, adverse childhood experiences, and suicide ideation and attempt among sexual minority adults, United States, 2016–2018. *American Journal of Public Health*, 110(7), 1024–1030. https://doi.org/10.2105/AJPH.2020.305637.

Calder, A. J., Novak, L. F., & Lane, A. (2020). We're all going crazy now: How the covid-19 pandemic can promote more compassionate clinical perspectives. *Journal of Humanistic Psychology*, 60(5), 639–646. https://doi.org/10.1177/0022167820938615.

Çalişkan, G., Müller, A., & Albrecht, A. (2020). Long-term impact of early-life stress on hippocampal plasticity: Spotlight on astrocytes. *International Journal of Molecular Sciences*, 21(14), 4999. https://doi.org/10.3390/ijms21144999.

Çoban, A., & Tan, O. (2020). Attention deficit hyperactivity disorder, impulsivity, anxiety, and depression symptoms mediating the relationship between childhood trauma and symptoms severity of obsessive-compulsive disorder. *Archives of Neuropsychiatry / Noropsikiatri Arsivi*, 57(1), 37–43. https://doi.org/10.29399/npa.23654.

Colich, L. N., Rosen, M. L, Williams, E., & McLaughlin, K. A. (2020). Biological aging in childhood and adolescence following experiences of threat and deprivation: A systematic review and meta-analysis. *Psychological Bulletin*, 1–44. http://dx.doi.org/10.1037/bul0000270.

Cozolino, L. (2014). *The neuroscience of human relationships: Attachment and the developing social brain* (2nd ed.). W. W. Norton & Company.

Cozolino, L. (2020). *The pocket guide to neuroscience for clinicians*. W. W. Norton & Company.

Dhongde, S. (2020). Multidimensional economic deprivation during the coronavirus pandemic: Early evidence from the United States. *PLoS ONE*, 15(12), 1–15. https://doi.org/10.1371/journal.pone.0244130.

Eigenhuis, E., Waumans, R. C., Muntingh, A. D. T., Westerman, M. J., van Meijel, M., Batelaan, N. M., & van Balkom, A. J. L. M. (2021). Facilitating factors and barriers in help-seeking behaviour in adolescents and young adults with depressive symptoms: A qualitative study. *PLoS ONE*, 16(3), 1–20. https://doi.org/10.1371/journal.pone.0247516.

Fegert, J. M., Vitiello, B., Plener, P. L., & Clemens, V. (2020). Challenges and burden of the Coronavirus 2019 (COVID-19) pandemic for child and adolescent mental health: A narrative review to highlight clinical and research needs in the acute phase and the long return to normality. *Child & Adolescent Psychiatry & Mental Health*, 14(1), 1–11. https://doi.org/10.1186/s13034-020-00329-3.

Folayan, M. O., Oginni, O., Arowolo, O., & El Tantawi, M. (2020). Internal consistency and correlation of the adverse childhood experiences, bully victimization, self-esteem, resilience, and social support scales in Nigerian children. *BMC Research Notes*, 13(1), 1–6. https://doi.org/10.1186/s13104-020-05174-3.

Francica, C. (2020). Did you receive the post? Heideggerian leaps into online therapy with children during the COVID-19 pandemic. *Existential Analysis: Journal of the Society for Existential Analysis*, 31(2), 237–246.

Franzen, A., & Wöhner, F. (2021). Coronavirus risk perception and compliance with social distancing measures in a sample of young adults: Evidence from Switzerland. *PLoS ONE*, 16(2), 1–13. https://doi.org/10.1371/journal.pone.0247447.

Herrington, O. D., Clayton, A., Benoit, L., Prins-Aardema, C., DiGiovanni, M., Weller, I., & Martin, A. (2021). Viral time capsule: A global photo-elicitation study of child and adolescent mental health professionals during COVID-19. *Child & Adolescent Psychiatry & Mental Health*, 15(1), 1–18. https://doi.org/10.1186/s13034-021-00359-5.

Houtepen, L. C., Heron, J., Suderman, M. J., Fraser, A., Chittleborough, C. R., & Howe, L. D. (2020). Associations of adverse childhood experiences with educational attainment and adolescent health and the role of family and socioeconomic factors: A prospective cohort study in the UK. *PLoS Medicine*, 17(3), 1–21. https://doi.org/10.1371/journal.pmed.1003031.

Johns Hopkins University and Medicine (2021, March 20). Coronavirus resource center. Johns Hopkins University and Medicine. https://coronavirus.jhu.edu.

Kalia, V., & Knauft, K. (2020). Emotion regulation strategies modulate the effect of adverse childhood experiences on perceived chronic stress with implications for cognitive flexibility. *PLoS ONE*, 15(6), 1–18. https://doi.org/10.1371/journal.pone.0235412.

Kumar, M., Karpaga Priya, P., Panigrahi, S., Raj, U., & Pathak, V. (2020). Impact of COVID-19 pandemic on adolescent health in India. *Journal of Family Medicine & Primary Care*, 9(11), 5484–5489. https://doi.org/10.4103/jfmpc.jfmpc_1266_20.

Lorenc, T., Lester, S., Sutcliffe, K., Stansfield, C., & Thomas, J. (2020). Interventions to support people exposed to adverse childhood experiences: Systematic review of systematic reviews. *BMC Public Health*, 20(1), 1–10. https://doi.org/10.1186/s12889-020-08789-0.

Luiggi-Hernández, J. G., & Rivera-Amador, A. I. (2020). Reconceptualizing social distancing: Teletherapy and social inequity during the Covid-19 and loneliness pandemics. *Journal of Humanistic Psychology*, 60(5), 626–638. https://doi.org/10.1177/0022167820937503.

Maunder, R. G., Hunter, J. J., Tannenbaum, D. W., Le, T. L., & Lay, C. (2020). Physicians' knowledge and practices regarding screening adult patients for adverse childhood experiences: a survey. *BMC Health Services Research*, 20(1), 1–5. https://doi.org/10.1186/s12913-020-05124-6.

Mead, V. P. (2020). Adverse Babyhood Experiences (ABEs) increase risk for infant and maternal morbidity and mortality, and chronic illness. *Journal of Prenatal & Perinatal Psychology & Health*, 34(4), 285–317.

Mirkovic, B., Cohen, D., Garny de la Rivière, S., Pellerin, H., Guilé, J-M., Consoli, A., & Gerardin, P. (2020). Repeating a suicide attempt during adolescence: Risk and protective factors 12 months after hospitalization. *European Child & Adolescent Psychiatry*, 29(12), 1729–1740. https://doi.org/10.1007/s00787-020-01491-x.

Moustakas, C. E. (1961). *Loneliness*. Prentice Hall.

Organisation for Economic Co-operation and Development. (2020, June 11). Youth and COVID-19: Response, recovery and resilience. OECD. https://www.oecd.org/coronavirus/policy-responses/youth-and-covid-19-response-recovery-and-resilience-c40e61c6/.

Panchal, N., Kamal, R., Cox, C., & Garfield, R. (2021). The implications of COVID-19 for mental health and substance abuse. Kaiser Family Foundation. https://www.kff.org/coronavirus-covid-19/issue-brief/the-implications-of-covid-19-for-mental-health-and-substance-use/.

Park, Y. M., Shekhtman, T., & Kelsoe, J. R. (2020). Effect of the type and number of adverse childhood experiences and the timing of adverse experiences on clinical outcomes in individuals with bipolar disorder. *Brain Sciences (2076–3425)*, 10(5), 254. https://doi.org/10.3390/brainsci10050254.

Pinchoff, J., Santhya, K., White, C., Rampal, S., Acharya, R., & Ngo, T. D. (2020). Gender specific differences in COVID-19 knowledge, behavior and health effects among adolescents and young adults in Uttar Pradesh and Bihar, India. *PLoS ONE*, 15(12), 1–13. https://doi.org/10.1371/journal.pone.0244053.

Pretorius, T. (2021). Depression among health care students in the time of COVID-19: The mediating role of resilience in the hopelessness–depression relationship. *South African Journal of Psychology*, 51(2): 269–278. https://doi.org/10.1177/0081246321994452.

Purkey, E., Davison, C., MacKenzie, M., Beckett, T., Korpal, D., Soucie, K., & Bartels, S. (2020). Experience of emergency department use among persons with a history of adverse childhood experiences. *BMC Health Services Research*, 20(1), 1–10. https://doi.org/10.1186/s12913-020-05291-6.

Read, J., Morrison, T., & Waddingham, R. (2020). Traumas, adversities, and psychosis: Investigating practical implications. *Psychiatric Times*, 37(7), 48–51.

Reinhardt, M., Horváth, Z., Morgan, A., & Kökönyei, G. (2020). Well-being profiles in adolescence: Psychometric properties and latent profile analysis of the mental health continuum model—a methodological study. *Health & Quality of Life Outcomes*, 18(1), 1–10. https://doi.org/10.1186/s12955-020-01332-0.

Sapolsky, R. (2017). *Behave: The biology of humans at our best and worst.* Penguin Press.

Sun, S., Goldberg, S. B., Lin, D., Qiao, S., & Operario, D. (2021). Psychiatric symptoms, risk, and protective factors among university students in quarantine during the COVID-19 pandemic in China. *Globalization & Health*, 17(1), 1–14. https://doi.org/10.1186/s12992-021-00663-x.

Szasz, T. S. (1970). *Ideology and insanity: Essays on the psychiatric dehumanization of man.* Anchor Books.

Tsehay, M., Necho, M., & Mekonnen, W. (2020). The role of adverse childhood experience on depression symptom, prevalence, and severity among school going adolescents. *Depression Research & Treatment*, 1–9. https://doi.org/10.1155/2020/5951792.

van de Groep, S., Zanolie, K., Green, K. H., Sweijen, S. W., & Crone, E. A. (2020). A daily diary study on adolescents' mood, empathy, and prosocial behavior during the COVID-19 pandemic. *PLoS ONE*, 15(10), 1–20. https://doi.org/10.1371/journal.pone.0240349.

Warner, E. T., Zhang, Y., Gu, Y., Taporoski, T. P., Pereira, A., DeVivo, I., Spence, N. D., Cozier, Y., Palmer, J. R., Kanaya, A. M., Kandula, N. R., Cole, S. A., Tworoger, S., & Shields, A. (2020). Physical and sexual abuse in childhood and adolescence and leukocyte telomere length: A pooled analysis of the study on psychosocial stress, spirituality, and health. *PLoS ONE*, 15(10). https://doi.org/10.1371/journal.pone.0241363.

Watters, E. (2010). *Crazy like us: The globalization of the American psyche.* Free Press.

Williams, J. R., Cole, V., Girdler, S., & Cromeens, M. G. (2020). Exploring stress, cognitive, and affective mechanisms of the relationship between interpersonal trauma and opioid misuse. *PLoS ONE*, 15(5), 1–19. https://doi.org/10.1371/journal.pone.0233185.

Yağci, I., Taşdelen, Y., & Kivrak, Y. (2020). Childhood trauma, quality of life, sleep quality, anxiety and depression levels in people with bruxism. *Archives of Neuropsychiatry / Noropsikiatri Arsivi*, 57(2), 131–135. https://doi.org/10.29399/npa.23617.

Yalom, I. D. (1980). *Existential psychotherapy.* Basic Books.

Yalom, I. D. (2012). *Love's executioner and other tales of psychotherapy.* Basic Books.

2

MULTICULTURAL HUMANISTIC PSYCHOLOGY

A Global Framework

To guide us through the darkness that young adults face within existential concerns (i.e., death, anxiety, fear, loss, and the abyss of meaninglessness), we will utilize multicultural humanistic psychology as a theoretical lens for understanding the self-actualizing power of relationships. We will utilize this framework to construct a praxis that facilitates the formation of growth-promoting relationships and the creation of meaning. The meanings that are created amongst relationships with the world cultivate mental well-being and flourishing in the face of hardships. The existential trauma caused by the pandemic has left many youth in despair, without direction or hope. A multicultural humanistic psychological praxis supports young adults' meaning-making processes to create opportunities for healing, growth, and enlightenment. These processes are most profound amongst relationships with others and the world. To explore multicultural humanistic psychology, this chapter surveys a brief history of humanistic psychology to give us an appreciation of its existential and phenomenal foundations, as well as its relevance to a multicultural society.

During the late nineteenth to mid-twentieth centuries, psychoanalysis and behaviorism were the two leading schools of psychology in Western society. Psychoanalysis was developed by Austrian psychologist Sigmund Freud as a way to remedy mental disturbances by first understanding a person's unconscious mind. Freud's theories and practices were historically important for making the field of clinical psychology a widely accepted and credible science. However, psychoanalysis argued that people were driven by unconscious desires that usually stemmed from failures to satisfy developmental needs in childhood. Clinical engagement meant exploring clients' relationships with parents, dreams, and

DOI: 10.4324/9781003251651-4

forbidden desires. On the other hand, behaviorism, championed by John B. Watson and B. F. Skinner, studied human behavior and believed that human beings are reflexive and reactionary beings to stimuli/conditions; entirely conditioned by their circumstances. Cognitive processes and emotions were rejected in behaviorism. Animals were mostly viewed as animated objects, devoid of thought or emotion. Behaviorists believed that conditioning can determine the outcome of every being.

During the mid-twentieth century, the limitations of psychology and Western culture were challenged by a group of rogue psychologists in the U.S. that were dissatisfied with psychoanalysis and behaviorism. Their intellectual backgrounds of study and clinical realities did not reflect the mainstream (i.e., psychoanalysis and behaviorism) psychological conclusions and clinical diagnostics. The popular deterministic and fatalistic view of human nature removed the phenomenal qualities of the person. These rebellious psychologists were versed in the works of existentialists such as Sartre and Camus, while also having deep understandings of phenomenology from Husserl and Heidegger. In 1964, as the U.S. Civil Rights Movement gained momentum and social unrest grew in the face of discrimination, racism, and prejudice; these psychologists met at the Castle Inn at Cornfield Point on Old Saybrook's coast in Connecticut to create their own movement, another school of psychology—a third force.

Third force psychology was a radical approach to the person. It utilized existential and phenomenological principles to break free from the determinisms, reductionisms, and fatalisms that psychoanalysis and behaviorism established. This movement later became known as *humanistic psychology*. Each humanistic psychologist helped usher in a new "vision of psychology as a holistic, phenomenological exploration of the processes that organically promote psychological health and growth in accordance with people's innate nature and potentials" (Bland & DeRobertis, 2017, p. 1). A few elements from psychoanalysis and behaviorism would be adopted, but the overall approach to the person would become radically different. According to Smrtic (2010), humanistic psychology

> stresses the unique quality and innate goodness of every human being. Humanism is ever mindful of the importance of personal integrity, autonomy, and freedom for the effective functioning of man. It is concerned with our existential dilemmas, and is relevant in a society where many ask, "Who am I? What is the meaning of life?" This perspective is very much concerned with the subjective experience of the individual.
>
> *(p. 3)*

Furthermore, humanistic psychology did not ignore the destructive aspects of humanity, where selfishness, violence, and ignorance reside, but rather developed a person-centered focus on growth potentials and possibilities. As the social fabric of the U.S. began to change, humanistic psychology developed into a flexible, adaptive, and inclusive paradigm that would learn about phenomena from humans living in the here-and-now (Bühler, 1974).

The humanistic psychologists' philosophies and clinical methods were revolutionary for the mid-twentieth century, but over the years have become widely accepted across the world and have even influenced medical and educational paradigms. In this person-centered revolution, the humanistic psychologists had an extraordinary amount of condemnation, resistance, as well as pressure to conform to the two dominant schools of psychology. For many years countless professors, clinicians, philosophers, teachers, and researchers firmly rejected humanistic psychology's ideas and practices, without consideration. The humanistic psychologists were disregarded or ostracized, even labeled as hippies and beatniks. Fortunately, the humanistic psychologists persisted and advocated for their paradigm's place into a society that was opening its mind to new possibilities. Humanistic psychology gained momentum through the years, even though some humanistic psychologists would only have their ideas accepted posthumously.

James Bugental summarized humanistic psychology in five tenets: The greater whole of a human being will always be more than the sum of its parts (anti-reductionist); human beings are a distinctive, phenomenal entity within unique contexts; each person has conscious awareness of the self and its relational contexts with others; human beings have free will and the responsibility to make meaningful choices that determine their lives; each person has intentionality to seek meaning and a place to be valued and creative. These pillars guide humanistic psychology to adapt and retain relevance to diversifying human contexts. In addition, the paradigm's tenets are inclusive of cultural meanings in order to open possibilities for exploring existential and phenomenological understandings.

Humanistic psychology dismantled the limitations of erudite philosophies that atomized, reduced, and minimalized human potentials and phenomena. To accomplish this, they removed the bureaucratic and disenfranchising methods of psychology where the therapist or mental health professional retained ultimate authority over the client (Bland & DeRobertis, 2017). Instead, the goal was to utilize the client's autonomy, inner directions, meaning-seeking motivations, and decision-making abilities in order to empower the client to make growth-promoting changes. These changes would have rippling effects, as an empowered person is more apt to be a democratic agent of social change. Unlocking potentials of the person would be the first step toward a democratic and socially just community.

Humanistic psychological praxis is a holistic engagement where the subject in contexts matters; instead of solely focusing on one analytical aspect of the person in isolation. The humanistic psychologists believed that human dilemmas, such as racism, discrimination, relationships, meaning, existential concerns, and emotional disturbances were important areas to explore with the person living within complex circumstances.

The world of the twentieth century accelerated global migration, cultural blending, and multiculturalism. Human diversities were not only blending but clashing as well, as many people felt uncomfortable to have the world around them transform at an extraordinary rate. It was the work of the humanistic psychologists to remove the barriers to personal and societal growth in order to cultivate and realize the potentials of a multicultural global community.

Multicultural Beginnings in Humanistic Psychology

Human diversity is fundamental for humanistic psychology to actualize its potentials as a paradigm. Diversity includes elements of ability, culture, religion, spirituality, beliefs, values, sexuality, interests, and heritage, to name a few. The dynamics of diversities have the potential to expand the depths of understandings of the human condition, while providing resources for creating a humanistic society that is open to change and cultural building. Nevertheless, diversity is not to be implied as a two-dimensional category because it is an infinite and evolving spectrum (DeRobertis, 2015).

Humanistic psychology paved the way for other paradigms in psychology to form, such as transpersonal psychology, which focuses on spirituality (Bland & DeRobertis, 2017; Gavin, 2019). Transpersonal psychology was built upon humanistic psychology by exploring the psycho-spiritual dimensions of Eastern paradigms, such as Buddhism, along with Western ones, such as Christianity and Judaism. The paradigm examines the state in which a person can be aware and transcend self-actualizing needs by erasing the illusion that the self is a distinct entity to be realized.

Humanistic psychology seeks to learn and explore existential worlds of meaning with other paradigms. For example, cultural paradigms such as Zen, Buddhist philosophy, and Taoism became important for expanding the existential and phenomenological philosophies of humanistic psychology (Bland & DeRobertis, 2017). Humanistic psychology is a paradigm of inclusion and possibility that reflects the nature of human beings, which is adaptable, community oriented, trustworthy, complex, and phenomenal. The success of the paradigm has historically proved relevant and successful in times of civil unrest. For example, Alfred Adler advocated for social justice and equality for women and minorities, as his theories were used in the Brown v. Board of Education Supreme Court decision (Watts & Bluvshtein, 2020). Van Deurzen (2019) recommended that youth need to value and engage the paradox of being human, where there are contradictions, struggles, vagueness, and intersectionality. Coming to appreciate the positive and negative forces within humanity allows young adults to form diverse relationships that can provide strength, wisdom, and enlightenment, where Being and becoming are synonymous (Bühler, 1974).

The Potential of Humanity: Growth-Promoting Relationships

The humanistic psychologists argued that if an organism is to flourish, it must seek or establish the growth-promoting conditions in which to actualize potentials. Thus, the humanists sought to understand the unique relational conditions that would cultivate human growth, healing, and actualization. They agreed that social relationships were the natural habitat for human beings (a characteristic shared with other primates). A growth-promoting relationship is an encounter in the here-and-now, where one organism has the intentionality to support the actualization of potentials in another organism, the self, and the relationship. In addition, there is a developing value for, exploration of, expression of, and application of the inner potentials and resources of the organism (Rogers, 1989). There are infinite possibilities to find relationships with organisms—the use of the word *organism* can designate any form of life. Humans actualize growth potentials with other people, but also with dogs, cats, trees, plants, and even fish. Diversities in relationships are key for helping people unlock personal potentials and abilities, such as empathy and socio-emotional intelligence.

Within the growth-promoting relationship, young adults are encouraged to be genuine, express themselves spontaneously, and explore rhythms and patterns that help connect one to another (Bühler, 1974; Moustakas, 1956). However, in almost every society there are barriers to achieving these types of encounters. Ethnocentrism, xenophobia, racism, imperialism, or even ageism are detrimental for human growth and potential. During the U.S. Civil Rights Era, humanistic psychologist Carl Rogers knew that regardless of human setbacks, "A quiet revolution is under way in almost every field. It holds promise of moving us forward to a more human, more person-centered world" (Rogers, 1977, p. 290). Although the destructive elements of ignorance are still present in modern society, there are greater global forces exposing and dismantling them to champion equity, social justice, and empathy. Founding member Charlotte Bühler described, "The conviction that people all over the world felt this need and that closer human relationships might help preventing devastating hostilities..." (Bühler, 1974, p. 7).

Worldwide, social institutions have largely supported the move toward multiculturalism, diversity, and inclusion. Many educational institutions have begun to prepare students to engage a diversifying and interconnecting human community—which has left the static curricular models to the past (Rogers, 1969). The skills needed to adapt to the complexities of a global community are more relevant than rote memorizations. The humanistic psychologists knew that the *process of learning* must become equally important as the curricular content if we are to grow with a changing world.

Humanistic psychology works to bring inclusion and prevalence of minority voices into the discourse. However, there still needs to be greater representation from diverse groups of people around the world in order to understand of how race, politics, sexuality, economics, and culture factor into the human experience (Hoffman et al., 2019; van Deurzen, 2019). Some believe that, since its inception, humanistic psychology has been limited to the ideas of middle- and upper-class White males, where privileged socio-economic status has influenced interpretations on what it means to be fully human and self-actualize (Schneider, 2019). However, this critique of humanistic psychology is limited. The humanistic psychologists, as Bland and DeRobertis (2017) stated, "emphasize the often-unheeded adaptive qualities available within marginalized populations. Furthermore, this criticism overlooks the wealth of humanistic literature involving multiculturalism, cross-cultural studies, and gender studies...which arose out of its constructivist focus" (p. 16). Therefore, the criticism of it being oppressive, male-dominated, and White neglects the fact that humanistic psychologists were advocates for minorities, anti-racist, and actively developed partnerships with diverse cultural communities. Humanistic psychologists were some of the first scholars in Western psychology to appreciate the intersectionality of identity. Intersectionality means that all people carry an infinity of historical, racial, and cultural traces that are interdependent within social and cultural positionalities for comprising an identity (Bradford, 2020; Guilfoyle, 2016; Johnson & Vallejos, 2019; Watts & Bluvshtein, 2020).

Third Force—Third Dimension

Western social institutions for learning have compartmentalized our understandings of culture, relationships, the brain, body, and biology into specific discourses (Cozolino, 2020). People, especially young adults, have become filtered through these lenses to become valued for what they represent, such as with their abilities for academic achievement, social status, career, or accolades (Moustakas, 1956). The young adult is judged, reduced, or distorted through absurd criteria of evaluation. They then come to value themselves against the same external criteria, experiencing estrangement from inner-core values.

Over the mid- to late twentieth century, humanistic psychology developed its philosophy and clinical approach. Concurrently, other sciences were inquiring and producing research data on brain structures involved in humanistic areas of study, such as empathy. The sciences had difficulty elaborating on such phenomena. Compartmentalizing quantitative and qualitative research diminished the progress for understanding. However, in recent years, scholars from across disciplines have collaborated through phenomena-based inquiry, where their consilience have produced enlightened findings (Bland & DeRobertis, 2017).

Nevertheless, there is still a major trend in pop psychology to use biological neuroscience to validate all psychological phenomena, such as how a young adult's motivation is *just* the result of dopamine, or depression is the *just* result of a neurochemical imbalance, and so on. (DeRobertis, 2015). Reductionists claim that if all is well in one's neurobiology, then there is no reason to be depressed or anxious. Pigeonholing psychological disturbances into neurological explanations is quick and convenient, such as saying empathy is *just* the activation of mirror neurons. In such a myopic approach, the young adult is only a mere shell to the neurons that conduct socialization and consciousness. According to DeRobertis (2015),

34   Part I

The mainstream of neuroscientific thought has successfully popularized a new, watered-down and muddled form of Cartesianism. According to this view, all aspects of worldly experience are perpetually suspect and subject to doubt until or unless some internal, neurological activity can be found to both justify and explain away their existence.

(p. 2)

For those that have once more separated mind and body, there is a privilege given to materialistic sciences that invent diagnostic categories based in quantitative research, which ultimately disregard the subjectivity of the person (Bradford, 2020).

Humanistic psychologists worked to break the person free from philosophical and empirical determinisms. As Wilson (2014) argued, free will exists "if not in ultimate reality, then at least in the operational sense necessary for sanity and thereby for the perpetuation of the human species" (p. 170). Otherwise, human beings would not have survived by being bounded and determined by the walls of a genetic or ontological fatalism. Any conclusion of human behavior that is judged by a certain event, gene, neurotransmitter, or hormone, is incomplete because it is one part of a greater whole that can never be reduced to part-function (Sapolsky, 2017). Empirical research is vitally important but if it becomes solely used to create reductionist conclusions or a disconnected praxis, then it will only serve the theories and not the living person (Schneider, 2019). Although the modern Cartesians of pop psychology and other sciences have once again worked to estrange mind from body, there are many scholars in the field of neuroscience that work to develop a humanistic neuroscience that utilizes neuroscientific findings to *enhance* (and not determine) our understanding of human phenomena (DeRobertis, 2015).

Historically, Western medicine has atomized the mind and body. One must question the limitations as to how Western psychology and psychiatry outlined what constitutes a "healthy" or "normal" brain (Bradford, 2020). Do the various Western psychological approaches understand the complexity of the sanity they are seeking to enhance? The psychological theories and methods are pieces to understanding a phenomenal whole of human experience, which always remain unfinished or incomplete. Limits of understanding are inherent in every field and focused study may leave out more than it includes. Findings may misapprehend the nature of the object of inquiry entirely, ultimately doing more detriment (Schneider, 2019). However, humanistic psychology has a history of consilience by welcoming in or reaching out to other fields of study.

For Buddhist philosophy and Tibetan medicine, the organism is interrelated and cannot be separated into parts if it is to flourish (Bradford, 2020). Similarly, humanistic psychology aligns with a holistic clinical engagement of the person. Humanistic psychology has been cautious of neuroscientific research conclusions for fear of reductionisms, atomization, or taking away from other organismic functions necessary to experience the world (DeRobertis, 2015). Developing a humanistic psychological and neuroscientific awareness for how brains are influenced, interconnected, function, and develop helps young adults to appreciate the complex nature of their emotions, cognition, and behaviors (Cozolino, 2020). Neuroscience and humanistic psychology can enhance each other in ways that educate young adults to explore phenomena mindfully.

Human beings are more than the complex result of social, cultural, political, environmental, and biological history. The intricacy of the person, as Bradford (2020) explained,

> does not necessarily have a singular, self-mind, but may be of many minds, have mixed feelings, contradictory ideas and diverse responses depending on the situation they are in. This view envisions a fluid, malleable self that is neither fixed nor reified, but always in a process of becoming: evolving, devolving or stagnating.
>
> *(p. 339)*

Humanistic psychology reconsidered Western psychology with Eastern philosophies in order to understand the illusory "self" within a stream of eternity, where a person has the freedom to choose how to be and what to become (Spinelli, 2019).

Developing a Multicultural Humanistic Psychology

The world is hyper-connecting at a pace never before seen in human history. There are many schools of thought that are understanding these changes through their historical canons. Humanistic psychology's tenets were not meant to bring anachronistic conclusions to current realities, but rather provide an adaptive premise in which to *learn with* the changingness of the world. However, the dizzying pace at which the complex technological and cultural advances take place means that a new paradigm is needed to reflect modern realities. By synthesizing the principles of multiculturalism with the tenets of humanistic psychology, a stronger praxis is created in which to empower young adults with critical literacies for understanding and acting within global complexities.

Multicultural humanistic psychology is a modern theoretical framework that emboldens young adults with the critical capacities to engage existential, multicultural, phenomenological, and humanistic themes in order to dismantle injustices and work toward developing an equitable global community that supports the self-actualization processes for all life and environments. By utilizing critical pedagogies and culturally responsive methods, educators, mental health professionals, and caring adults focus on culturally relative self-actualization processes to support young adults in realizing existential potentials for creating meaning within relationships. Multicultural archetypes inherent in the global community

36 Part I

are vital resources in this process. The goal of multicultural humanistic psychology is to promote holistic well-being for the person and cultivate the necessary conditions for growth-promoting relationships to actualize the potentials of a human community. In *Empowering Children: A Multicultural Humanistic Approach*, the guiding principles for this theoretical consilience/praxis were outlined as follows:

- Diverse and complex cultural paradigms are integral resources for expanding perspectives on what it means to actualize potentials of humanity.
- Human diversities cannot be reduced to their parts. Cultures are complex, intersectional, and constantly evolving. Cultural differences are traces of human phenomena, in which there is an infinite amount. These cultural phenomena are explored to reveal the human condition.
- It is the responsibility of human beings to establish dignity, equity, social justice, and freedom for all groups, especially for those that are marginalized. It is necessary to empower communities with a critical consciousness to become literate in local and global realities.
- Multicultural education, critical pedagogies, and culturally relevant curriculum are humanistic vehicles that empower children to dismantle inequities, prejudices, and discriminations that marginalize and subjugate people in the community and worldwide.
- It is our responsibility to empower children with the skills and knowledge in which to take responsibility of an interdependent and interconnecting global community, where not only human societies are cultivated to flourish, but also include animal, ecological, fish, and insect communities.
- Human beings are able to make choices and determine meaningful ways of living that are constructive, growth promoting, and inclusive. All cultural meanings are valuable when they promote meaning-making, well-being, growth, community, and holistic health. Collective meaning-making generates cultural expressions which explore existential concerns.
- Culturally relative self-actualization processes are promoted and achieved in the cultural paradigm that defines its terms. Each culture provides a valuable perspective on what means to be fully human and the processes necessary to achieve potentials.
- Identity is intersectional, interdependent, and based upon the meanings we choose to create. Multiculturalism enhances our understanding of ourselves, our ability to be empathic, and enlightens us on what it means to be fully human.

(Kazanjian, 2021, p. 39)

Humanistic multicultural psychology is intended to facilitate the realization of young adults' abilities and potentials as explore existential phenomena and create meaning amongst their relationships with the world.

A multicultural humanistic framework is important in a post-pandemic world because it supports young adults in making sense of existential trauma. This framework uncovers subjugated and marginalized knowledges/experiences from populations that were deeply affected by existential trauma in order to develop partnerships that work to dismantle inequities and oppression (Savery, 2019). Within diverse relationships, young adults develop a multi-axial positionality in which to understand the experience of others, especially in liminal spaces (Guilfoyle, 2016; Hoffman et al., 2019). Inclusiveness is imperative for developing multicultural humanistic psychology, not only from diverse groups of people or other fields of study, but with all forms of life, where each organism can provide unique insight into the phenomenon of Being.

Culturally Relative Self-Actualization

The diversities of encounter and in relationships are holistically stimulating for the young adult and promote enhanced growth and/or healing. The pandemic limited social interactions, in which the years to come after are crucial for reconnecting with others. In these engagements, young adults must learn to greet the world with a phenomenological attitude, which means to "return to the beginnings, to the things themselves as they give themselves in lived through experience—not as externally real or eternally existent, but as an openness that invites us to see them as if for the first time" (van Manen, 2016, p. 43). As young adults learn to re-engage the world with a fresh perception, they become mindful of the privilege for how relationships open possibilities to create meaning. Through diverse relationships cultural paradigms expand in meaning and potential.

Cultural paradigms are foundational processes for meaning-making that reflect a community's shared experience. In the contemporary interconnecting world, young adults are finding more cultural connections across the world. Cultural creations contain phenomenal essences that reflect human experiences, interests, concerns, and realities. Although never to be fully grasped, cultural phenomena are gateways into a phenomenology of humanity. Exploring cultures through diverse relationships helps reevaluate and redefine their meanings ascribed to human phenomena. This opens up possibilities for creating new inter-cultural meanings, but also realizing potentials of the self.

Humanistic psychology modernized the philosophical discussions of *self-actualization* through the principles of third force psychology. Their conception was most notably championed by Abraham Maslow, who argued that self-actualization is a process of sequential need fulfillment in order to achieve self-integration, authenticity, and discovery of aptitudes (Maslow, 1971). Basic needs were identified as elements/conditions for which without their fulfillment would result in a decline in well-being. The prevention of ill-health is established by fulfilling these needs, and when the choice is given they will be a priority to the organism. Needs can be classified into Basic, Psychological, and Self-fulfillment, which

Maslow (1998) claimed are generally satisfied for people with high levels of well-being and life satisfaction. The processes of need transcendence were outlined by Maslow in a pyramid known as the Hierarchy of Human Needs: physiological needs and safety needs (Basic Needs), love and belonging and self-esteem (Psychological Needs), and self-actualization (Self-fulfillment Needs).

The Hierarchy has served as an effective guide for mental health professionals, educators, and parents to support the successful development and well-being of youth. It has been an intergenerational resource for helping communities of people flourish; however, it may need an update for times more complex and diverse than what Maslow knew. Therefore, multicultural humanistic psychology advocates that a *culturally relative self-actualization* is an appropriate update for a diversifying global human community.

Culturally relative self-actualization is defined as the transcendence of basic physiological, psychological, and self or group-fulfillment needs that are meaningful and defined by a person's cultural paradigm. Within a cultural paradigm, the person's specific living contexts must be taken into account, as many do not have the privilege or ease of satisfying needs as readily as others. For example, some young adults with home insecurities have difficulty transcending basic needs (Best et al., 2008). A compassionate educator may seek to find ways in which to provide conditions in which to satisfy home security needs by contacting the appropriate school or community services that are in alignment with their cultural paradigms. However, even though students are settled into residential care, they may still not feel safe. How do we understand what safety and security means to an individual that has had a history of insecurities, estrangement, or trauma? The needs taken for granted are phenomena, in which have been vastly overlooked. Many caring adults try to satisfy young adults' needs from their own cultural paradigm's meanings. Often times, adults are seeking to generate well-being for young adults without truly understanding the phenomenon first.

The collectivistic and individualistic cultural paradigms have differences in meaning that must redefine the processes of self-actualization. Self-esteem for a person in a collectivistic paradigm may have elemental variations that someone in an individualistic culture may not experience. For example, "areas of the medial prefrontal cortex associated with self-evaluation and self-knowledge respond differently according to the degree to which individuals endorse individualistic versus collectivistic values" (DeRobertis, 2015, p. 11). Collective self-esteem or group esteem has different values, meanings, and practices than the self-esteem realized in individualistic cultures. Group esteem is where a person feels worth and dignity through identification, contributions, and service to the collective group—the need for esteem is satisfied and defined by the well-being and success of the group. A young adult from a collectivistic culture is not likely to find need fulfillment by engaging in self-esteem practices of an individualistic culture, where the focus/meaning of the self is separated from the group.

Self- or group esteem is an important part of culturally relative self-actualization and appreciating cultural relativity can help facilitators and professionals gear activities to align with a broad spectrum of paradigms (Hocoy, 2019). Knowing that collectivistic cultural orientations seek to develop esteem through group activity, caring adults can open spaces for young adults to meaningfully contribute to a group function by working together and sharing success, while also providing components for individualistic orientations to find esteem by giving opportunities to work alone or compete with themselves for individual achievement.

Culturally relative self-actualization is open to new meanings and values that understand/engage phenomena in each component of Maslow's revised Hierarchy. In addition, culturally relative self-actualization is an ongoing process in which the person can satisfy needs through meaningful experiences that promote integration, self or group-esteem, and processes of creativity and contribution.

Regardless of cultural orientation, relationships are integral to realizing transcendence in the culturally relative hierarchy of needs. People need others in which to realize potentials and integration; as Cozolino (2014) stated, "*Relationships are our natural habitat*" (p. 4). The meanings created in relationships are essential for need transcendence. Inclusion redefines foundational elements of Maslow's Hierarchy or could even add new levels. If human relationships are necessary for human growth and development, perhaps the basic needs area of the pyramid should contain growth-promoting relationships as a core component. We need relationships in which to stimulate brain growth and integration—a basic physiological need for flourishing.

Opening spaces for young adults to experience culturally relative self-actualization means establishing the conditions of growth-promoting relationships, such as empathy, congruence, positive regard, safety, and freedom (Moustakas, 1956). Only when young adults feel safe to explore, experiment, and express can they truly meet another in an encounter. Otherwise, the artificiality, mimicry, and masks they have learned to wear to survive will further estrange them from their selves (even though they appear to have all the necessary components of socio-emotional well-being). Culturally relative self-actualization opens limitless possibilities for diverse groups of young adults to achieve peak experiences and perhaps even find geometric possibilities for understanding the processes of actualization beyond the pyramid.

Processes of Young Adulthood in Multicultural Humanistic Psychology

Experiencing young adulthood in a hyper-connecting world means that the intersectionality of identity reflects global contexts. Cultures, economies, societies, educational institutions, and many other spheres of human life are integrating and diversifying across the world. The contexts of young adulthood have become vastly complex. Although there will be superficial changes in popular culture, young adults will find that multicultural humanistic psychology is a helpful guide for developing diverse relationships and exploring new worlds of meaning.

40   Part I

The processes of learning and value formation are integral at every developmental phase of life. When secondary and higher education aligns with (culturally relative) personal values and interests, it brings about a mindful awareness of the emotional aspects of learning. This emotional awareness is excited by the curricular material being adventurous and aligning to cultural values and realities (Moustakas & Perry, 1973). Young adults seek to understand the complexity of their circumstances as well as explore diverse relationships. School populations are increasing in cultural diversity which reflects an integrating global community. Establishing positive values in the classroom for forming new relationships with diverse others will have lifelong influences, as "numerous studies have shown that ethnocentrism may decrease over time, as group members develop experience with both the in-group and out-groups, and views of out-groups may become more positive with experience" (Keith, 2011, p. 24). Classrooms can reflect global realities and become safe spaces where young adults learn from each other as their knowledge becomes part of the curricular content.

One key component to the process of multicultural learning is tolerance. Tolerance is, as Moats (2019) discussed, "not intended as *tolerating other people,* but rather *tolerating the discomfort* necessary for understanding and change. Even if one does not accept the other person's perspective, it is vital to empathize and work to understand them" (p. 98). The discomfort in realizing that knowledges and perceptions of the world are limited is an important feeling for young adults to appreciate as they explore new relationships with people that have differing cultural paradigms.

When young adults become tolerant of life's impermanence, they can realize the curricular relevance of existential lessons. Learning to grow older and experience the existential concerns, such as accepting one's own mortality can cause great discomfort. Tolerating change is an ability that translates from existential enlightenment to multicultural realization, where human communities and cultures are not static, but impermanent or ever-evolving. Young adults do not have to agree or change themselves with every life discomfort, but can become mindfully aware of other paradigms, meanings, and impermanence. Tolerance needs to be cultivated in a safe atmosphere for young adults by establishing limits of communication and expression to help them learn new information and interpersonal communication skills during times of discomfort or disagreement. Socio-emotional skills are important to develop interoceptive awareness, empathy, and relationship building during encounters. Identifying and exploring emotions during unsettling conversations or experiences opens spaces for learning that the judgments, prejudices, biases, and categories have always been limiting.

Whether in virtual or real-life worlds, young adults need time and opportunities to reflect on how existential concerns affect their perceptual abilities and curiosities for knowing others. Fostering these processes for growth must include the abilities to cope and adapt with uncertainty. The pandemic forced many to adapt frantically, where some were driven by reactions or impulse. Young adults can learn that existential concerns run deeply within people, and certain triggers can cause them to act in ways that do not necessarily reflect their character. Seeking to adapt mindfully and thoughtfully to intense and immediate change is an important multicultural humanistic psychological life skill. Even adapting to the discomfort that the unsolvable conundrums of life present is an enriching process, where Rilke (2000) recommended, "Try to love the *questions themselves*...At present you need to *live* the question. Perhaps you will gradually, without even noticing it, find yourself experiencing the answer, some distant day" (p. 35). The existential questions themselves are the most profound and beautiful, even if they may appear as the scariest places for young adults to live through. Answers to existential questions can only be realized in the living moment.

The world that young adults will inherit has been deeply marred by COVID-19. Multicultural humanistic psychology is meant to empower them to share the responsibility for where to go with it all—to be able to care for not only human life, but animals, ecosystems, plants, insects, and even microorganisms (Jackson, 2019). Responsibility is important in an existential paradigm because it is through creating meanings and making decisions that one determines a life story. Young adults must also realize their responsibilities to communities of life in the world (i.e., not only humans, but plant and animal life as well), seek out injustice, discrimination, and suppression in order to alleviate suffering and promote life's well-being.

In multicultural humanistic psychology, the cultural contexts in which people experience young adulthood is important. The challenges, barriers, or privileges of race and socioeconomics are imperative for understanding subjective meanings. This is why being *colorblind*, where one actively ignores race or racial appearances, limits and deteriorates growth-promoting relationships. The reverse can also be detrimental, where overcompensation to racial aspects leads to engaging the race first and ignoring the person (this also happens with other diversities as well, such as with for people living with disabilities). Either avenue removes empathy from the encounter—as the subjectivity is removed in favor of superficial objectivity. Denying the racial aspects of a person's reality or focusing too much on a condition ultimately prevents an encounter of the whole person (Hocoy, 2019; Moats, 2019).

Contexts frame a subjective experience, but do not define the person's potentials. Within cultural contexts, young adults seek to create meaning, which "involves having an aim or purpose toward which we strive in the daily activities of life, the cognitive ability to understand our circumstance, and the capacity to emotionally appraise the value of a given situation" (Calder et al., 2020, p. 642). Cultural meanings have a reciprocal relationship with establishing cultural norms for behaviors, goals, roles, and understandings. Young adults are mostly reared in cultural world(s) where meanings and values are predetermined to help guide their decision-making processes. Over time, young adults may realize the absurdity of these meanings, typically when their inquiries posed to adults are met with, "That is just the way we do it," "That's just how it has always been," or the dreaded, "I don't know, ask your mother (or the Internet)." Of course, there are norms and values that are not growth promoting (i.e., violence, discriminations, prejudices), which will always cause inner havoc within the person.

Norms and values that promote kindness and empathy align with the human condition, in which most young adults will not find any distress. The elements in question are the superficial and absurd norms, such as the way to dress, social acceptability of career choice, materialisms, cultural gender traits, violence to other forms of life, names of things, and so on. These can be questioned, removed, or changed without damaging the well-being of the person that is dissatisfied. Rebelling against destructive cultural norms may be seen as delinquent. Yet, in a deep sense, these young adults are beginning to free themselves from cultural barriers to enlightenment.

According to DeRobertis (2015), "Culture becomes an integral part of the individual organism as part of a lifespan developmental process that involves many time scales and is highly plastic in nature" (p. 18). The natural plasticity of youth culture seeks new ways of expressing and relating with peers that promotes inclusive values, self/group-esteem, belonging, and well-being. Many times, the plasticity of youth culture will harden in adulthood and become nostalgic. Pop-cultural music demonstrated this idea as young adults of the mid-twentieth century had a cultural paradigm shift when they saw Elvis Presley perform. Expressing freedom of movement through dance, creating new hair and fashion styles that mimicked "The King," and other cultural norms that felt good to teenagers shocked and disgusted older generations. Over the years, they became facets of a time of innocence and wholesome values.

The hyper-connecting world has offered innumerable cultural resources for youth, creating new interactions and processes that have brought forth new phenomena in young adulthood. New forms of music, dance, art, animation, fashion, literature, and online interactions from differing cultural paradigms have opened possibilities for how one creates meaning. Marginalized groups of young adults can represent themselves through virtual spaces, while finding and creating larger communities in which to find empowerment. Groups are able to experiment with cultural fusions as a way to discover possibilities in meaning-making. Some experimentations may result in failure or misperceptions, misrepresentations, disagreements, and rifts. However, the majority of global interactions of youth have progressed a global culture—not to be reduced in a singular sense, but an opening of possibility for multiplicity. There are smartphone applications for games and talking, mental health, cultural learning, language learning, sharing photos, or combining images with music, sharing triumphs and tragedies, while new arenas develop each year. Young adults utilize these avenues as ways for relating, understanding, and creating.

Although there are new developments in technology that promote cultural integration, these may also cause side effects that decrease well-being. As it was

Multicultural Humanistic Psychology   43

discussed in the previous chapter, social media disorder and problematic internet use are real threats to young adulthood. The misuse of technology can cause cultural othering and destruction to certain groups. Developing literacies in global phenomena will give young adults the tools to keep destructive and oppressive factors from forming, while dismantling existing ones.

Multicultural humanistic psychology develops the necessary abilities that can realize the potentials of a diverse and complex global culture. This framework empowers young adults with the cultural humility in which to transform themselves in lifelong cultural exploration and critical self-reflection (Johnson & Vallejos, 2019). Within cultural humility the person seeks to form partnerships with diverse groups in order to collaborate in the processes of learning and social justice. Cultural humility is parallel to what DeRobertis and Bland (2020) discussed as a process that,

> engenders an intellectual humility in the learner in which one is no longer quick to maintain assumptions and make prejudgments concerning the others' culture. The learner becomes better able to shift from an avoidance orientation to a relative openness orientation through deepening intrapersonal and interpersonal dialogue. This is, however, a process and it takes varying amounts of time to unfold. Even after the learning has occurred, the others are still relatively new to the learner and thus in ways still unknown. The learner will struggle to keep assumptions and stereotypes in check and work to resist the temptation to pass judgement as an ongoing task.
>
> *(p. 9)*

There are no ends to learning about people or their cultural paradigms. A critical consciousness brings forth biases, misperceptions, and preconceived notions of one's culture. Realizing positionality, privilege, and power is important as young adults learn to explore differing paradigms with empathy and sincerity. With cultural humility, young adults discover relationships that inspire partnerships in democratic action for social justice. To overcome the challenges of a multicultural global society, young adults must begin by opening their doors of perception to an infinity of connections with others, the world, and the universe that are found within the nothingness of existential darkness.

References

Best, D., Day, E., McCarthy, T., Darlington, I., & Pinchbeck, K. (2008). The Hierarchy of Needs and care planning in addiction services: What Maslow can tell us about addressing competing priorities? *Addiction Research & Theory*, 16(4), 305–307. https://doi.org/10.1080/16066350701875185.

Bland, A. M, & DeRobertis, E. M. (2017). Humanistic perspective. In V. Zeigler-Hill & T.K. Shackelford (Eds.), *Encyclopedia of personality and individual differences* (pp. 1–19). Springer International.

Bradford, K. (2020). The subject matter of psychology: Psyche, Dasein, non-self. *Existential Analysis: Journal of the Society for Existential Analysis*, 31(2), 336–350.

Bühler, C. (1974). The scope of humanistic psychology. *Education, 95*(1), 3–8.

Calder, A. J., Novak, L. F., & Lane, A. (2020). We're all going crazy now: How the covid-19 pandemic can promote more compassionate clinical perspectives. *Journal of Humanistic Psychology*, 60(5), 639–646. https://doi.org/10.1177/0022167820938615.

Cozolino, L. (2014). *The neuroscience of human relationships: Attachment and the developing social brain* (2nd ed.). W. W. Norton & Company.

Cozolino, L. (2020). *The pocket guide to neuroscience for clinicians*. W. W. Norton & Company.

DeRobertis, E. M. (2015). A neuroscientific renaissance of humanistic psychology. *Journal of Humanistic Psychology*, 55(3), 323–345. https://doi.org/10.1177/0022167814536617.

DeRobertis, E. M., & Bland, A. M. (2020). From personal threat to cross-cultural learning: An eidetic investigation. *Journal of Phenomenological Psychology*, 51, 1–15. https://doi:10.1163/15691624-12341368.

Gavin, V. J. (2019). Moving on creatively: Creative existential therapy for children, adolescents and adults. *Existential Analysis: Journal of the Society for Existential Analysis*, 30(1), 45–58.

Guilfoyle, M. (2016). Subject positioning: Gaps and stability in the therapeutic encounter. *Journal of Constructivist Psychology*, 29(2), 123–140. https://doi.org/10.1080/10720537.2015.1034815.

Hocoy, D. (2019). The challenge of multiculturalism to humanistic psychology. In L. Hoffman, H. Cleare-Hoffman, N. Granger Jr., & D. St. John (Eds.), *Humanistic approaches to multiculturalism and diversity: Perspectives on existence and difference* (pp. 18–28). Routledge.

Hoffman, L., Cleare-Hoffman, H., Granger, N., & St. John, D. (2019). History and critique of humanistic psychology from a multicultural perspective. In L. Hoffman, H. Cleare-Hoffman, N. Granger Jr., & D. St. John (Eds.), *Humanistic approaches to multiculturalism and diversity: Perspectives on existence and difference* (pp. 3–14). Routledge.

Jackson, T. (2019). The history of black psychology and humanistic psychology. In L. Hoffman, H. Cleare-Hoffman, N. Granger Jr., & D. St. John (Eds.), *Humanistic approaches to multiculturalism and diversity: Perspectives on existence and difference* (pp. 29–44). Routledge.

Johnson, Z. & Vallejos, L. (2019). Multicultural competencies in humanistic psychology. In L. Hoffman, H. Cleare-Hoffman, N. Granger Jr., & D. St. John (Eds.), *Humanistic approaches to multiculturalism and diversity: Perspectives on existence and difference* (pp. 63–75). Routledge.

Kazanjian, C. J. (2021). *Empowering Children: A Multicultural Humanistic Approach*. Routledge.

Keith, K. D. (2011). Ethnocentrism. In K. D. Keith (Ed.), *Cross-cultural psychology: Contemporary themes and perspectives* (pp. 20–33). Guilford Press.

Maslow, A. H. (1971). *The farther reaches of human nature*. Viking Press.

Maslow, A. H. (1998). *Toward a psychology of being*. J. Wiley & Sons.

Moats, M. (2019). White privilege: A multifaceted responsibility. In L. Hoffman, H. Cleare-Hoffman, N. Granger Jr., & D. St. John (Eds.), *Humanistic approaches to multiculturalism and diversity: Perspectives on existence and difference* (pp. 90–102). Routledge.

Moustakas, C. E (1956). *The self: Explorations in personal growth*. Harper & Brothers.

Moustakas, C. E. & Perry, C. (1973). *Learning to be free*. Prentice Hall.

Rilke, R. M. (2000). *Letters to a young poet.* Joan M. Burnham, Trans. New World Library.

Rogers, C. R. (1969). *Freedom to learn: A view of what education might become.* C. E. Merrill Pub. Co.

Rogers, C. R. (1977). *Carl Rogers on personal power.* Delacorte Press.

Rogers, C. R. (1989). *On becoming a person: A therapist's view of psychotherapy.* Houghton Mifflin.

Sapolsky, R. (2017). *Behave: The biology of humans at our best and worst.* Penguin Press.

Savery, D. C. (2019). Recognising echoism as a phenomenon in existential therapy: A Daseinsanalytic hermeneutic approach. *Existential Analysis: Journal of the Society for Existential Analysis, 30*(1), 144–154.

Schneider, K. J. (2019). Foreword. In L. Hoffman, H. Cleare-Hoffman, N. Granger Jr., & D. St. John (Eds.), *Humanistic approaches to multiculturalism and diversity: Perspectives on existence and difference* (pp. x–xi). Routledge.

Smrtic, J. D. (2010) *Abnormal psychology: Classic perspectives the text/anthology.* Linus Publications.

Spinelli, E. (2019). What's so existential about existential therapy? *Existential Analysis: Journal of the Society for Existential Analysis, 30*(1), 59–79.

van Deurzen, E. (2019). Facing an uncertain future: The next 30 years of existential therapy. *Existential Analysis: Journal of the Society for Existential Analysis, 30*(1), 4–17.

van Manen, M. (2016). *Phenomenology of practice: Meaning-giving methods in phenomenological research and writing.* Routledge.

Watts, R. E., & Bluvshtein, M. (2020). Adler's theory and therapy as a river: A brief discussion of the profound influence of Alfred Adler. *Journal of Individual Psychology, 76*(1), 99–109. https://doi.org/10.1353/jip.2020.0021.

Wilson, E. O. (2014). *The meaning of human existence.* Liveright.

3

EXISTENTIAL TERROR AND THE NECESSARY DISTRACTIONS

Being the Center of the Universe

The meanings of existential concerns (death, meaninglessness, isolation, and freedom) that young adults create are important elements for how they choose to live. Those that feel death is the ultimate end may be living as intensely as possible, often getting lost in a world of intense stimulation that is mistaken for meaningful experiences. While others may feel that the *you only live once* (maybe *twice* if you are James Bond!) attitude is an existential attitude designed to make sure that they never miss an opportunity. The Western conception of death as the end of life can motivate one to live to the fullest potential, but what if young adults revised their existential stories to include other cultural paradigms—to where death is not an end, but a necessary interval in the stream of eternity?

The COVID-19 virus has removed the veil of invincibility people across the world. However, young adults that exhibit the developmental concept of *adolescent egocentrism* may have denied their risk of mortality through the fable of invincibility, where they feel invulnerable to harm or death (Moshman, 2011). The young adults that demonstrated this fable disregarded the gravity of a deadly pandemic, while many others taunted death itself. For instance, during 2020, there were countless house parties that violated CDC and state health guidelines as a way to assert power over death or dismiss its finality (i.e., "it could never happen to me"). For instance, in Texas there was a gathering of 300 teenagers to have a "pong fest" (Chavez & Lemos, 2020). Others gathered because they believed that the virus was not as deadly as the scientists and doctors claimed. In addition, the pandemic's severe threat to mortality has shown that egocentrism, especially with the fable of invincibility, is not limited to young adulthood. Adults exhibited similar death denial as they attended super-spreader events,

DOI: 10.4324/9781003251651-5

parties, and activities that put them and others at greater risks of infection (Majra et al., 2021).

Egocentrism was a concept developed by developmental psychologist Jean Piaget (Hanna, 2017). Piaget argued that egocentrism is most prominent during adolescence and entails a self-centeredness that cultivates a preoccupation with the self, where the person believes that others are just as interested in their appearance, goals, and behaviors. This inflated sense of importance leads to the personal fables, where individuals believe they are extraordinarily unique so that no one can understand them or could ever experience a negative emotional state as they have. Around the mid-teen years, egocentrism is less prevalent as adolescents develop a greater sensitivity to the needs, realities, and emotions of others. Understanding the experiences of others cultivates self-reflection and a more realistic self-perception.

In addition to egocentrism, there are many other variables that influence young adults' decisions to deny or defy mortality—cultural values, education, the quality of supportive relationships, and so on. The person has contextual influences for how or what to choose, but the decision is their own—not left to history, brain development, peers, society, parents, or fate. An egocentric lens reveals populations of youth (and adults) that deny death, but this lens disregards populations that fully acknowledge and appreciate mortality. For instance, Shahbaz et al. (2021) conducted a phenomenographic study that surveyed 25 university students in Pakistan in order to understand how young adults perceived the COVID-19 pandemic and lockdowns. The researchers found four major themes amongst the sample's interview data: escape into peace, hope for personal freedom, fear of falling victim to the virus (mortality awareness), and concerns pertinent to school and careers. Shahbaz et al. (2021) found that these themes revealed perceptions that seek hope and life amongst a prevalent fear of infection (most notably one's mortality). This study discovered a population of young adults that were sensitive to the existential significance of their mortality.

Managing the Terror of Death

Many young adults find themselves intimidated by the immensity of the reality of existentialism, especially if they are without growth-promoting relationships or coping strategies to promote understanding, learning, and well-being (Dewa et al., 2014; Mikulincer et al., 2004). The result is a sense of loneliness anxiety, where the idea of being alone (i.e., the concern of isolation) causes excessive amounts of distress. Temporary therapy is achieved through escapism by immersion in what young adults feel are necessary distractions. These include such things as social media, Internet and smartphone use, materialism, or over-identification with cultural features. What exactly motivates young adults is more complex than solely existential terror, but how they manage the terror is important for understanding the essences of experience.

Terror management theory (TMT) argues that the terror of death is managed by immersion in culture, relationships, and even career labors, all of which offer a sense of symbolic death transcendence. Death anxiety is thwarted by upholding cultural or in-group values that sustain self-worth, so that when people die they can rest assured that their identity will live on through their contribution (Dewa et al., 2014). Cultural groups reify identities, which become buffers against death anxiety. The social labors that generate self-esteem help manage existential terror (Lifshin et al., 2017). TMT proffers that these human activities are necessary so that people can function in society, otherwise they would be immobilized by the anxieties from the inevitable process of dying and the finality of death.

Furthermore, TMT holds that human beings are unique in that they generate cultural paradigms, social institutions, artefacts, and expressions as a way to lessen death anxiety (Greenberg et al., 2004; Solomon et al., 2004). Culture therefore became an evolving process to manage the terror of death. There are rules and norms within a culture that mitigates the terror by denying realities. For instance, most women in Western culture are required to conceal the processes of aging, adhere to impossible standards of beauty, as well as conceal their menstrual cycle processes, all of which are reminders of mortality (Goldenberg & Roberts, 2004).

TMT also understands that the risky behaviors from young adults (and adults) exhibit

> a way to resolve their existential fear of death. It is not that they consciously decide whether they want to live or to die when they engage in a risky behavior, rather what guides the behavior is the "walking on the edge," limit testing, and a sense of aliveness.
>
> (Taubman-Ben-Ari, 2004, p. 104)

Surviving or succeeding risks increases self-esteem and illusions of mastery over life, which promotes future risk-taking. For young adults, managing risks and promoting habits conducive for well-being can be accomplished by focusing on the preciousness of life instead fear of death.

Healing from trauma means having spaces to comprehend the events as well as finding their significance for appreciating the miracle of life. Many survivors of trauma have reported that "recognition of meaninglessness in the first sense—incomprehensibility—that appears to serve as a catalyst for the creation of the meaning in the second sense—significance" (Janoff-Bulman & Yopyk, 2004, p. 122). Creating meanings that offer significance to traumatic events move young adults beyond certainties once known. Overestimating security and certainty means minimizing exposure to uncertainty, randomness, and things that cannot be controlled (i.e., nature). However, even though one can heal and choose to move forward from trauma, the direct experience (such as the death of a loved one) has become a psychological touchstone, where loss and death are readily available reminders.

Existential Terror and the Necessary Distractions   49

In addition, TMT explores multicultural possibilities where people can redefine their cultural paradigms and practices to create inclusive meanings (Salzman & Halloran, 2004). Multicultural practices, labors, and identities will create new avenues in which people can manage the terror of death.

Although TMT makes important contributions for understanding existential terror, some conclusions have limitations. TMT's principal argument is that a person's motivation for forming relationships and engaging in social efforts is to manage their existential terror. Although TMT is relevant to the topic of this book, humanistic psychological foundations are more pertinent to consider the possibilities and potentials of human motivation (i.e., altruism, empathy) and the self-actualizing power of relationships.

Knowing the Night

An enlightened existential awareness generates a deep valuing of life, to where one is attuned to the world in compassionate and loving ways. Reaching out to the world and developing growth-promoting relationships helps young adults come to know the impermanent nature of life (Yalom, 2009). Appreciating impermanence means the willingness to face existential concerns as a darkness without form or end—an eternal source of mystery and wonder. There are some that misperceive shadows as fearful or terrifying. However, as Camus (1991) said, "There is no sun without shadow, and it is essential to know the night...The struggle itself toward the heights is enough to fill a man's heart" (p. 123). The shadows of existentialism are not separate from ourselves. They are a necessary part of Being. Our human ability to face, explore, and create meaning within realities is a triumph in and of itself. A multicultural humanistic paradigm blossoms from existential awareness—where people across the globe enter dialectics and creations of new meanings. In the realm of relationships, human beings actualize their potentials.

However, young adults may not have perceived a triumphant human community in 2020, as the death tolls from COVID-19 accumulated into the millions. The disturbing reality became tangible when family members were lost, virus testing centers became a neighborhood staple, schools transitioned to online learning, facemasks became mandatory, businesses shutdown, and curfews enacted (Calder et al., 2020; Bland, 2020). Perhaps some misperceived that the race to develop a vaccine was just a way to keep humans from becoming extinct, or an obligatory act from scientists and the government. In this case, young adults need an empowering existential framework that is based in multicultural humanistic psychology—where a perceptual shift reveals a different reality to what human lessons can be derived from the pandemic.

Within the shadows of the pandemic's reality were stories of healthcare professionals that worked overtime in dangerous conditions, psychologists that sought to reach clients in quarantine via video conference, teachers that labored

50   Part I

and innovated new ways to reach their students in the online environment, and scientists that worked tirelessly to discover breakthroughs in virology. These efforts show that the story of the pandemic is one of a united human community which actualized potentials for compassion, empathy, courage, and discipline to alleviate suffering and preserve life. The extreme existential reminders of death, meaninglessness, isolation, and freedom of choice realigned the world with the realities of existence and a clearer portrait of human nature.

Existential philosophy is at the heart of multicultural humanistic psychology. It is a framework that provides unique insights and directions for a global community that is fatigued from death anxieties. The power to live forward lies in the ability to embrace the existential realities of the human condition.

Expanding an Inclusive Existential Philosophy

In the nineteenth and twentieth centuries, European and American philosophers, writers, and artists developed a Western canon of thought called existentialism. This paradigm became a mode of inquiry into the human experience of Being. The foundational issue was not understanding why we exist but, rather, exploring a fascination that we exist. The writings of Søren Kierkegaard, Martin Heidegger, Jean-Paul Sartre, Friedrich Nietzsche, and Fyodor Dostoevsky were influential for developing a Western paradigm based in subjective meanings and the finiteness of existence; while placing the power of choice in the hands of people instead of fates or mystical powers. Existentialism was to be more than just a philosophy, as it sought to develop a praxis to empower individuals to determine their own lives and meanings.

There have been scholars in the humanities and sciences that have understood existence by means of reductionist conclusions and fatalisms, which minimalized phenomena as a means to gain power over them (Martin et al., 2004; Merleau-Ponty, 2002). Existentialists were radical in that they dismissed these conclusions in a way to give existence back its phenomenal qualities. Each philosopher offered a new perspective that developed this Western philosophy, as "Kierkegaard's Christian existentialism emphasizing freedom and choice; Nietzsche's iconoclastic determinism; Heidegger's focus on temporality and authenticity; Camus' sense of absurdity; Jean Paul Sartre's stress on commitment in the fact of absolute gratuitousness" (Yalom, 2009, p. 200). Existential philosophy acknowledged that, "*we humans are the only creatures for whom our own existence is the problem*" (Yalom, 2009, p. 200). In this problem, we are able to find possibilities and potentials in a *science of being*, for how to live and create meaning (May, 1983).

Existentialism is not a burdensome reminder that one has the arduous task of making countless decisions or that mortality looms in the shadows ready to snatch one up. Rather, existentialism is a soft whisper at any given moment to remind us: *experience sounds, sights, smells, feelings, sensations, and tastes of this moment; for there will be nothing like it ever again; take a moment to appreciate it but then let go and be*

Existential Terror and the Necessary Distractions 51

in it; the purpose of you is to Be, so Be; go; move with it all and make it count! Within the moment is the power of decision. A person can decide how to engage a circumstance and create its meanings. The existential orientation frees the person from having to accept the conclusions and meanings of others.

, Once an existential awareness is embraced the absurdity of predetermined conclusions comes into view; where cultural norms, social practices, judgments, and especially materialism become tenuous. As described by Camus (1991),

> The absurd man thus catches sight of a burning and frigid, transparent and limited universe in which nothing is possible but everything is given, and beyond which all is collapse and nothingness. He can then decide to accept such a universe and draw from it his strength, his refusal to hope, and the unyielding evidence of a life without consolation.
>
> *(p. 60)*

Acceptance of existentialism can be difficult for many young adults that have misperceptions or misunderstandings of the paradigm. Caring adults can provide spaces, resources, and partnership guidance in order to help young adults create meanings and decide how to write their life story. Otherwise, "there are many people who reach their conclusions about life like schoolboys; they cheat their master by copying the answer out of a book without having worked out the sum for themselves" (Kierkegaard, 1959, p. 53). Living according meanings determined by others causes despair or a sickness unto death, in which life no longer resonates with the person (Kierkegaard, 2004). Rather, existentialism reveals the absurdity of predetermined meanings and that we can work to create possibilities in the here-and-now, accepting *what is*.

Developing an existential attitude means becoming fascinated that we exist. Heidegger (1962) explored the phenomenon of *Being* and its problem of definition—because it cannot be contained to the limits of an entity, as our logic determines for things. Being is not an entity and thus cannot be stated as a meaning but, rather, as Husserl (2012) described, Being is *"fundamentally something that is defined otherwise than as that which is given in perception as corporeal reality, which is given exclusively through its sensory determinations, among which must also be reckoned the sensori-spatial"* (p. 75). As Sartre (2007) described, to realize Being "is simply *to be there*; those who exist let themselves be encountered, but you can never deduce anything from them" (p. 131). When young adults may wonder how death factors into Being. The greatest surprise happens when one realizes,

> you don't die because you were never born. You had just forgotten who you are...In death we doff the *persona*, as actors take off their masks and costumes in the green room behind the scenes. And just as their friends come behind the stage to congratulate them on the performance, so one's own

52   Part I

friends should gather at the death-bed to help one out of one's mortal role, to applaud the show, and, even more, to celebrate with champagne or sacraments (according to taste) the great awakening of death.

(Watts, 1966, pp. 40–41)

Within existentialism, one appreciates the phenomenological nature of existence, where essences exist within a phenomenon and death is not the end of essence, but rather its impermanence and transient nature.

There are four major and universal existential concerns that Yalom (1980) outlined as "death, freedom, isolation, and meaninglessness" (p. 10). Yalom (2015) explained that within these concerns people develop narratives that "deal with anxiety about death, about the loss of loved ones and the ultimate loss of oneself, about how to live a meaningful life, about coping with aging and diminished possibilities, about choice, about fundamental isolation" (p. 211). These ideas became foundational for the development of existential psychology. Since then, it has reached new depths and expanded into other fields of study. Existential psychological principles have been adopted by many discourses, such as education, counseling, and nursing. The praxis of existential psychology is achieved by:

1. Recognizing that life is at times unfair and unjust.
2. Recognizing that ultimately there is no escape from some of life's pain and from death.
3. Recognizing that no matter how close I get to other people, I must still face life alone.
4. Facing the basic issues of my life and death, and thus living my life more honestly and being less caught up in trivialities.
5. Learning that I must take ultimate responsibility for the way I live my life no matter how much guidance and support I get from others.

(Yalom, 1985, p. 92)

Although accepting these parameters may cause stress for young adults, growth-promoting relationships provide the necessary resources and opportunities to make them achievable. Taking responsibility for living means that the young adult "is nothing else but that which he makes of himself" (Sartre, 1948, p. 28).

Young adults experience rifts amongst inner-core values and culturally determined ones when the external values no longer satisfy inner existential angst. To question one's own cultural paradigm can be a disconcerting process, as the world that was known is no longer as it appeared. The person realizes that the meanings of others do not reflect a fluid, intersectional identity that seeks unique directions.

Peers and adults may disapprove, disregard, or remove meanings that young adults have created and offer no substitutions (Moustakas, 1995). For instance, spiritual meanings can be a major factor in well-being for one person, while having no value for another. Young adults that experience violence against the meanings they have created begin to question their self-worth. The meanings that develop throughout young adulthood that seek to know, keep sacred, give purpose, and are growth promoting are valid.

To safeguard against the violence toward personal meanings, people must be proactive in developing an awareness of the cultural ideas and practices that do not resound within. To develop a critical awareness offers perspective on meaning, absurdity, and purpose. Existential philosophy is a supportive guide for forming values and exploring inner directions. The praxis comes in the form of making decisions on how to live in the here-and-now. This important for young adults to practice as they will have (if not already experience) complex situations where decisions must be made. Developing trust in oneself for making choices is integral for realizing existential lessons (Kierkegaard, 1959; Sartre, 1966). Existentialism empowers young people to create meaningful relationships so that the angst deep within can find an avenue to be lived out, understood, and appreciated as a relational factor to the rest of the universe. Failures, shame, regret, guilt, and limitations are just natural parts of being human and their intensities are related to the spectrum of cultural absurdities (Gnaulati, 2020).

Discovering Relationships with the World

Young adults may be inclined to compare future experiences to those they had during the pandemic. Trauma does not allow the subject to forget. The pandemic will become an existential reference for future circumstances. Many are preoccupied with memories, haunted by anxieties, or even form certain habits, all of which seek to make sense of an extremely disturbing event. Although young adults can give the impression of equanimity and having moved on, the terror of death of the self and for loved ones continues to shake beneath feigned smiles and empty words. The power of mortality awareness encourages young adults to either move forth to accept reality, or resist (which can also include forms of apathy). Resistance will disorient and disrupt the unfolding processes of self-actualization (Yalom, 1985).

Cultural transcendence is not a deconstruction that leaves one with nothing, but rather a wider awareness of the no-thing-ness, which opens opportunities to become not only one thing, but many things; inclusive of other paradigms and beings. Young adults may wish to explore other cultural ideas and customs that are aligned with their values—in this manner young adults become cosmopolitan—finding a self in relation to a greater global paradigm. Existentialism and humanistic psychology were not designed to solely align people to upper-class values, assuming that young adults have the resources, time, or opportunities to travel, explore, and readily meet all of needs in Maslow's Hierarchy. Rather, the existential foundations of humanistic psychology are meant to encourage young adults to live within a diversity of circumstances and situations in order to become attuned to the world around them and the impermanent nature of life.

With peers, nature, animals, teachers, coaches, or plants, young adults can attune themselves to the space between things and create meanings therein. Although young adults cannot (or have great challenges to) change certain circumstances, the one inalienable right is the freedom to determine what things mean (Frankl, 2006). This right is exercised best in growth-promoting relationships, which provide equitable opportunities for young adults to achieve culturally relative self-actualizing processes.

Existentialism encourages young adults to develop an inclusive multicultural paradigm. This is important for a rapidly interconnecting world, where there are more opportunities to create meanings across paradigms. The lines between Eastern and Western cultures have blurred considerably since the beginning of the twenty-first century, as the Internet has connected more people and ideas across the world than ever before. Many of the existentialists and humanistic psychologists in the mid-twentieth century advocated for multicultural inclusivity in their existential frameworks. In fact, Heidegger was influenced by Zen Buddhism and Taoism in his understanding of the non-self *Dasein,* which is "the nature of human selfhood...the freedom of this nature allows us to see, or more commonly to ignore, the unnerving mystery of self-existence" (Bradford, 2020, p. 44). The Eastern metaphor of the self in the stream of eternity was the basis for Heidegger's understanding of human essence.

The momentum of the late twentieth century's multicultural movement in the U.S. challenged the Western canon for its cultural exclusiveness, especially in existential thought. Cultural paradigms of Eastern, Native American, Aboriginal, and indigenous peoples had been historically marginalized, and many groups and scholars advocated for equality. There were meaningful ways of knowing existence that have been completely destroyed, while others assimilated—the choice was made by those in power. The death of an existential paradigm was not only a loss of knowledge, but also of coping strategies that created meanings of death, meaninglessness, isolation, and freedom—this violence has had harmful epigenetic effects for indigenous people (Salzman & Halloran, 2004). Equity for cultural paradigms means acknowledging the damage and destruction that colonizers and imperialists did to non-Western cultures' existential paradigms (Mika, 2015; Spinelli, 2019). As a result of the diversity within an inclusive existential philosophy, our understandings of existence have expanded.

Young adults must come to realize that their cultural paradigm has not been static, but has had historical influences and interactions with others cultures over millennia. There is an infinity of historical cultural traces within paradigms. Critically analyzing one's cultural paradigm through histories, values, and norm formation is important for understanding relationships to others. This is why multicultural humanistic psychology seeks to affirm subjugated and marginalized forms of existential knowledge. With more cultural resources to create meanings and explore existential concerns, a young adult can find out for oneself what it means to die; then there is no fear, therefore every day is a new day—and I really mean this, one *can* do this—so that your mind and your eyes see life as something totally new. That is eternity.

(Krishnamurti, 1973, p. 84)

Finding oneself in eternity means recognizing the resplendence of sharing existence with other beings. Furthermore, the absurdity of a static self is given up in favor of an enlightened realization.

Cultivating an existential awareness begins, as Watts (1979) stated, with such a question as, "Where do I begin and end in space? I have relations to the sun and air, which are just as vital parts of my existence as my heart" (p. 49). Seeing or hearing deeply, touching things with wonder, experiencing the space between oneself and others, and letting go into full pre-reflective experiences places young adults in positions to realize that life and death are two intervals in the stream of eternity. The essences of phenomena are unique but also share spaces with everything. For young adults to develop a phenomenological attitude toward relationships, they must begin to dismantle the static images of things and greet phenomena as they truly are. The silence of the moment and the space between things hold potential to enlighten youth to the phenomenon of existence. Existential awareness is not something to be fought, conquered, ignored, or destroyed—because the only modicum of sense anything makes is through the living moment, in which loses its profundity upon consideration.

Relationships with caring adults and peers offer young adults opportunities to express their emergent understandings of existential concerns, while exploring new themes. However, they may not be aware of constructive strategies for expression in order to empower the relationship, nor have the vocabulary yet to share such thoughtful insights (Gavin, 2019). Existentialism places the absurd, socially determined formalities for expressing emotions, knowledge, or realizations in question. How deeply can a young adult express an existential insight through a multiple-choice test or as a short-spoken response? It is better to open up different modalities of expression, which in turn will strengthen the relationship and promote personal growth. There are limitless ways to express and explore existential concerns and themes. Avenues for expression may include: writing abstract poetry or haiku, film-making, animation, daily drawing to learn how to *see* things, mindful awareness practices, hiking, caring for animals, or even expression through dancing. All of these avenues reflect a loving embrace of the world, in which self-expression is meant to strengthen the relationships.

The inner flow of creativity and authenticity of the person experienced many obstacles during the pandemic. Returning to normal must now mean sensitively checking in with the person to see if this flow has been obstructed or disrupted. If so, caring adults such as educators and mental health professionals can work to provide opportunities so young adults can resonate with their environment and experiences—unblocking a flow of meaning and expression toward self-actualization (Bland & DeRobertis, 2017). Relationships with the world hold powerful healing forces and are depthless sources of awe, resilience, and faith, where Being is the purpose (Moustakas, 1956). Existential awareness within a relationship can happen by staring at the clouds, a flower, walking a dog, dancing with another, eating, exercising, or creating.

The Loneliness of Death

Western culture has typically promoted mourning as an individual, solitary process, unless the community has suffered collective trauma (Testoni et al., 2021). The opportunities for youth to collectively cope with personal experiences with mortality have been limited. During the pandemic, the time to cope with dying loved ones had been shortened due to the violent nature of the virus's effects on the body. As a result of the quick and tragic deaths, the time to explore and develop existential meanings was limited. Many young adults did not have enough time to prepare their hearts. The goal now is to return to make peace with the past and within the living moment. Existentialism means removing the veil of invincibility.

Young adults of all age brackets have a natural curiosity of death, but the pandemic cultivated death anxiety. Death for the self is "an always possible nihilation of my possibles which is outside my possibilities" (Sartre, 1966, p. 657). The death anxiety was reinforced by the constant state of emergency, as well as disturbing images of body bags and overcrowded hospitals.

The loss of family members or friends fundamentally disrupted young adults' support systems for well-being and equanimity. Over one million people in the U.S. experienced the loss of a loved one during the pandemic. Moreover, Verdery et al. (2020) discovered the "bereavement multiplier," which estimated that for every one death caused by COVID-19, nine people experienced bereavement. The researchers found that young adults are,

> at comparably high risk of losing parents and grandparents, the subset of the population with the highest documented COVID-19 fatality rates. Tracking these differences will illuminate some of the broader population health challenges that COVID-19–associated deaths will leave in their wake, and the potential for them to act as future sources of disparities among youth (18–20).
> *(Verdery et al., 2020, pp. 17695–17696)*

Whether through the fear of losing someone or the actual grief from loss, COVID-19 has had traumatic emotional impacts on youth.

Many people will protect themselves from further emotional turmoil by denying new relationships or distancing themselves from existing ones (with other people and the world). Koole and Van Den Berg (2004) reported:

Existential Terror and the Necessary Distractions **57**

Individuals who are chronically prone to experience high levels of threat or anxiety may be driven by self-defense needs to a greater degree than are low-anxious individuals. When self-defense needs predominate, people will respond highly defensively to nature, for instance, by psychologically distancing themselves from nature or by seeking out cultivated environments...Moreover, individuals who are reminded of death are especially likely to support beliefs that humans are distinct from animals and to report being disgusted by animals.

(p. 92)

Denying relationships with nature and animals has deleterious effects for young adults' well-being and development. Relationships are needed to support coping strategies and exploration of existential concerns. Animals and plant life do not have the death anxieties that humans experience; only humans have created paradigms that make death into something other than the nature of itself. Disgust or denial of animals and plants seeks to abstractify life into a hierarchy of value, worth, and intelligence. Empathy in this scenario can be dangerous to the illusion that humans are exempt from death and decay, because it leads one into the lived experience of other beings, opening relational possibilities. Young adults must then suppress their empathy, so the perceptual/sensational union can be withheld in order to escape reality. The deterioration of empathic abilities with animals and nature will naturally extend into the human world, creating inner- and intra-personal destruction like no other.

Death anxiety is common during states of emergency. Young adults observe how adults cope and manage through the events. If they see influential adults in panic, reject nature and animals, distance themselves from relationships, then young adults are highly likely to develop similar values toward those ideas and behaviors—as if to learn: *perhaps this is how it is done, and I can give it a try too*. If observed values greatly conflict with inner values, the young adult may reject those ideas, ways of behaviors, and even the adult.

During emergencies, the adults that once provided certainty and guidance (as if they had authority on the proper way to live) are seen to have frailties and faults. It can be overwhelming for young adults to realize that they share the same existential givens as adults. The person must take responsibility for how to live and to determine what it will mean to die. As existentialists believe, living well means dying well. Dying with grace and without fear can be difficult for those in a Western paradigm, because death was historically believed to be the end and not the beginning of another journey.

As Yalom (2009) described,

Adults who are racked with death anxiety are not odd birds who have contracted some exotic disease, but men and women whose family and culture have failed to knit the proper protective clothing for them to withstand the icy chill of mortality.

(p. 117)

One is able to test the tensile strength of cultural apparatuses to buffer death anxiety the closer the great transition looms or the greater the threat of a deadly virus. No other existential concern can haunt like death does; as its tremors can be felt at our deepest levels of Being and at the outermost edges of our knowings (Yalom, 1980). Many young adults worldwide had (or continue to have) trouble coping with the grief of death or home trauma brought on by the COVID-19 pandemic (Organisation for Economic Co-operation and Development, 2020). Some were required to take on financial responsibilities of their parents that lost employment or even passed away. Although the existential earthquake may be over for now, its aftershocks can take place for the rest of this generation's lives, influencing character and lifelong habits. The maladaptive coping methods will fail to realize that *"death is the condition that makes it possible for us to live life in an authentic fashion"* (Yalom, 1980, p. 31)

Existential Loneliness: Solitude and Broken Life

Throughout young adulthood a sense of loneliness may increase from the early teens to the early twenties, as individuals seek to increase the number of close relationships in complex social spheres (van Roekel et al., 2018). Loneliness is an experience that is typically associated with undesirable negative emotions, where there is a disjunction between the actual number and quality of one's relationships with what is personally desired.

A person's life has periods of loneliness and each phase or circumstance may bring about new experiences or meanings. However, in young adulthood loneliness oscillates in intensity, as development and circumstance may be (un)favorable for developing the desired relationships (i.e., issues of privacy, immaturity, failures to establish relations, etc.) (Çakir & Çetinkaya, 2020). Although not many young adults would not seek to be lonely, Moustakas (1961) found that it is an essential element of the human condition. The incomparable emotions of emptiness, angst, and disappointment, which make up the negative sides of loneliness, are gateways to creating the meanings of isolation. Loneliness can be found in many life experiences, such as loss, rejection, illness, failure, as well as in success, creativity, or meditation. Young adults cultivate enlightenment if they switch their perception of loneliness from something to be avoided or defended against to a necessary exploration of their solitude in the universe.

Loneliness provides opportunities for young adults to explore potential values, meanings, and paths to take. Initially, submitting entirely to loneliness can be terrifying, but this pain and anguish will pass one into a realm of authenticity and inner resources that bring awe and vibrancy to life. Loneliness can be an emancipatory experience, as Moustakas (1961) explained:

Loneliness involves a unique substance of self, a dimension of human life which taps the full resources of the individual. It calls for strength, endurance, and

Existential Terror and the Necessary Distractions   **59**

sustenance, enabling a person to reach previously unknown depths and to realize a certain nakedness of inner life.

(p. 8)

The empowering qualities of loneliness help young adults dismantle social norms,
cultural demands, and stereotypes to live and express themselves as they always
wished to, even if that means exploring these processes day to day. Tolerance of
loneliness means accepting uncomfortableness or uncertainties to courageously
embrace the solitude. Loneliness will then take one back to life, where all relationships are a privilege and each day is lived diligently.

The Icy Chill of Death

The genre of young adult fiction can be a powerful tool in helping youth explore
existential themes. Within the stories, young adults empathically relate to characters so that they reflectively explore the meanings of their own life experiences.
For this generation of young adults, the popularity of comic book superhero or
villain characters has allowed authors to reach large audiences.

For instance, Lauren Myracle's *Victor and Nora: A Gotham Love Story* (2020)
(illustrated by Isaac Goodhart) is a graphic novel where readers follow two young
adults named Victor Fries and Nora Kumar through their romantic relationship.
This graphic novel is the backstory to the Batman series villain Mr. Freeze.
However, this story follows the influence of one of the most successful reima-
gining for a villain in the D.C. comic universe—with the authorship of Paul Dini
and direction of Bruce Timm in *Batman: The Animated Series* (1992) episode
"Heart of Ice" (first aired on September 7, 1992).

In "Heart of Ice," a new villain appears in Gotham City using his freezing gun
(that literally turns anything to ice in its sights) to steal technology from Goth-
Corp's science laboratories. Batman realizes that the stolen pieces are meant to
build a giant freeze cannon, but for what purpose? The detective finds evidence
that the perpetrator known as Mr. Freeze is a cryogenic scientist named Victor
Fries, who invented a deep-freeze chamber that holds his wife until a cure can be
found for her inoperable life-limiting illness. The CEO of GothCorp, Ferris
Boyle, discovers the secret project, confronts Victor, and ultimately causes an
altercation that results in the destruction of the cryogenic chamber holding Nora.
Victor's physical composure is irreparably changed by the chemical spills, so that
he can now only survive in subzero temperatures. Batman has to bring Boyle to
justice before Mr. Freeze serves Boyle a dish of cold revenge.

"Heart of Ice" won a Daytime Emmy Award for Outstanding Writing in an
Animated Program. Timm and Dini turned a clichéd, comical, and campy villain
from the 1960s into one of tragedy and depth; reflecting the fear of losing loved
ones to illness, the grief of loss, and what the icy chill of death can mean for
people's lives. The graphic novel *Victor and Nora* is the backstory to this storyline,

but it is set in contemporary Gotham City, where Victor and Nora are both two lonely young adults exploring their existential concern of mortality.

In Myracle's (2020) novel, Victor Fries is a gifted young scientist, particularly for cryogenic research. He works as an intern at Boyle Labs seeking to achieve a technique that can fully suspend the animation of life. Nora has been diagnosed with a life-limiting neurological illness called Chrysalisis, in which she is mindful of her remaining time. She plans to commit suicide on her next birthday in order to save her father and brother from the grief of having to see her deteriorate. She also does not want to suffer from a neurological demise. Both young adults had suffered early deaths of family members, Victor's older brother and Nora's mother. They serendipitously meet while visiting their deceased in a graveyard.

The character of Nora is full of life and love as her illustrated panels show vibrancy and warm colors. She has decided to live her remaining year in this life with no reservations and a mindful appreciation of life's beauty and wonder. Nora's inner dialogue is filled with excitement and passion. Victor's panels are drawn with colder tones, with text bubbles that show logical thinking and reflections in solitude. The two fall in love quickly. Their mindfulness of mortality allows them to encounter each other with authenticity, which deepens the quality of relationship in a short period of time. Readers find that their relationship does not form out of loneliness anxiety or fear of death. Nora and Victor did not seek a relationship in order to fill a need or be distracted from inner angst. Instead, both young adults have an existential awareness and chose to create meanings that motivated them to live more diligently, for each other.

In their growth-promoting relationship, Nora helps Victor *warm up* and find authentic ways of expressing himself and relating. Victor offers Nora love, in that regardless of her diagnosis and shortened time on earth, they could choose to endure the illness together. He offers presence for her in ways that do not distract or give false hope; but rather to hold her hand and face the darkness of mortality together. Secretly, Victor has hope of discovering a cure, and works tirelessly to save his beloved from death.

The reader is emotionally moved by seeing how Victor loves Nora for the unique person she is and not as a static image labeled with an illness. Victor and Nora's tragic story haunts readers because it forces us to face the reality of death of our loved ones, and for ourselves. This is a cautionary tale to where if we deny death, we may end up in a frozen and rigid state, as Victor does—no longer living in this world, but as an observer behind frosted glass. Or, as Nora shows us, death is a reality that can teach us how to live more diligently, authentically, and intensely. She ultimately does not choose suicide, but accepts her fate as an act of love for Victor, to show him that beautiful things must also pass.

At the end of the novel there are mental health resources for young adult readers to gain support if they are having suicide ideation. Suicide is not normalized in the book, but rather demystified in a way that offers perspective into someone that has these thoughts due to a life-limiting illness. Young adult readers can dispel feelings of shame or guilt for having thoughts about death as they relate to Nora. She rejected the option of suicide, which demonstrates to readers that no matter the circumstance, life is always the right choice. The imperative need for stories like this comes from the fact that for young adults worldwide suicide is the second leading cause of death (Ibrahim et al., 2019).

Many works in young adult fiction, such as *Victor and Nora*, facilitate an exploration of existential concerns in safe ways, where the characters and story-universes provide meaningful backdrops to interests. The existential loneliness that Victor and Nora experienced placed them in a position to form a growth-promoting relationship, rather than a loneliness anxiety, where they needed the other to fill an inner void. The difference between existential loneliness and loneliness anxiety is important to understand in young adulthood because one can be growth promoting, while the other bitter cold.

According to Moustakas (1961) the experience of existential loneliness is designated by "an intrinsic and organic reality of human life in which there is both pain and triumphant creation emerging out of long periods of desolation. In existential loneliness man is fully aware of himself as an isolated and solitary individual" (p. 24). Acceptance of the condition of isolation is key to existential loneliness, as one can find equanimity in solitude, where the person, the world, and the mysteries of the universe are in perfect harmony. The irreversible changes in what Moustakas (1972) designated as the *loneliness of a broken life* can come from the experience of trauma, injury, sickness, or crisis. These can each become gateways into existential loneliness. COVID-19 caused *loneliness of a broken life* for many individuals that were infected or experienced the death of loved ones. The terror of mortality can bring one in touch with the universe and motivation to create new meanings and purposes of life. Solitude provides opportunities for enlightenment, even though it may be the result of tragedy or sadness.

Solitude is important for understanding the experience of existential loneliness. Although its circumstances and meanings may vary, young adults can appreciate solitude as a place to find inner resources and abilities to determine how to move forward or grow from an experience. Some young adults may prefer to explore meanings with peers or adults, while others may prefer to search alone. Regardless of preference, the experience of existential loneliness can only happen within a solitary being. In the aftermath of the pandemic, especially in the *loneliness of a broken life*, there is a need to figure out what disturbing experiences could mean and how to accept the reality of existential isolation. If young adults reject the reality of isolation and do not explore their solitude, they may be lost in a torrent of escapism, dissolving themselves into cultivated environments, materialism, and intense stimulation. This is the path into the disorienting, dizzy depths of loneliness anxiety.

Loneliness Anxiety: Streaming in the Darkness

When loneliness generates intense angst that exceeds psychological and social resources for coping, habits form to provide momentary escape from negative emotional states. This motivation to escape reality is due to *loneliness anxiety*—an estrangement of the self, where one is desperate to find immediate gratification, a sense of power or status, material accumulation, fusion into conformity, or rigid patterns of life and meaning. These motivations are for the purpose of evading the reality of existential isolation (Moustakas, 1961).

Many young adults sit up at night starring at a smartphone screen, scrolling through pictures, videos, or steaming content, as if to believe this is a true connection to reality. Cyberspace can promote the illusion of a world with inherent meaning, ageless identities, and immortality, when in fact the night around them silently waits for the screen to turn off. Starring at a bright screen and then clicking off into darkness hurts one's eyes. Being left alone in the darkness with wandering thoughts and unpleasant feelings can bring greater discomfort. The remedy? Click the phone back on, and push oneself to the point of exhaustion. Then, loss of consciousness in what appears to be sleep can skip the terrors of night. This over-simplistic scenario seeks to demonstrate that many young adults seek to cure loneliness anxiety by denying the existential reality of solitude.

The motivation to immerse oneself into prefabricated virtual worlds to mitigate loneliness anxiety is more complex than just warding off existential isolation or death anxiety (Bland & DeRobertis, 2017). There are stimulating and supportive resources that the Internet has to offer, but when it becomes a dependence or problematic use, then the seeds of loneliness anxiety begin to flourish. Loneliness anxiety is a much older phenomenon than the technological revolution. Historically, there have been many social avenues for people to distract themselves, such as overworking, shopping, sporting events, alcohol and substances, cultural immersion, and so on. Loneliness anxiety has been around since Western culture has hurried folks along to achieve progress, gain material wealth, and keep up with the Joneses.

However, with the invention/development of the Internet, people have constructed virtual worlds in which to grant higher global accessibility into realms of digital possibilities. As technologies progress at exponential rates, many have lost a mindful appreciation for the nourishment that food offers, spiritual connections to nature and animals, encountering others with empathy, and the joys of cultivating community. Keeping busy has cut many people off from natural occurring sources for mental well-being. In the social reproduction theory, adults that were raised to overwork, over-consume, and seek intense distractions, transfer these values to children, who will transfer them on to their children, who perhaps may one day become computer programmers and transfer them to artificial intelligence. In 2021, there are countless avenues in which to escape loneliness anxiety; but it is as if trying to escape the dark of night, where it is ever-present outside of the virtual worlds illuminated by LED screens. Online shopping, social media feeds, streaming shows, and posting selfies of strained smiles are just a few activities that can temporarily distract one from loneliness anxiety, as its effects begin to take a toll on well-being.

Loneliness Anxiety's Effects on Well-Being

Researchers around the world are investigating how young adults experience emotional disturbances and the conditions/potentials in which they are fostered. However, cultural paradigms for understanding emotional disturbances vary, as well as their research designs. These differences provoke questions of construct validity—does the study actually measure what it intends? Also in question are the studies' generalizability—would the outcomes or results be similar in different countries? Emotional phenomena do not have direct objects for observation, so it is difficult to assess depression or loneliness when there are such differing conceptions, meanings, and tools of inquiry. However, research efforts largely contribute to understanding emotional phenomena, not because they grasp them entirely, but for the reason that they offer a better understanding of the essence of experience. Husserl (2021) stated that the essences of a phenomenon are not the thing entirely, but only one side, only to find an infinity of sides, which can never be completed. Researchers are exploring phenomena in a way that represents the reality for that specific sample population. The more studies that are produced and interact within the global research community, the more enlightened our understandings will become.

The challenges in young adulthood for developing an identity independent of the family as well as taking on new social roles were intensified by the effects of the pandemic's social distancing, isolation, and threats to life. Home situations became difficult as families faced unemployment and decreases in household income. Youth were also exposed to closer and longer contact with family members that suffer from mental disturbances, had higher exposure to domestic violence, as well as other distressing situations that increased incidence rates of substance abuse, anxiety, depression, and suicide ideation (Biondi & Poduti, 2020; Blosnich et al., 2020; Fegert et al., 2020; Luiggi-Hernández & Rivera-Amador, 2020).

There are about 7.2 billion people in the world, in which 1.2 billion are young adults—this number is a global record for the amount of young people in the world. Out of the entire world population, one out of five young adults have been found to have an emotional disturbance (Çakir & Çetinkaya, 2020). In particular, of the 1.2 billion youth, almost 5% experience depression that has decreased well-being, removed them from enjoyable interests, disturbed sleep, and caused fatigue and diet problems. Two notable types of depression are state and trait. State depression is a period of depression caused by a certain event or circumstance, such as seasonal affective disorder (the state changes with time and circumstance). In trait depression, the symptomology (i.e., an intense and disabling sadness) lasts for six months or longer. Depression of both sorts has been found to have a correlation with loneliness.

In a study of demographic, well-being, and social situations, Franssen et al. (2020) sought to understand if there were life-stage differences for loneliness between 19 years old and 65 years old. The researchers found "an association between psychological factors and loneliness among adults irrespective of life stage. This is in line with prior research showing no age-related differences in the association between depression and loneliness" (p. 7). Young adulthood is victim to intense loneliness just as people in advanced age, so why is it often minimized for youth? An important question to consider: Is loneliness a cause of depression, or perhaps depression removes one from socializing so it leads to loneliness? In Flanders, Danneel et al. (2019) studied the loneliness, social anxiety, and depressive symptomology for young adults in secondary school. The researchers investigated if these challenges were distinguishable, separate phenomena for adolescents. They found that each were independent of the next but had crossovers in symptomology and were usually comorbid. Young adulthood is just as susceptible to the complex and damaging effects of loneliness, but it is often viewed as just a temporary phase of growing up.

Loneliness anxiety affects social well-being and development, so that the intricate interpersonal processes for learning to adapt and function amongst peers are disrupted (Segerstrom et al., 2019). In turn, socio-emotional developments are thrown off balance with the correlative nature of loneliness with depression and/ or anxiety. Perceptual balance of the self and world, where acceptance, meaning, and esteem are developed is important for young adults to try out new behaviors or ways of relating to peers (Portillo & Fernández-Baena, 2020).

There is more to the effects of loneliness in young adulthood than just an increased chance of emotional disturbances; there are physical consequences that pose significant developmental concerns. Loneliness anxiety has been discovered to have strong correlations with obesity, substance abuse, sleep irregularities, pain, disease, premature aging, and early death (Segerstrom et al., 2019; Reinhardt et al., 2020). Young adults that suffer from these challenges to well-being typically remove themselves from the age-normative goals or social activities, which worsens their sense of loneliness anxiety. Loneliness is intense when the social support circle has fewer individuals or the depth of support is minimal. Without them growth-promoting relationships, overall well-being deteriorates. Loneliness anxiety exacerbates the severity of mental disturbances for young adults, which can lead to thoughts of self-harm or even suicide ideation.

To Be or Not to Be

Distorted perceptions of reality may lead a young adult to believe that suicide is a valid solution to an unsolvable life challenge. When coping mechanisms are no longer effective and all available resources and support have been exhausted, a young adult may think there is no other option or way out than to take one's life. Although Albert Camus stated that the only serious philosophical problem is that of suicide, he did not promote it as a solution or option.

According to Gwin et al. (2020), "suicide is a maladaptive coping strategy for which individuals seek to find relief from severe pain of mental hardships"

Existential Terror and the Necessary Distractions   **65**

(p. 275). There are many aspects and circumstances of a young adult's life (i.e., financial hardships, loss of loved ones, relationship challenges, illness, physical conditions) that may lead to the lonely places of suicide ideation, making vulnerability a key factor. As Mirkovic et al. (2020) described,

> Vulnerability is linked to life-long traits such as a personal or family history of [suicidal behavior], early adversity such as childhood sexual abuse, family dysfunction, serotonin dysfunction, and stress regulation by the hypothalamo-pituitary-adrenergic axis, as well as certain deficits in emotional, cognitive or metacognitive processes. Social factors include social isolation and victimization via bullying, sexual discrimination poor social adjustment and low peer connectedness. Among the psychiatric disorders, the strongest associations have been found with all mood dysfunctions, including major depression, dysthymia and bipolar disorder.
>
> *(p. 1730)*

In the philosophical sense, the person has developed a distorted perception that life has a rationalized or materialized purpose, rather than life being a natural process of itself. Failure at "living" in this sense places one in the thought process of: *what is the point of continuing?* Negating the purpose of living is just as absurd and rationalizing why one must go on living—the reasoning should not focus on if one should live, but how to live.

Young adults are curious to explore thoughts of suicide and what the death of loved ones might mean. A young person who experiences the loss of someone through suicide often imagines what it might be like to take their own life. Suicidal ideation is a complex psychological disturbance that has sociological, cultural, and economic underpinnings. These are dark and often ignored realities are in every human society. When people are experiencing a weariness or despair from living mechanically, their consciousness arises for "the gradual return into the chain or it is the definitive awakening. At the end of the awakening comes, in time, the consequence: suicide or recovery" (Camus, 1991, p. 13).

Caring adults can remain beside young adults experiencing difficult times in order to offer support and presence. Adults may also provide appropriate psychological resources so that recovery is chosen. The generalized apathy, fear, or neglect toward young adult suicide ideation needs to be removed from cultural paradigms. The resources that empower adults to feel confident in addressing the issues of suicide are only effective if there is motivation from young adults to engage the issues. Many authors, artists, actors, and musical artists take a proactive approach to raising awareness by creating spaces/opportunities for youth to engage uncomfortable issues. This is why the graphic novel *Victor and Nora* is an example of a creative way to engage young audiences in the issue of suicide and mortality.

In addition, Steven Page and Ed Robertson of the alternative musical group Barenaked Ladies wrote a song that addressed the social apathy toward suicide in their 2003 album *Everything to Everyone*. The song "War on Drugs" contains lyrics that reference the Bloor Street Viaduct in their hometown of Toronto, which is a notorious place for suicide. In addition to the artists and authors that raise awareness, there are many agencies, resources, and professionals meant to serve as safety nets, to catch young adults—but it is everyone's social responsibility to face this neglected darkness. It is also important that a collaborative approach must not cause the problems it seeks to remedy. Overly focusing on issues and quickly labeling young adults places them within stigmas and two-dimensional categories. Many adults seek to cure suicide ideation or associated mental disturbance, when they have not fully understood the contexts and subjectivities in which these phenomena exist. Cautiously, we must explore together and be inclusive in our approaches and methods.

Loneliness anxiety can cause many forms of death and destruction for young adults, as it does for all age groups. In the BBC Loneliness Experiment, researchers studied data on how age, gender, and culture interacted with reported states of loneliness (Barreto et al., 2020). The data came from 237 countries and territories, where participants were between 16 and 99 years of age. The cultural classifications for collectivism and individualism showed no significant distinction for the incidence rate of loneliness. This challenged the idea that people from individualistic cultures experience more rates of loneliness because they promote values of self-reliance, small intimate networks, and individual success. Cultural differences for loneliness cannot be determined by the classification categories, because there are too many confounding variables. Barreto et al. (2020) explained that "cultural differences are sometimes studied by comparing the responses of individuals with different cultural ancestry, but residents in the same country" (p. 2). There are spectrums of difference within cultures that contain unrecognized meanings and coping methods for loneliness and loneliness anxieties. Cross-cultural studies would need to determine differences by investigating multicultural categories and accounting for varieties to gain greater insight.

A study by Ansion and Merali (2018) investigated the diverse populace of Canada, where the 2006 Canadian census reported that 20% of the entire population identified themselves as being born in a different country. The researchers focused the study on Latinx populations because they are the largest population of immigrants in Canada. Of the Latinx population, 29% have at least a bachelor's degree and are between 25 and 44 years of age, and the 60% have a child between 0 and 4 years of age. Ansion and Merali (2018) sought to understand the meanings and adjustment processes of Latinx immigrant parents that were raising children without extended family members.

In the collectivistic values of Latinx culture, the role of the family is integral for child rearing. These include resources and knowledge for cultural socialization, self-actualization, and socio-emotional development opportunities; empathy, love, compassion, and the informational side that accesses previous knowledge, relevant information, and direction for how to manage life situations. This is known as *familia*—where the family (immediate and extended) is a central component to the culture. *Familia* promotes values of community, solidarity, sharing, and loyalty. However, Canadian immigration policy prevents Latinx parents from bringing extended family into the country (Ansion & Merali, 2018). Migration to Canada without extended family may disturb the natural cultural processes of *familia*.

Migrant families generally have greater economic pressures in urban centers and limited access to social and material resources. This causes migrant children to be more susceptible to emotional disturbances, such as loneliness, anxiety, and depression (Ying et al., 2019). Financial hardships have a negative impact on children's ability to adjust to new life situations, as well as for the quality of relationships with caregivers. Many migrant children report psychological distress, most notably loneliness when their guardians are facing economic challenges (Ying et al., 2019). Family units are important for coping with loneliness because they are influential in developing socio-emotional intelligences and behaviors.

Ansion and Merali's (2018) study of immigrant Latinx families in Canada found that without extended familial support there were greater responsibilities placed upon on the parents/guardians, which resulted in higher reported levels of loneliness, anxiety, sadness, and feelings of exhaustion or despair. Only when participants adjusted their lifestyles and created new relationships and support networks (i.e., through school and healthcare resources), were they able to cope and manage the excessive stressors. Some families experienced greater parental involvement, which became a benefit to the family unit. Community support was important in fulfilling the cultural needs of Latinx parents because it compensated for the absence of extended family. Ansion and Merali (2018) found:

> The shifts the parents in this study made appear to have moved them towards Canadian family cultural norms in terms of shared parental responsibility between mothers and fathers and nuclear family cohesion, consistent with the cultural learning perspective on acculturation.
>
> *(p. 421)*

As global migration increases, it is important to be open and receptive of immigrant populations' cultural paradigms, because inclusion will open greater existential perspectives on the experience of loneliness.

Loneliness in a Cyber-Youth

Most social institutions, such as with education, business, or public services, adapted to the social distancing guidelines by creating fully online services. In 2021, as rates of infected persons declined, people slowly started to make an in-person return to classrooms, after-school spaces, stores, restaurants, and workplaces. Virtual components continued to be an essential part of many institutions' operational plans. The pandemic forced people, places, and services to adapt. Those that could not (due to limited resources) adapt struggled considerably or closed. Prior to the pandemic, young adults utilized the Internet and virtual technologies as fundamental resources for learning, informational research, and social interaction. Just over 3 billion people, or 42% of the world's population that used the Internet for social media, reported daily use for an average of 6 hours (Ergun & Alkan, 2020). In a survey of university students, Prievara et al. (2019) found that 82% used the Internet daily, where social media comprised most of the usage. As Internet use was a daily activity for young adults prior to the pandemic, the quarantines and social distancing increased the rates significantly. This was especially so for students that had to switch to virtual learning. Public libraries and colleges provided free Wi-Fi and computer use for underserved populations. A year of habitual online use created lifelong habits and rituals for young adults that factor into long-term well-being.

Virtual worlds helped many institutions and businesses survive the extreme conditions of the pandemic. However, they may have caused developmental setbacks for socio-emotional growth in groups of young adults dependent on the Internet for social interaction, as "loneliness plays a central role in youth's problematic Internet use that may also stem from the lack of social support from peers as well as from parents" (Prievara et al., 2019, p. 1017). The Internet can be an important source of virtual interaction, but when it is a young adult's only sphere, dependency is present, and time spent interacting online exceeds real-world interaction, it becomes a source of loneliness anxiety. Belonging to virtual groups can be of interest and stimulation, but real-world dynamics are irreplaceable for exploring and creating identity, empathy, and interpersonal communication skills. Without a balance of real life and virtual interaction, young adults may experience loneliness and low self-esteem during a critical developmental phase (Çakir & Çetinkaya, 2020).

The more time that young adults spend on social media increases the chance for developing social media disorder (SMD) and problematic Internet use (PIU) (Ergun & Alkan, 2020; Prievara et al., 2019). PIU and SMD are not exclusive to young adulthood, but researchers are finding that they have significant effects on well-being and growth during crucial developmental phases. Both of these phenomena have been shown to resemble addictive-type behaviors, where there is a compulsive need to use the Internet, the habituation and need for more usage, comorbidity with emotional disturbances, and deterioration of real-life social interactions. Most young adults will access the Internet via a smartphone or computer for social media, videos, entertainment, connecting to shared interest groups, research, school work, or even gaming. When the smartphone use becomes the only avenue for social interaction, it has been shown to cause greater feelings of loneliness anxiety and social estrangement (Garakouei et al., 2020).

If young adults spend a disproportionate time in front of a screen, they increase their risks of physical problems, such as obesity and sleep disturbance. Sun et al. (2021) found that a sample of young adults during the pandemic, self-reported an average of 6 h of daily screen media time outside of school and work purposes in the past 2 weeks. In the context of the pandemic, young adults may consume more screen media due to restricted access to other avenues of entertainment, increased media exposure related to COVID-19 (e.g., news, report), and the need for connection with peers.

(p. 11)

The pandemic has created habits and rituals for screen time that virtually fulfills the need for social stimulation. The content and information that they viewed on the Internet were also major factors in well-being. The news about COVID-19 and death tolls caused death anxieties, as disturbing images of hospitals and mobile morgues were shown daily.

In Bolivia, in an online study carried out by Zeballos Rivas et al. (2021), 866 young adults (between the ages of 18 and 25) were surveyed during the pandemic in order to measure how exposure to social media information on COVID-19 impacted risk perception attitudes and preventative behaviors. The researchers found that females that had greater exposure to COVID-19 related information via social media adopted a greater number of higher risk preventative behaviors (e.g., social distancing, wearing masks, washing hands frequently). Zeballos Rivas et al. (2021) recommended, "Understanding the role of social media during the pandemic could help policymakers and communicators to develop better communication strategies that enable the population to adopt appropriate attitudes and behaviors" (p. 2). Social media has gained powerful influence in the lives of young adults and it can become a wider platform to promote well-being and education. As we understand *what* is important to young adults in the social media experience, it is equally important to understand *why* it has such high value.

One's cultural paradigm is important for understanding the value of experience in virtual technologies. Especially during the pandemic, the Internet was a connection to a vast array of virtual worlds, when most of the real world was under quarantine. In this sense, cultural technologies, such as social media platforms, provided resources and tools in order to remedy loneliness, but it also become a foundation for it. Cultural norms and standards have the potential to lower self-esteem for young adults— as social media predominantly shows others' academic or career success, happiness, physical achievements, loving relationships, and opportunities many cannot afford. Critical analysis quickly puts these images and updates into perspective, because one realizes all the failures, trials, challenges, hard work, privileges, or performances that are behind them. Although comparing oneself to successful and happy peers may lower self-esteem, one must realize many of these images are performative, with staged smiles and artificial enactments. When engaging young adults in conversations about social media, it is important to attune empathically, because

we can only understand the subjective experience of another to the extent that we are aware of our own subjectivity. If we are unaware of our own subjective experience, we will remain unaware of how our individual experience partly shades and shapes our understanding of other people's experience.

(Calder et al., 2020, p. 643)

Many adults that log in to social media do well to manage their time, while there are also those that exhibit the same SMD and PIU as those in young adulthood. Our subjective experiences within virtual worlds are important to reflect on—exploring our own feelings and emotions will allow us deeper information as we seek to relate to youth.

There are factors that can help prevent youth from developing PIU, such as growth-promoting relationships, social emotional learning, and supportive social circles. The pandemic altered these spheres, so that the safety nets above mental disturbance and physical ailments were compromised. In addition, young adults that were shy no longer had the positive social dynamic to encourage them to socialize and establish satisfying relationships with peers (Prievara et al., 2019). Contrarily, for some youth victimization and bullying were removed from the school experience which eliminated anxieties and fears for going to school. With the overuse of the Internet, however, the chances and opportunities for cyber-bullying have increased.

The social environments of young adulthood are rapidly changing. The exploration of the self and world must now factor in the virtual spaces (Ergun & Alkan, 2020). During the pandemic, many have had a year of cyber-young adulthood where the only realm to develop and know others was through the Internet. Cyber-victimization, PIU, and SMD have shown to have negative effects on holistic development (Garakouei et al., 2020). One such negative aspect is the development of social anxiety. Simply stated, "social anxiety is characterized by a prominent fear of one or more social situations in which the person is exposed to possible scrutiny by others" (Danneel et al., 2019, p. 1237). Social anxiety caused by online scrutiny, cyber-bullying, or the return to social atmospheres taxes the body's stress systems at the cost of growth and development.

Researchers have found that "lonely adolescents were motivated to use online communication significantly more frequently than others to compensate for their weaker social skills to meet new people" (Ergun & Alkan, 2020, p. 142). PIU and SMD are phenomena that are cultivated by loneliness anxiety, victimization, and rejection. Although PIU and SMD are not necessarily unique to young adulthood, they have greater developmental consequences during this time. The need is for young adults to develop interpersonal skills and socio-emotional intelligences to balance both virtual and real-life spheres. Before helping people learn socio-emotional management strategies, it is important to understand what has motived young adults to develop PIU and SMD and the conditions in which they were cultivated. The focus must always be on the subjective here-and-now: why do they feel the need to do them at this moment? This question will have more valuable information that a historical inquiry.

Existential Terror and the Necessary Distractions **71**

The pandemic cultivated anxieties which influenced many young adults to give into the worlds of constant distraction and intense stimulation. Without psychological resources or social support, many turned to the bright screens for guidance, distraction, or entertainment. The searching was inexhaustible, the scrolling was incessant, and what were they exactly looking for—or looking away from? The pandemic caused trauma to young adulthood which bred new phenomena—where virtual worlds created real world consequences. Within the trauma, intense periods of loneliness have had compounding effects, to where the depths and reaches of loneliness are yet to come. Those without the psychological tools or resources to understand and cope with death and dying may develop death aversion or even become obsessed with death. Creating meaning within relationships is what brings young adults out of the daze of distraction and into an existentialism for living in the here-and-now.

Existential loneliness is fundamental to development. Young adults in social circles need to support one another for allowing solitude its place, while being able to recognize and heal loneliness anxieties. Solitude is not a darkness to be feared, but one that can bring healing and strength, so that when reentering real-life social situations there is greater perspective and courage to face realities. Relationships bring about daily opportunities to create enlightened meanings that motivate young adults to live more diligently and to take better care of themselves and others.

The shock caused by the existential trauma resonates with young adults as they grow and mature. The memories are engrained and emotions still fresh, but "life must be lived forwards," where the forward is in the here-and-now (Kierkegaard, 1959, p. 89). The existential loneliness that is found within existential trauma may hold the courage to turn off digital screens and face the night—only then can young adults experience enlightenment and transcendence.

References

Ansion, M., & Merali, N. (2018). Latino immigrant parents' experiences raising young children in the absence of extended family networks in Canada: Implications for counselling. *Counselling Psychology Quarterly*, 31(4), 408–427. https://doi.org/10.1080/09515070.2017.1324760.

Barreto, M., Victor, C., Hammond, C., Eccles, A., Richins, M. T., & Qualter, P. (2020). Loneliness around the world: Age, gender, and cultural differences in loneliness. *Personality and Individual Differences*, 169, 1–6. https://doi.org/10.1016/j.paid.2020.110066.

Biondi, G., & Poduti, E. (2020). Self-harm behavior in preadolescence: An integrated intervention model pediatric-psychologist. *Pediatric Reports*, 12(2), 15–16.

Bland, A. M., & DeRobertis, E. M. (2017). Humanistic perspective. In V. Zeigler-Hill,& T.K. Shackelford (Eds.), *Encyclopedia of personality and individual differences* (pp. 1–19). Springer International.

Bland, A. M. (2020). Existential givens in the Covid-19 crisis. *Journal of Humanistic Psychology*, 60(5), 710–724. https://doi.org/10.1177/0022167820940186.

Blosnich, J. R., Henderson, E. R., Coulter, R. W. S., Goldbach, J. T., & Meyer, I. H. (2020). Sexual orientation change efforts, adverse childhood experiences, and suicide ideation and attempt among sexual minority adults, United States, 2016–2018. *American Journal of Public Health*, 110(7), 1024–1030. https://doi.org/10.2105/AJPH.2020. 305637.

Çakır, O., & Çetinkaya, A. (2020). Time spent on the Internet, blood pressure, and loneliness in adolescents: A cross-sectional study. *Erciyes Medical Journal / Erciyes Tip Dergisi*, 42(1), 30–36. https://doi.org/10.14744/etd.2019.68815.

Calder, A. J., Novak, L. F., & Lane, A. (2020). We're all going crazy now: How the covid-19 pandemic can promote more compassionate clinical perspectives. *Journal of Humanistic Psychology*, 60(5), 639–646. https://doi.org/10.1177/0022167820938615.

Camus, A. (1991). *The myth of Sisyphus and other essays*. J. O'Brien, Trans. Vintage International.

Chavez, N., & Lemos, G. (2020, July 1). Hundreds of teens at 'pong fest' party exposed to coronavirus, officials say. CNN. https://www.cnn.com/2020/07/01/us/texas-teens-party-coronavirus/index.html.

Danneel, S., Bijttebier, P., Bastin, M., Colpin, H., Van den Noortgate, W., Van Leeuwen, K., Verschueren, K., & Goossens, L. (2019). Loneliness, social anxiety, and depressive symptoms in adolescence: Examining their distinctiveness through factor analysis. *Journal of Child & Family Studies*, 28(5), 1326–1336. https://doi.org/10.1007/s10826-019-01354-3.

Dewa, L. H., Ireland, C. A., & Ireland, J. L. (2014). Terror management theory: The influence of terrorism salience on anxiety and the buffering of cultural worldview and self-esteem. *Psychiatry, Psychology & Law*, 21(3), 370–384. https://doi.org/10.1080/13218719.2013.818520.

Ergun, G., & Alkan, A. (2020). The social media disorder and ostracism in adolescents: (OSTRACA- SM Study). *Eurasian Journal of Medicine*, 52(2), 139–144. https://doi.org/10.5152/eurasianjmed.2020.19076.

Fegert, J. M., Vitiello, B., Plener, P. L., & Clemens, V. (2020). Challenges and burden of the Coronavirus 2019 (COVID-19) pandemic for child and adolescent mental health: A narrative review to highlight clinical and research needs in the acute phase and the long return to normality. *Child & Adolescent Psychiatry & Mental Health*, 14(1), 1–11. https://doi.org/10.1186/s13034-020-00329-3.

Frankl, V. E. (2006). *Man's search for meaning*. Beacon Press.

Franssen, T., Stijen, M., Hamers, F., & Schneider, F. (2020). Age differences in demographic, social and health-related factors associated with loneliness across the adult life span (19–65 years): A cross-sectional study in the Netherlands. *BMC Public Health*, 20 (1118), 1–12. https://doi.org/10.1186/s12889-020-09208-0.

Garakouei, S. A., Mousavi, S. V., Rezaei, S., & Lafmejani, A. Q. (2020). The examination of mediating effects for self-control and time management in relationship among problematic cellphone use with loneliness and educational performance of high school students. *Journal of Educational Sciences & Psychology*, 10(1), 127–140.

Gavin, V. J. (2019). Moving on creatively: Creative existential therapy for children, adolescents and adults. *Existential Analysis: Journal of the Society for Existential Analysis*, 30(1), 45–58.

Gnaulati, E. (2020). Fostering mirthful acceptance in couples therapy: An existential viewpoint. *Existential Analysis: Journal of the Society for Existential Analysis*, 31(2), 368–379.

Goldenberg, J. L., & Roberts, T. (2004). The beast within the beauty: An existential perspective on the objectification and condemnation of women. In J. Greenberg, S. L.

Koole, & T. Pyszczynski (Eds.), *Handbook of experimental existential psychology* (pp. 71–85). Guilford Press.

Greenberg, J., Koole, S. L., & Pyszczynski, T. (2004). Experimental existential psychology: Exploring the human confrontation with reality. In J. Greenberg, S. L. Koole, & T. Pyszczynski (Eds.), *Handbook of experimental existential psychology* (pp. 3–9). Guilford Press.

Gwin, S., Branscum, P., Taylor, E. L., Cheney, M., Maness, S. B., Frey, M., & Ying Zhang. (2020). Associations between suicide behaviors and religiosity in young adults. *American Journal of Health Studies*, 35(4), 257–269.

Hanna, J. L. (2017). Adolescents, egocentrism, and mortality. *Clearing House*, 90(1), 30–33. https://doi.org/10.1080/00098655.2016.1249751.

Heidegger, M. (1962). *Being and time*. Harper & Row.

Husserl, E. (2012). *Ideas: General introduction to pure phenomenology*. Routledge.

Ibrahim, N., Che Din, N., Ahmad, M., Amit, N., Ghazali, S. E., Wahab, S., Abdul Kadir, N. B., Halim, F. W., & A Halim, M. R. T. (2019). The role of social support and spiritual wellbeing in predicting suicidal ideation among marginalized adolescents in Malaysia. *BMC Public Health*, 19(1), 1–9. https://doi.org/10.1186/s12889-019-6861-7.

Janoff-Bulman, R., & Yopyk, D.J. (2004). Random outcomes and valued commitments: Existential dilemmas and the paradox of meaning. In J. Greenberg, S.L. Koole, & T. Pyszczynski (Eds.), *Handbook of experimental existential psychology* (pp. 122–138). Guilford Press.

Kierkegaard, S. (1959). *The journals of Kierkegaard*. A. Dru, Trans. Harper & Row.

Kierkegaard, S. (2004). *The sickness unto death*. A. Hannay, Trans. Penguin Classics.

Koole, S. L., & Van Den Berg, A. E. (2004). Paradise lost and reclaimed: A motivational analysis of human–nature relations. In J. Greenberg, S. L. Koole, & T. Pyszczynski (Eds.), *Handbook of experimental existential psychology* (pp. 86–103). Guilford Press.

Krishnamurti, J. (1973). *The awakening of intelligence*. HarperCollins.

Lifshin, U., Helm, P. J., Greenberg, J., Soenke, M., Ashish, D., & Sullivan, D. (2017). Managing the death of close others: Evidence of higher valuing of ingroup identity in young adults who have experienced the death of a close other. *Self & Identity*, 16 (5), 580–606. https://doi.org/10.1080/15298868.2017.1294106.

Luiggi-Hernández, J. G., & Rivera-Amador, A. I. (2020). Reconceptualizing social distancing: Teletherapy and social inequity during the Covid-19 and loneliness pandemics. *Journal of Humanistic Psychology*, 60(5), 626–638. https://doi.org/10.1177/0022167820937503.

Majra, D., Benson, J., Pitts, J., & Stebbing, J. (2021). SARS-CoV-2 (COVID-19) super-spreader events. *The Journal of Infection*, 82(1), 36–40. https://doi.org/10.1016/j.jinf. 2020.11.021.

Martin, L. L., Campbell, W. K., & Henry, C. D. (2004). The roar of awakening: Mortality acknowledgement as a call to authentic living. In J. Greenberg, S. L. Koole, & T. Pyszczynski (Eds.), *Handbook of experimental existential psychology* (pp. 431–448). Guilford Press.

May, R. (1983). *The discovery of being: Writings in existential psychology*. W. W. Norton & Company.

Merleau-Ponty, M. (2002). *Phenomenology of perception*. Routledge.

Mika, C. (2015). Counter-colonial and philosophical claims: An indigenous observation of Western philosophy. *Educational Philosophy & Theory*, 47(11), 1136–1142. doi:10.1080/00131857.2014.991498.

74 Part I

Mikulincer, M., Florian, V., & Hirschberger, G. (2004). The terror of death and the quest for love: An existential perspective on close relationships. In J. Greenberg, S. L. Koole, & T. Pyszczynski (Eds.), *Handbook of experimental existential psychology* (pp. 287–304). Guilford Press.

Mirkovic, B., Cohen, D., Garny de la Rivière, S., Pellerin, H., Guilé, J.-M., Consoli, A., & Gerardin, P. (2020). Repeating a suicide attempt during adolescence: Risk and protective factors 12 months after hospitalization. *European Child & Adolescent Psychiatry*, 29(12), 1729–1740. https://doi.org/10.1007/s00787-020-01491-x.

Moshman, D. (2011). Adolescents are young adults, not immature brains. *Applied Developmental Science*, 15(4), 171–174. https://doi.org/10.1080/10888691.2011.618098.

Moustakas, C. E (1956). *The self: Explorations in personal growth*. Harper & Brothers.

Moustakas, C. E. (1961). *Loneliness*. Prentice Hall.

Moustakas, C. E. (1972). *Loneliness and love*. Prentice Hall.

Moustakas, C. E. (1995). *Being-In, being-for, being-with*. Jason Aronson.

Myracle, L. (2020). *Victor and Nora: A Gotham love story*. Detective Comics.

Organisation for Economic Co-operation and Development. (2020, June 11). Youth and COVID-19: Response, recovery and resilience. OECD. https://www.oecd.org/coronavirus/policy-responses/youth-and-covid-19-response-recovery-and-resilience-c40e61c6/.

Page, S., & Robertson E. (2003). War on drugs. On Everything to Everyone. Reprise.

Portillo, M., & Fernández-Baena, J. (2020). Social self-perception in adolescents: Accuracy and bias in their perceptions of acceptance/rejection. *Psicologia Educativa*, 26(1), 1–6. https://doi.org/10.5093/psed2019a12.

Prievara, D. K., Piko, B. F., & Luszczynska, A. (2019). Problematic internet use, social needs, and social support among youth. *International Journal of Mental Health & Addiction*, 17(4), 1008–1019. https://doi.org/10.1007/s11469-018-9973-x.

Reinhardt, M., Horváth, Z., Morgan, A., & Kökönyei, G. (2020). Well-being profiles in adolescence: psychometric properties and latent profile analysis of the mental health continuum model—a methodological study. *Health & Quality of Life Outcomes*, 18(1), 1–10. https://doi.org/10.1186/s12955-020-01332-0.

Salzman, M. B., & Halloran, M. J. (2004). Cultural trauma and recovery: Cultural meaning, self-esteem, and the reconstruction of the cultural anxiety buffer. In J. Greenberg, S. L. Koole, & T. Pyszczynski (Eds.), *Handbook of experimental existential psychology* (pp. 231–246). Guilford Press.

Sartre, J. P. (1948). *Existentialism and humanism*. P. Mairet, Trans. Haskell House.

Sartre, J. P. (1966). *Being and nothingness: An essay on phenomenological ontology*. Washington Square Press.

Sartre, J. P. (2007). *Nausea*. L. Alexander, Trans. New Directions Paperbook.

Segerstrom, S. C., Boggero, I. A., King, C. D., Sturgeon, J. A., Arewasikporn, A., & Castro, S. A. (2019). Associations of pain intensity and frequency with loneliness, hostility, and social functioning: Cross-sectional, longitudinal, and within-person relationships. *International Journal of Behavioral Medicine*, 26(2), 217–229. https://doi.org/10.1007/s12529-019-09776-5.

Shahbaz, S., Ashraf, M. Z., Zakar, R., Fischer, F., & Zakar, M. Z. (2021). Psychosocial effects of the COVID-19 pandemic and lockdown on university students: Understanding apprehensions through a phenomenographic approach. *PLoS ONE*, 16 (5), 1–30. https://doi.org/10.1371/journal.pone.0251641.

Solomon, S., Greenberg, J., & Pyszczynski, T (2004). The cultural animal: Twenty years of terror management theory and research. In J. Greenberg, S. L. Koole, & T. Pyszczynski (Eds.), *Handbook of experimental existential psychology* (pp. 13–34). Guilford Press.

Spinelli, E. (2019). What's so existential about existential therapy? *Existential Analysis: Journal of the Society for Existential Analysis*, 30(1), 59–79.

Sun, S., Goldberg, S. B., Lin, D., Qiao, S., & Operario, D. (2021). Psychiatric symptoms, risk, and protective factors among university students in quarantine during the COVID-19 pandemic in China. *Globalization & Health*, 17(1), 1–14. https://doi.org/10.1186/s12992-021-00663-x.

Taubman-Ben-Ari, O. (2004). Risk taking in adolescence: "To be or Not to be" is not really the question. In J. Greenberg, S. L. Koole, & T. Pyszczynski (Eds.), *Handbook of experimental existential psychology* (pp. 104–121). Guilford Press.

Testoni, I., Palazzo, L., Ronconi, L., Donna, S., Cottone, P. F., & Wieser, M. A. (2021). The hospice as a learning space: A death education intervention with a group of adolescents. *BMC Palliative Care*, 20(1), 1–11. https://doi.org/10.1186/s12904-021-00747-w.

van Roekel, E., Verhagen, M., Engels, R. C. M. E., Scholte, R. H. J., Cacioppo, S., & Cacioppo, J. T. (2018). Trait and state levels of loneliness in early and late adolescents: Examining the differential reactivity hypothesis. *Journal of Clinical Child & Adolescent Psychology*, 47(6), 888–899. https://doi.org/10.1080/15374416.2016.1146993.

Verdery, A. M., Smith-Greenaway, E., Margolis, R., & Daw, J. (2020). Tracking the reach of COVID-19 kin loss with a bereavement multiplier applied to the United States. *Proceedings of the National Academy of Sciences*, 117(30), 17695–17701. https://10.1073/pnas.2007476117.

Watts, A. (1966). *The Book: On the taboo against knowing who you are*. Vintage Books.

Watts, A. (1979). *The wisdom of insecurity: A message for an age of anxiety*. Vintage Books.

Yalom, I. D. (1980). *Existential psychotherapy*. Basic Books.

Yalom, I. D. (1985). *The theory and practice of group psychotherapy* (3rd ed.). Basic Books.

Yalom, I. D. (2009). *Staring at the Sun*. Jossey-Bass.

Yalom, I. D. (2015). *Creatures of a day and other tales of psychotherapy*. Basic Books.

Ying, L., Yan, Q., Shen, X., Jia, X., & Lin, C. (2019). Economic pressure and loneliness in migrant children in China: The mediating roles of parent–child communication and parental warmth. *Child Psychiatry & Human Development*, 50(1), 142–149. https://doi.org/10.1007/s10578-018-0827-3.

Zeballos Rivas, D. R., Lopez Jaldin, M. L., Nina Canaviri, B., Portugal Escalante, L. F., Alanes Fernández, A. M. C., & Aguilar Ticona, J. P. (2021). Social media exposure, risk perception, preventive behaviors and attitudes during the COVID-19 epidemic in La Paz, Bolivia: A cross sectional study. *PLoS ONE*, 16(1), 1–12. https://doi.org/10.1371/journal.pone.0245859.

4

CONSTELLATIONS WITHIN THE DARKNESS

Growth-Promoting Relationships

For young adults that continue to experience the effects of existential trauma in the wake of COVID-19, high-quality growth-promoting relationships are therapeutic and promote holistic well-being. In this chapter, we will explore how the meanings that young adults create in their relationships help alleviate death and loneliness anxieties. With the autonomy of existentialism, they can greet concerns with compassion and sincere curiosity.

There is no prescribed pedagogy, method, or technique that can predict what "profound awakenings and discoveries that will occur in a person's inner searching" (Moustakas, 1972, p. 5). For young adults and adults alike, there is a search for inner discoveries that take place within relationships with the world. With friends, classmates, coworkers, loved ones, animals, and the environment, we find meaningful relationships that illuminate more of what is within us. This self-realization comes with an enlightened awareness that we share the existential givens, such as death and isolation.

However, caring adults, such as mental health professionals, teachers, and professors that seek to facilitate the actualization of young adults' inner potentials do not want to overstep boundaries of privacy. Violating levels of private thought and meaning may prevent young adults from achieving greater levels of self-awareness. These reservations also come with the curiosity for how to establish a climate free from imposition or restriction, and how to cultivate a space that promotes meaningful connections with the world. Once trauma sets in, there is a labyrinth of defenses that preclude young adults from establishing growth-promoting relationships. How do we find young adults within these mazes where we can share a living appreciation of existential givens through empathy and encounter? Moreover, how can we help young adults transcend the labyrinth walls of trauma if no exits are to be found? Few would think of the existential

DOI: 10.4324/9781003251651-6

darkness as a beacon of hope and source of vitality; it is hard to realize that sometimes we must seek to the darkness as much as we follow the light.

Rhythms and Rituals of Being Together

To begin appreciating the phenomenon of relationships, we must examine its boundaries in philosophical discourse. This review will establish parameters for understanding and recognizing the essence of the phenomenon. The etymology of the word *relate* stems from the Latin *refero* (Moustakas, 1995). *Refero* breaks down to its word root of *fero* which means to bear with—which is also found in a similar word *suffero*, or to suffer. This indicates that the Latin origin of relate means to endure with. Rilke (1930) aptly stated, "To be loved is to pass away, to love is to endure" (p. 234). Relating in this sense means to endure realities with another.

The relationship is not solely what is given or taken, but how two beings establish rhythms and rituals for enduring life and creating meaning. Relationships in this manner are not for possession, as a materialist understanding would have it, but more of a faith to *let go*. In the faith of relationship, the façades and rigid patterns of living can be given up in favor of being authentic and open to possibilities. There are rifts, stressors, and confrontations in the meeting of two wills but the established limits and intentions are meant to bring about commitment, repair, growth, and potential. Moustakas (1995) described that courage in a relationship will allow "one to face the old patterns of criticism, adversity, and rejection; enables one to live with the negative feelings and thoughts while creating new images and meanings in the process" so that "one discovers new perspectives and new meanings, no matter how many new and positive relationships have been formed" (p. 70).

When relationships are formed, they hold the potential for possibility in personal and relational growth, while also holding the chance for emotional pain, immobility, and expiration. When an encounter takes place between two beings and there is an intent for it to be significant, there are patterns of thought, behavior, and communication that create the foundation of that relationship. This can influence the relationship's quality as well as future encounters (Moustakas, 1995). There must be a mutual determination and labor to identify, as early as possible, the patterns that are not conducive toward growth. The two must dispel the patterns established from previous relationships that prevent one from encountering the other in the here-and-now. The person must be open to new ways of relating with each new encounter.

For an operational definition of growth-promoting relationships, Rogers (1989) defined it as a relationship "in which one of the participants intends that there should come about, in one or both parties, more appreciation of, more expression of, more functional use of the latent inner resources of the individual" (p. 40). Rogers' (1989) description of the growth-promoting relationship allows us to appreciate his ecological approach—where the love and care for another drives the efforts to help promote growth and actualize inner potentials. Each participant in the growth-promoting relationship is granted a deep sense of self-esteem so that identity is affirmed and experience is validated. Within the relationship both find that they have significant meaning and value to this world (Mikulincer et al., 2004).

The motivation to establish growth-promoting relationships is more than a defense mechanism against the terror of death or an innate drive to perpetuate genes. Those aspects are parts to a greater phenomenon. Human beings can form relationships out of need, but those are not growth promoting. Rather, growth-promoting relationships predominately reflect an inner motivation to care for others in order to increase their quality of life. There is a sincere desire to empathically create meaningful rhythms and rituals in order to endure life together. The rewards of self-actualizing potentials in the relationship are the by-products of care and love.

Founding humanistic psychology member Carl Rogers developed a unique person-centered approach for establishing and cultivating growth-promoting relationships. This was revolutionary during the mid-twentieth century when there were two dominant schools in Western psychology: psychoanalysis and behaviorism. Both placed the power of therapy in the hands of the therapist. Rogers (1939, 1969, 1970, 1980, 1989), whose childhood was spent on the family farm, developed an affinity for the agricultural sciences. When he later studied clinical psychology in college, Rogers applied an ecological philosophy to the person. This means if the appropriate conditions conducive to human growth and development were cultivated, then the person would be able to actualize inner potentials for healing, creating meaning, and decision-making that aligned with inner-core values. Rogers' (1977) person-centered approach was radical in Western psychology because he argued that the person is "a trustworthy organism, capable of evaluating the outer and inner situation, understanding herself in its context, making constructive choices as to the next steps in life, and acting on those choices" (p. 15). Trusting the person to align with inner values and directions also meant that Rogers, as the therapist, would provide the necessary conditions, resources, knowledge, and support in order to empower the client with existentialism to make decisions and create a meaningful life story.

The universal human conditions in which the person needs to heal, grow, learn, and actualize potentials within relational contexts are, as Rogers (1980) found, empathy, congruence, and unconditional positive regard (Moon & Rice, 2012; Murphy & Cramer, 2014). The Rogerian conditions are foundational aspects in humanistic psychology's concept of relational *encounter*, where there is "a joyous experience of self-discovery, a real meeting of self-to-self. It contains an exciting flow of feeling connected with life. It includes a sense of harmony and well-being" (Moustakas, 1972, p. 21). Encounters happen intentionally or unintentionally throughout life with other people, animals, and the environment.

There is a broad spectrum of empathic abilities for mammals that allow us to feel or understand the experience of another being. Empathy can be experienced automatically, such as when we cringe if someone takes a nasty fall; or it can be experienced mindfully, as we intentionally seek to know the depths of someone's grief through conversation. Although the neuroscience of empathy will be discussed later in this chapter, we will first explore how Rogers understood empathy for his ecological approach to healing, growth, and learning. Rogers was primarily focused on encounters between two people (or more if in group therapy settings) that intended to explore worlds of meaning, experience, and emotion. For example, in an educational setting, the teacher would seek to know what an experience was/is like for the young adult student, *as if* it was the teacher's own personal experience (de Waal, 2009).

Empathy is an intricate and delicate process where the adult checks understandings with the young adult, as a means to insure an alignment to his/her/their perspective. To achieve an empathic encounter, the adult must first be satisfied in his/her/their own personal needs. This is so that the person does not to overly identify with the young person or seek to remedy one's own uncomfortableness. The caring adult is a confident companion for exploring the meanings just below the young adult's awareness (Rogers, 1977). As this companion, the adult travels the inner worlds of experience with the person, gently calling forth meanings that may have been overlooked or disregarded.

Empathy supports personal growth and strengthens the growth-promoting relationship. Rogers resolutely argued that empathy is *not a technique* used to achieve a hidden agenda or externally determined goal—because that intention would cause the encounter to be disingenuous, inauthentic, and would not empower the person with the autonomy to make decisions. Rather, he argued that empathy is *a way of being*, where people unlock empathic potentials naturally within an encounter. The freedom within empathy encourage people to determine their own goals. Having a phenomenological attitude in the empathic encounter allows one to realize that we must "be receptive to another human being who is struggling to find a way to live seems to be present, to be open, to listen with love, and to hear and receive whatever manifests itself" (Moustakas, 1995, p. 79).

Congruence is the second Rogerian condition needed to cultivate growth, learning, or healing in the encounter. When the person's inner perceptual worlds (i.e., feelings, emotions, thoughts) are aligned with outer expressions, it is said that the person is congruent (Bugental, 1965; Rogers, 1980). Empathy becomes deeper and relationships are more apt to grow when people are congruent. When others sense the honesty of congruence, they are encouraged to align their own inner and outer worlds. Living incongruently causes rifts within the person. Hiding or distorting the inner world so that the outer expressions can achieve an ulterior goal leads to emotional turmoil and identity crisis.

Thirdly, the element of unconditional positive regard is necessary to build a growth-promoting relationship (Rogers, 1989). Unconditional positive regard is a sincere valuing of the person without any condition of thought or behavior. The person is prized for being someone of value that has the potential to make growth-promoting decisions. Unconditional positive regard is important for minorities and culturally diverse youth, because it reassures them that they are not being engaged through negative stereotyped lenses (Spencer & Rhodes, 2014). When a young adult is given evaluation or judgment, the majority of power in the relationship is redistributed to the adult—leading to dependency. Although the adult does not have to agree with certain thoughts or behaviors, it is established that the young adult is worthy of value and dignity regardless of how one chooses to live. The fact that the young adult is seeking a growth-promoting relationship means that the person has an intention to heal, grow, or change from what may be an unsatisfying or destructive way of life.

The Rogerian method is highly relevant for youth living in the aftermath of the pandemic, especially for underserved and minority populations that have experienced greater incidences of discrimination and levels of trauma. For minority populations, dignity has been scarce, voices ignored, and knowledges discounted. Establishing Rogerian conditions nurtures encounters to promote growth, healing, and learning. The diverse partnerships formed are gateways for advocacy, social justice, and social change.

From growth-promoting relationships adults and young adults learn from one another as they empathically explore issues of race, economics, and social adversities. There is no one-size-fits-all standardized method for exploring the psychology of another person, especially when there are cultural differences (which is why the processes of cultural humility are critical). The competence for establishing the Rogerian conditions is not an academic or technical achievement, but rather an emergence of personal abilities or *ways of being* that seek to understand, learn, and contribute to the growth of others. Furthermore, as Cozolino (2020) wrote of the Rogerian effects:

> Via sociostasis, a positive therapeutic relationship can modulate arousal, activate the biochemistry of bonding, enhance neuroplastic processes, and support neural network integration. By treating clients as worthy of our attention and care, we activate mirror neuron systems that allow for learning through imitation, support plasticity, and boost the courage to try new ways of being. Rogers' emotional stance toward his clients parallels parenting attitudes supportive of secure attachment. Nurturing connections have been shaped by evolution to create a state of brain and mind that opens us to learning, self-reflection, experimentation, and exploration.
>
> *(p. 9)*

Caring adults, such as mental health professionals and educators, can cultivate the Rogerian conditions in order to explore worlds of meaning with young adults and build growth-promoting relationships. This discovery process will have moments of failure, but if both parties are committed to seeing the journey through, they can recover and repair from rifts and misunderstandings in order to explore new directions.

The Space between the Stars

Once the Rogerian conditions are established in a relationship, adults and young adults learn to discover possibilities for creating meanings together. The very search for meaning alleviates existential anxieties by promoting agency. Accepting existentialism means to discover enlightened perspectives and positions to greet realities with compassion and sincere curiosity. Although suffering happens, it is not required to have a fulfilling life (Frankl, 2006). Searching for meaning "cares for *existential* realities, such as the potential meaning of his existence to be fulfilled as well as his *will* to meaning" (Frankl, 2006, p. 103). This *will* to meaning is the force behind the processes of creation.

Providing the conditions and opportunities for young adults to establish meaningful encounters are necessary to explore existential concerns. It is in these spaces that offer a deeper sense of purpose. One key purpose is to create meanings in a life shared with others. Relationships are the foundations for creating meaning. Developing growth-promoting relationships means both parties are courageous to challenge previous associations, in order to find new rhythms and patterns of living that are relevant to the moment. As Moustakas (1995) wrote of new relationships with caring others:

> The new relationship is anchored in the reality of one person's presence to another, in being there, and in the safety, security, compassion, and acceptance of this other person...Going through a relationship means facing polarities within oneself. It means challenging the desire to call onto fixed patterns rather than let go; the desire to repeat rather than to risk new experience; to remain passive rather than be assertive; to live in the past rather than in the present. It means facing the fear of trying again, undergoing the dangers, facing the old suffering; the fear of going around and around, awakening the old tortures of darkness.
>
> *(p. 71)*

It is through this openness to possibility that two beings create meaningful relationships that endure existential darkness.

Relationships hold potentials for emergence of the self. They are unique opportunities to become a *firebrand*, in which the young adult discovers what makes a relationship unique and cultivates those elements to bring about vitality and emergence. Young adult firebrands dispel roles that do not align with inner values; by problematizing and dispelling irrelevant categories, suppositions, hierarchies, and permanent routines (Moustakas, 1995). The choices are geared toward finding new

82 Part I

rituals, rhythms, and networks with other beings, where secrets can be sacred and kept, trust is foundational, and where conflict or intimate encounters are equally enriching experiences. Young adults with this disposition will find more capabilities to be open-minded, creative, trustworthy, candid, and adventurous.

Offering *presence* is integral to all growth-promoting relationships. It is a gentle yet highly powerful act. To offer presence means to encounter another being in the living moment with unconditional value, openness, sympathy or empathy, and the willingness to express the self authentically. Or as Moustakas (1995) described, "Presence means receptiveness to all that is, readiness to enter fully and be part of all that happens, to recognize the child in the moment, without judgment, but with full support and unconditional valuing" (p. 153). The reason presence is different than offering mindfulness or mere friendship, is that it entails a phenomenological attitude in being with another being. Presence includes both harmony and divergence. This is different than transcendental mindfulness and Zen, because it is not necessarily aiming to dissolve the self into no-thing-ness, but rather focuses on an expanding ontology of the self to compassionately encounter another. Simply, offering presence means to exist with another being—not a detachment of suffering, but enduring life together in a living and growing relationship.

The relationship should not dissolve one party into the other where the self is lost, dependent, or fused so that another's world is abstractly adopted as one's own. There are limits to a relationship that keep it within growth-promoting bounds, such as ways of showing respect, language used, behaviors, rules as to what is off-limits, or even personal requests. There are moments of what Martin Buber described as *I-Thou* and *I-It* encounters.

An *I-It* encounter takes place during times of reflection in an experience, where the person has mindful introspection and the self becomes relational to an *it*, or other being (e.g., I am having fun, I love you). There are also times of *I-Thou*, when the person engages an encounter wholeheartedly, without reflection—where there is a deep and phenomenal meeting between two beings that are the experience. One can never force the other, yet in an authentic relationship they occur naturally, mutually; as Buber (1958) stated,

> Concentration and fusion into the whole being can never take place through my agency, nor can it ever take place without me. I become through my relation to the *Thou*; as I become *I*, I say *Thou*. All real living is meeting.
>
> *(p. 11)*

Not every meeting has an *I-Thou* encounter, but the elements of unity, empathy, value, and honesty provide a significant occurrence to know the self and the other being in a way that grows the relationship. Moustakas (1972) described,

> When unity of self and other is experienced and communication reaches a heightened, personal meaning, life is being lived at a peak level. At times it

seems unbelievable, almost beyond reach, but when it happens it is something of awesome beauty.

(p. 102)

The *I-Thou* experience is important to realize that the most powerful relationships are in the living moment.

The Pursuit of Meaning

As the young adult attains more responsibilities and seeks to enter complex social relationships, the motivations to try new things, take risks, and meet new people is present. Often times, new social roles are experimented with. Young adults will explore social aspects they are drawn to in order to see if a certain element aligns with inner-core values and actualizes inner potentials. The motivations of the young adult are sometimes influenced by mass media which propagandizes that the ultimate goals of relationships are to achieve unrealistic representations of love and happiness. Failures in relationships then cause the person to question: *what is wrong with me* or *why can't I find someone to make me happy*? Self-esteem usually deteriorates in this deficit frame of mind. The growth-promoting relationship is meant to enlighten the young adult that "a human being is not one in pursuit of happiness but rather in search of a reason to become happy, last but not least, through actualizing the potential meaning inherent and dormant in a given situation" (Frankl, 2006, p. 138). The challenges of encounters are plenty, especially when values differ, but happiness is a byproduct of meaningful relationships.

Socialization through meaningful groups or relationships, in which socio-emotional intelligences and skills are utilized have vital importance for developing areas of the young adult's brain, such as the limbic region (which facilitates emotional regulation, learning, and memory) (Sapolsky, 2017). Growth-promoting relationships have shown to be fundamental for interconnecting brain hemispheres and regions—this ultimately allows young adults more brain power to critically analyze and understand complex situations (Presti, 2016). Stimulating brain growth can be accomplished in relationships with guardians, peers, and teachers/professors as well as with animals, nature, and the universe.

When understanding and facilitating the creation of meaning in young adulthood, it is important to utilize a multicultural humanistic paradigm. As previously discussed, this paradigm focuses on the functions and conditions in which culturally relative self-actualization processes develop within a diversity growth-promoting relationships (Kazanjian, 2021). This means that when young adults form positive attitudes and values toward diverse encounters, they are more apt to form partnerships within multicultural communities. Within these diverse relationships are the resources for accelerated personal development. Learning cultural humility, interpersonal skills, emotional management, empathy, and decision making within culturally diverse circumstances are skills that translate into academic success.

84 Part I

Furthermore, humanistic multicultural humanistic psychology advocates for young adults to develop a multicultural phenomenological attitude. This means critically reflecting on one's own cultural paradigm in order to understand the individualistic or collectivistic meanings and biases in order to be open to new cultural meanings. For example, growth-promoting relationships for collectivistic paradigms are mostly aligned to the greater group, where the person-to-person relationship takes on a collective meaning. The phenomenological attitude helps the person critically reflect on the paradigm to broaden the perception for what relationships can be/mean. Relationship paradigms can be widened to include nature, weather, animals, and the environment. Even the relationship with time can be growth promoting, as Moustakas' (1994) phenomenological study revealed:

> Time, oh time, you come so suddenly, entering my world, shaking and humbling me, teaching me of mysteries and agonies of living.
>
> Time, slow and gradual, swift and sure, too much of you when not needed, too little in hours of desire.
>
> Time, you linger and endure, you create a sense of now, of yesterday, of tomorrow, forever. You take with you all that is and has been and ever will be.
>
> *(p. 82)*

There are growth-promoting relationships that have gone unnoticed. The phenomenological attitude helps young adults to explore other perceptional worlds of meaning and recognize phenomena from different positionalities.

No person can achieve the processes of culturally relative self-actualize in isolation. There are strong correlations amongst the quality of our relationships with physical and psychological development (Cozolino, 2014; Presti, 2016). Just as our bodies need gravity to stand on earth, muscles to grow, and bones to harden, we need others to stimulate emotions, ideas, creativity, and the physical being. Relationships are necessary and people typically seek out others that provide safety, empathy, value, and honesty. The collectivistic and individualistic cultural paradigms each have spectrums of complexities. These have important elements for young adults in the processes of creating meaning as well as offering parameters for exploring what things *could* mean.

As young adults explore their worlds, cultural paradigms are ready-made systems for determining meaning parameters. These limits provide context and opportunities to develop empathy, compassion, and self-esteem. Cultural values and meanings are important for how existential trauma will affect the person. Without them, creating meaning for life's challenges can become intimidating and lead young people to despair. This is why cultural paradigms contain healthful ways to cope and create meanings for death, meaninglessness, isolation, and freedom.

Some may find it cathartic to dance in a group, sing, be alone, create something, or perhaps make a pilgrimage. However, many young adults seek to expand the limits of cultural paradigms through cultural blending via diverse relationship formation. Most young adults are naturally open to new experiences than compared to adults (more often if the child-rearing practices have cultivated open-mindedness by forming positive values toward human diversities, new activities, and different ideas). When young adults explore (through Rogerian principles) the different cultural worlds of others, they may challenge cultural rules that do not align with them. This generation has unique opportunities to create new cultural rules. As the world becomes progressively interconnected and interdependent, people move toward a global cultural paradigm, where they find greater instances of inter-paradigm interaction and cultural blending.

Growth-Promoting Brain Development

When understanding the abilities and potentials for relationship formation in young adulthood, many scientists are looking for a part in a function to explain why things exist. Although neuroscientific research into psychological phenomena like empathy or depression provide important findings, they explain more of an observable *what* is happening rather than the phenomenological experience. Even the *what* is limited as new technology is developed and current studies reveal that the brain is more interconnected and interdependent than previously found. A person does not need neuroscientific findings to justify an experience nor establish the value of a phenomenon. Instead, neuroscience can provide a knowledge base for understanding the complexity of the brain and what happens during certain processes. As long as we remain with the *whole is greater than the sum of its parts* tenet, neuroscientific findings provide important insights into how the young adult's brain is developing and factors that are conducive to growth or deterioration.

To illustrate, empathy is a mammalian characteristic that is studied by a number of research fields, such as primatology, biology, neuroscience, and psychology. The complex spectrum of biological, sociological, and psychological facets make inquiry into empathy an exciting venture, where we learn about ourselves and other animals. The Rogerian condition of empathy designates a partnership that focuses on dialectics to explore the meanings of experience. Although Rogers did not write extensively about human empathy for animals, or animals' empathic abilities, does not mean he denied its importance. He was in favor of opening our empathic awareness, abilities, and understandings for all forms of life—*empathy is a way of being*. In the mid-twentieth century, there were primatologists that revealed controversial empirical research findings, which demonstrated how human beings were not so different from other primates, such as bonobos and chimpanzees. Humans and monkeys alike displayed relationship building, politics, rituals, and society. Primatologists also observed that empathy was a shared trait amongst all primates. Empathy is a phenomenon where the body elicits internal processes (e.g., increased heart rate,

86 Part I

emotions) and external responses (e.g., blushing, facial expressions) to contextual circumstances/encounters (de Waal, 2009). The varying levels of empathy build social relationships, while also helping manage self-needs in order to recognize the feelings, needs, emotions, and experiences of others.

Although the origins of empathy are still under investigation (and still being disputed), research communities generally agree that its comeuppance was the result of complex mammalian social situations, particularly with the bonding of mothers and their newborn children. Those mothers that were empathic with their children were able to pass on their genes more than ones that were not sensitive to the needs of the babies. One result was the development of a neural network that could facilitate the sensing of emotional experiences of others, especially mother to child and child to mother (Cozolino, 2014). The limbic region of the brain developed as a facilitator for emotional and somatic responses in empathic experiences. However, the brain and body are interdependent and interconnected so that the organism could only experience empathy with the support of other areas, such as the amygdala, hippocampus, thalamus, and even the enteric nervous system (those gut feelings!) (Sapolsky, 2017).

Empathy is an innate response to environmental stimuli. The entire body is involved with empathy. For example, when witnessing a wrestling match where Macho Man Randy Savage is about to deliver an atomic elbow drop from the top rope to his opponent, audience members cannot help but tense up in suspense when the Macho Man is trying to balance high above the ring. Viewers then cringe when Macho delivers the blow to his opponent—imagining they were at the receiving end of the finisher. Or, seeing a lost dog creates the feeling of the stomach dropping, where we recognize the experience of being lost or helpless. We experience empathy in various depths and circumstances.

Certain people may seek to block empathic states, or choose to ignore or deaden empathic capacities. Whereas, some people that are sociopathic have low levels of empathy from birth. There are also those that are anomalies born without any empathic abilities. These people are usually the focus of serial killer documentaries. In addition, some media outlets promote that human beings are mostly selfish and uncaring creatures, only seeking to serve themselves. However, individuals with diminished empathy are a minority and cannot be representative of the human condition. As de Waal (2009) described:

> Economists prefer to imagine a hypothetical world driven by market forces and rational choice rooted in self-interest. This world does fit some members of the human race, who act purely selfishly and take advantage of others without compunction. In most experiments, however, such people are in the minority. The majority is altruistic, cooperative, sensitive to fairness, and oriented toward community goals. The level of trust and cooperation among them exceeds predictions from economic models.
>
> *(p. 162)*

Over 200 years of mammalian evolution have supported empathy as a genetic capacity. Empathy is an innate mammalian trait that allows the human community to take care of one another, thrive, and tend to those in need (Moustakas, 1972). The young adult is open to new experiences, which also means opportunities to empathically relate and learn about the self from how others experience the world (Sapolsky, 2017).

Empathy excites brain areas that are over a hundred million years old that allowed ancestors the abilities for motor mimicry and emotional contagion. Over the millions of years, subsequent layers of the brain were added, so that primates could not only just feel what others felt, but could also sense/anticipate desires and needs (de Waal, 2009). Many scientists agree that the capacity for empathy, emotional contagion, and motor mimicry were supported by *mirror neurons*. Mirror neurons are a system of neurons that concertedly activate a network of neural connections that mimic the patterned activation it would take to accomplish the observed emotional state or activity of another (Cozolino, 2020; 2014). These mirror neurons were, perhaps, the precursor or the prerequisite for empathy's evolution.

To illustrate mirror neurons, consider the following scenario: a young adult is watching Arnold Schwarzenegger in *Pumping Iron* (1977) lifting weights as he trains for the Mr. Olympia contest, the neural networks that it takes for Arnold to accomplish the motor movements of bicep curls are identically firing in the brain of the viewer. However, although mirror neurons are mimicking an observed activity they alone will not pump the viewer a set of 22-inch arms for a legendary front double bicep pose. Regardless, mirror neurons are essential for learning, navigating social situations, understanding physical and spoken languages, and, of course, empathy. Social encounters are important for young adults because mirror neurons fire when interacting with peers and caring adults. These encounters stimulate neurons and networks that promote empathic development and socio-emotional intelligences.

Socio-Emotional Intelligences for Relationship Building

Socio-emotional intelligences designate a continuum of emotional, social, behavioral, and cognitive processes that stimulate growth in abilities for interoception, social awareness, emotional regulation, empathy, positive-decision making, and the capacities for developing growth-promoting relationships (Domitrovich et al., 2017; Thomson & Carlson, 2017). Young adulthood is a critical phase of development to where socio-emotional intelligences are developing at an extraordinary rate in order to ensure long-term survival and success in diverse communities. The social and emotional learning (SEL) for young adults has been implemented in many public schools' curriculum to focus on the development of these skills in order to prepare youth for a rapidly changing world (Bowers et al., 2017; Haymovitz et al., 2018; Lemberger et al., 2018). SEL is correlated to academic success, engagement, and greater empathic abilities for identifying emotions of the self and others—leading to more effective emotional management and success in relationships (Eklund et al., 2018; Garner et al., 2018).

The curricular frameworks for SEL programs are largely created within the parameters and definition outlined by the Collaborative for Academic, Social, and Emotional Learning (2020) (CASEL) as a "Process through which children and adults understand and manage emotions, set and achieve positive goals, feel and show empathy for others, establish and maintain positive relationships, and make responsible decision" (para. 1). Lemberger et al. (2018) conducted a meta-analysis of roughly 200 SEL K-12 school-based programs to investigate how the five goals outlined by CASEL affected students. The findings revealed that SEL programs were highly effective in developing students' social and emotional skills, forming positive habits and relationships, and promoting academic success. SEL programs also had success for meeting multicultural and social justice objectives for equitable developmental opportunities for minority, marginalized, and special populations of students (Bowers et al., 2017). SEL is an investment in youth. Eklund et al. (2018) found that each dollar invested into an SEL program has on average, an 11 dollar return for communities, rates of substance abuse and juvenile arrests are lowered, and academic success correlates into a higher skilled workforce.

In a meta-analysis of 213 SEL programs that surveyed over 270,000 K-12 students, Rowe and Trickett (2018) found that programs concentrated on at least one CASEL component for developing an SEL competence. Many of the programs focused on relationship skill building, which had greater effects to school culture and classroom management. The focus of this meta-analysis sought to understand what conclusions can be made for diverse student populations. However, there were inconsistencies in the demographics reported because of the limited criteria for what was considered diverse. For example, most diversity surveys leave out sexual orientation and gender identity. Creating representational survey demographic identifiers can help researchers understand correlations better, in order to help schools develop interventions for victimization and promote mental well-being. Identification of diverse populations can be challenging in research because there are many that wish to keep their identities hidden (Jackman et al., 2020). This causes major holes in the SEL research which cannot identify the effects of interventions for victimized, marginalized, or hidden populations.

Young adults have an innate desire to form meaningful relationships, especially within their peer circles. SEL facilitates the success of relationships because it improves holistic functions for social awareness, emotional regulation, interpersonal communication, and interoception (Gresham et al., 2018; Morrish et al., 2018; Valosek et al., 2019; Vidic & Cherup, 2019). Many young adults have had a year of meaningful peer interactions that practice SEL placed on hold due to the pandemic. Now, returning to school each year or engaging in social situations may cause a sense of anxiousness or dread. Young adults that have experienced loss of family members or close friends may still be experiencing grief. Their mourning processes continue. As a result, grieving young adults may feel a sense of loneliness amongst happy-to-return peers and teachers. In the wake of pandemic's trauma it is important for young adults to develop the positive habits to cope with existential concerns, so that they can seek out meaningful social interactions.

The Tides of Emotions

Meaningful growth-promoting relationships encourage young adults to safely explore the gamut of human emotions through all intensities. Emotions are powerful states of being in which a circumstance or stimuli brings about physiological changes—these can be powerful, mysterious, and overwhelming at times.

Relationships reflect the flowing nature of life, whereby emotions are a necessary part of the living moment. When young adults deal with existential concerns or trauma, there may not always display consistency in what emotion is expressed or the meanings behind them. This is because the young adult is seeking to understand emotional experiences from various vantage points. New meanings are experimented with and emotional varieties are blossoming. Sometimes this experiential variance brings a sense of frustration, as it can be challenging to identify emotions or figure out constructive ways to cope with them. Socio-emotional intelligences are important for young adults to manage and understand the deep emotional forces happening within. Although many young adults may feel that no one understands them, they can come to appreciate that there are caring others willing to fare the ocean of emotional experience with them, no matter the temperament of the waves.

Commonly, young adults are motivated to find situations that elicit positive emotions. There are many circumstances in which one can feel positive emotions, even if they appear negative. For example, those that seek out sad movies or sorrowful music may feel a great sense of meaning in the solitude or sadness. Although the emotion of sadness is present, it does not always have to be destructive. Sadness can be enlightening and meaningful, offering discoveries of the self and world that have spiritual depth. Perhaps the parameters for what constitutes as *positive* needs to be widened because emotions are not as simple or distinct as previously considered.

Rather, there is a mélange of emotional experiences at any given time—much like the interaction of water colors on a canvas or the shifting nature of cumulous clouds. Positive emotions in this sense would mean experiential states that are favorable toward well-being or growth of the person. There is a motivating force to create meaning and explore potential. Negative emotions are unpleasant but necessary. They often cause pain, turmoil, confusion, and heaviness—and are of equal value to positive emotions for enlightenment and growth. At the heart of most cultural traditions is a motivation to elicit positive emotions, because "our capacity to manifest compassion, gratitude, and other prosocial emotions is a

90 Part I

testament to the deep interconnectivity and interdependence of human beings" (Presti, 2016, p. 253). Emotions connect people and the world. Although cultures have different meanings for emotional states, every person has the capacity to experience the same emotions (Adolphs & Anderson, 2018).

How emotions are interpreted and what meanings are created from them are unique to diverse cultural paradigms. For young adults around the world, emotions are powerful forces within social engagements that contain exciting, scary, boring, or even passionate encounters with peers. Young adults need to appreciate that strong emotional forces are necessary experiences for succeeding in diverse social/environmental circumstances. Survival and growth mean being able to listen to emotions in order to learn and adapt. Emotions are not separate entities that have their way with an individual's life. Rather, emotions are that person's innate ability to resonate with an experience. There is no separating the person from the emotional experience, but there is managing and learning within them.

By helping young adults deconstruct reductionist viewpoints of emotions, or even removing the widely advised strategy of *controlling emotions*, they can realize that emotions are a transcendental guide for knowing the phenomenology of Being. Conquering emotions is an ill-advised act for young adults. It would be as if one were to tell the clouds to hold their rain, the wind to stay back, or the ocean currents to flow somewhere else. Emotions are not to be dominated or controlled because they are a being's way of living. People cannot deny their emotions.

One must allow emotions to be experienced in order for them to pass. This does not mean to let emotions consume the individual, or even to always believe that the perception of them is correct while they happen. Rather, young adults that realize the necessity of positive and negative emotions open up opportunities to learn how to manage them; to direct flows and forces in ways that can constructively and compassionately express inner states in order to empower relationships. Emotional regulation for young adulthood means developing the awareness and abilities that help develop the deciding power for the manner of expression, the meanings created, and lessons to be learned. Reducing emotions to neurobiology through the belief that young adults are just a ticking time-bomb of negative emotions or raging hormones does not do well for building empathic growth-promoting relationships (Adolphs & Anderson, 2018).

Developing socio-emotional intelligences and a phenomenological attitude means removing the reductionist traces that were sown by social institutions and influential people. For example, there are still professors in higher education that believe the brain is set up exactly like a computer. This is false, outdated, and often misleading, because, as Cozolino (2020) stated:

Computers don't need to be programmed in ways that interrupt or impede other aspects of their programming; their programming is simply modified.

Alternatively, the brain has been organized and reorganized, piece by piece, over millions of years in response to the process of natural selection resulting from changing environmental and social demands. Sometimes, the adaptation to particular challenges in one era becomes a problem for later generations.

(p. 260)

The prefrontal cortices are relatively new in the human being's evolutionary history, where its development helped regulate older parts of the brain, such as the amygdala. The fear response that the amygdala elicits is powerful, but with the evolution of the prefrontal cortex, human beings could dispute and manage fearful states. Young adults need to realize that the brain is much more complex than any computer, as it has had millions of years of circumstances and genetic variations to adapt and evolve.

When it comes to appreciating the nature of emotions, the brain does not have contained centers for certain activities:

this is particularly the case with the limbic system and emotion. There is indeed a sub-subregion of the motor cortex that approximates being the "center" for making your left pinkie bend; other regions have "center"-ish roles in regulation breathing or body temperature.

(Sapolsky, 2017, p. 25)

The interconnectedness of brain layers reveals immeasurable complexity, where any focus on one hemisphere or region of the brain always leads to interdependence with another (Adolphs & Anderson, 2018). Emotions are facilitated by regions of the brain, but to say they are solely contained there is limited. Emotional orchestration takes a symphony of networks to create an experience relevant to a living moment (Damasio, 2018). To become mindful of emotions, young adults need to develop a sensitive awareness to the environmental triggers, behavioral, physical, cognitive changes, and how they create internal representations. To develop this mindful awareness, neuroscience has outlined which regions of the brain have important features in the experience of an emotion.

For example, the anterior cingulate cortex (ACC) is a region of the brain that facilitates the interweaving and interactions amongst regional layers of the brain so that emotions, perceptions, sensations, thoughts, and behaviors are coordinated to support the success of empathy, relationship encounters, and socio-emotional intelligences (Cozolino, 2014). The ACC supports decision-making processes so that the person can choose the appropriate course of action. Furthermore, the ACC is important for young adults to understand and appreciate because its stimulation/development promotes enhanced functioning of abilities to manage emotions.

Cozolino (2020) proposed the *social synapse* metaphor to illustrate that we need other people to self-actualize just as brain neurons need synaptic network stimulation in order to develop. The social synapse is

92 Part I

the space between us, the medium through which we communicate with and link to one another. When we smile, wave, and say hello, our behaviors are transferred across the social synapse to the send organs of others—their cell surface, if you will.

(p. 11)

Young adults learn to navigate the social synapse, where the psychobiological changes of one individual creates a response in another—both stimulating and learning about how to survive and succeed in a complex social sphere. This stimulation propagates socio-emotional intelligences to develop.

Negatively charged associations created through social interactions may motivate young adults to seek or avoid certain circumstances. For instance, an individual that has an overall negative schooling experience may associate school with unpleasantness, victimization, or shame. A young adult with such adverse experiences may develop unfavorable attitudes toward school and will avoid future contact with educational institutions. In addition, negative experiences within social interactions may discourage people from developing new relationships. Helping young adults appreciate the workings of the brain will help them challenge negative associations in order to be open to forming new relationships and seeking out educational experiences.

Canadian neurologist Donald Hebb (1904–1985) discovered that neurons are connected through vast systems of networks upon networks in the brain (e.g., memory, sensory, emotional, and motor networks). Hebb argued that when neurons fire together they will inevitably become wired together. The strength and frequency of simultaneous neuron activation creates neural networks. The Hebbian network principle was further developed in 1966 by Terje Lomo as *long-term potentiation*, in which "excitation between cells is prolonged, allowing them to become synchronized in their firing patterns and organized into neural networks" (Cozolino, 2014, p. 32). Thus, if young adults have negative associations to school, social encounters, or romantic partnerships, they must realize that networks were formed, where neurons that fired together were inevitably wired together. Creating new associations means being mindful of new stimuli in order to create new firings and associated wirings. Also needed is a determination to be optimistic and courageous so that previous experiences do not determine future possibilities. Associations can influence and guide, but the person has the power to decide how to be, what to value, and which path to take.

Late into young adulthood, the brain areas that facilitate decision-making and emotional regulation finalize their structural development, mainly in the prefrontal cortex. The prefrontal cortex facilitates many functions such as critical thinking, forethought, as well as memory organization for retrieval. This area develops last in the maturation of the brain, which makes it more influenced by experience than by genes. As Sapolsky (2017) stated:

by definition the frontal cortex is the brain region least constrained by genes and most sculpted by experience. This must be so, to be the supremely complex social species that we are. Ironically, it seems that the genetic program of human brain development has evolved to, as much as possible, free the frontal cortex from genes.

(p. 173)

The prefrontal cortices' freedom from genetics permits people to be highly adaptable to social contexts and new environments. Having it mature last helps people to determine which habits and qualities to cultivate that resonate with inner directions and values. Young adults have the ability to fundamentally change themselves in ways that are meaningful to them. The experiences during young adulthood are critical for influencing the development of the prefrontal cortices and neural networks. That is why growth-promoting relationships are paramount for long-term health and well-being. Regions of the brain, hormones (e.g., oxytocin), and neurotransmitters (e.g., dopamine) are important elements for growth and development but they do not determine or comprise the whole story. The story is of a whole person, a phenomenal being, that is exploring an infinity of possibilities in who to become.

Living Life in Widening Rings

Growth-promoting relationships are meaningful to young adults because they help make sense of confusing and unsettling experiences. These relationships provide the Rogerian conditions that support each individual to explore and create meaning. However, growth-promoting relationships are not just with peers and caring adults, but also with animals, nature, spaces between, and silences within. Young adults may wonder how to create meanings in experiences with, for example, a mountain. They may also wonder how one encounters a dog or cat as a phenomenal being that knows the universe in ways that they never could. Young adults may be curious about how they can create rhythms and rituals as a way to build relationships. When young adults develop relationships with the world, they must be mindful to greet the being as it is and not as a projection of an image or an unfulfilled need. Creating relationships in the manner of transference/projection will lead to un-fulfillment and ultimately relational failure, because the young adult is trying to use this other being to satisfy self-needs. Young adults need to learn how to satisfy their culturally relative needs in ways that do not use others (i.e., abstractly or materially). Growth-promoting relationships are not formed to satisfying a need, but as an intention to give and make better.

The self-esteem and confidence that blossoms within relationships supports the courage to face the existential concerns. The meanings created within relationships navigate young adults through what might seem like dreadful or scary realities. New realms of understanding are achieved as these dark and hostile areas are enlightened by existential themes. The relationship's meaning brings a fundamental integration for areas of understanding, confusion, interest, even previously unconnected areas of

94   Part I

the brain, so that holistic associations are made. Integration promotes healing. When young adults appreciate the phenomenon of encounter, the existential concerns become motivators for living with greater diligence. However, relationships are not sought as a panacea for trauma—it is only the meanings created within that establish the conditions which promote healing and equanimity.

Meaning-making with others promotes young adults' abilities for critical reasoning, imagination, creativity, and executive brain functioning. Previously learned knowledge is called forth, in which novel ideas interact with current knowledge and circumstances. Young adults recall decisions that they have made, challenge previous judgments, and analyze what the encountered phenomenon is all about. Meaning is a holistic experience, to where not only images are recalled and recreated, but the somatic associations are also remembered. From this, young adults begin to craft a personal narrative that has cultural contexts, where knowledge and contextual information take on structure. According to Cozolino (2014), narratives that are inclusive offer

> the executive brain with the best template and strategy for the oversight and coordination of the function of the mind. Narratives allow us to practice facing challenging experiences in imagination as our brains learn to cope with the emotions they stimulate.
>
> (p. 392)

The greater the depth of meaning in a relationship the more imagination is inspired to engage current and future challenges, no matter how emotionally taxing or harrowing they appear.

Many individuals base their definitions and parameters for relationships upon normalized stereotypes, values or standards of others, misrepresentations, distortions, or oversimplifications. These lessons may be learned from guardians, media, influential adults, peers, and social institutions, which will ultimately create inner turmoil for young adults as the organic components of the self are ultimately reduced, refuted, or denied (Bland & DeRobertis, 2017). A young adult may want to form a relationship with a peer that establishes unique rhythms and patterns that are different from social norms. As a result, shame or embarrassment may come from people that believe *that isn't the way it is done!* To what degree will a young adult that has created rituals with an animal friend appear strange to others that see it as *just a dog or cat* and reduce a meaningful relationship into one of lesser value than one that *should be?*

The inner conflicts also come from the incongruence of the social role demands and the young adult's inner-core values. This distress can be explicitly recognized or cause harm to the young adult in subversive ways, such as irritability or even somatization. Furthermore, the denial of a unique relationship or submission to social norms/practices precludes individuals from exploring possibilities for meaning. Young adults are developing complex intersectional identities in the contexts of cultural blending and global integration. Thus, as van Deurzen (2019) declared, "We must remain sensitive to the actual connections that make people's lives meaningful: their connections to nature, objects, their own embodied experience, other people, animals, their inner voices, their most sacred beliefs, their hopes and their fears" (p. 9). This sense of cultural humility is a gateway to understanding the existential concerns and meaning-making processes that are unique to a person in their cultural paradigm.

The meanings that are created within a growth-promoting relationship are powerful forces that can bring healing and enlightenment in the wake of trauma; as Frankl (2006) stated, "even the helpless victim of a hopeless situation, facing a fate he cannot change, may rise above himself, may grow beyond himself, and by so doing change himself. He may turn a personal tragedy into a triumph" (p. 146). This is important for young adults because they must develop self-esteem and confidence to create their own meanings in the midst and aftermath of existential turmoil. Denying the inner voices, values, and directions of young adults diminishes self-esteem, and always places them in doubt of their potentials.

In addition, *inclusiveness* is important when creating meaningful narratives. Inclusion signifies that meanings are most alive when they are crafted with others. Including cultural and personal elements into the shared meaning is important to value voice and affirm identity (Harari, 2015). Otherwise, if relationships are principally sought to fill in the loneliness, then it becomes a narcissistic or materialistic task, which amounts to an insatiable accumulation of abstractified things. Shared inclusive meanings can be cultivated to grow or left to wither.

Young adults exploring their potentials for creating an identity within relationships will find that the process is never complete. Appreciating the process of self-discovery is fulfilling in itself. Rilke (1995) wrote in *The Book of Hours*, that there is deep meaning and fulfillment living a life in widening rings, always expanding awareness of the self, never to find a static or distinct image. Growth-promoting relationships with other beings and phenomena offer young adults opportunities for appreciating the processes of self-discovery (Moustakas, 1995).

Thus, existential anxiety develops largely from a static or rigid definition of the self; one that has become estranged from the world. A young adult may seek to establish a static and reified identity that denies the changingness of existence and the interval of death. To deny that everything is constantly changing or flowing means to believe that the self can be material and can resist the passage of time. This rigid self will also deny relationships with nature and animals, as they are beings that are most attuned to the flow of existence and reminders of mortality. Death in this perspective is the end of the self and must be avoided at all costs. An identity that is unyielding to the forces of life cultivates potentials for emotional disturbances.

However, if young adults are to understand what their humanity is all about, then they should seek inclusive definitions with the world. Rilke (1995) illustrated this most aptly:

Take dogs: their confidential and admiring nearness is such that certain of them seem to have renounced their most ancient canine traditions, in order to adore our habits, and even our errors. This is precisely what makes them tragic and sublime. Their decision to admit us forces them to live, so to speak, at the very boundaries of their nature, which they constantly pass beyond their humanized gaze and their nostalgic muzzle.

(p. 304)

The willingness for young adults to encounter others, like in the nature of dogs, will encourage us to transcend the limits of human nature. Death is not the end in an inclusive existential paradigm, but rather an interval in the flow of a shared eternity. The relationships with people, animals, and nature dissolve lines of demarcation and remove rigid patterns so that inclusive meanings emerge to enlighten, heal, and help each other become.

References

Adolphs, R., & Anderson, D. J. (2018). *The neuroscience of emotion: A new synthesis*. Princeton University Press.

Bland, A. M, & DeRobertis, E. M. (2017). Humanistic perspective. In V. Zeigler-Hill & T. K. Shackelford (eds.), *Encyclopedia of personality and individual differences* (pp. 1–19). Springer International.

Bowers, H., Lemberger-Truelove, M. E., & Brigman, G. (2017). A social-emotional leadership framework for school counselors. *Professional School Counseling*, 21(1b), 1–10. https://doi.org/10.1177/2156759X18773004.

Buber, M. (1958). *I and Thou* (2nd ed.). R. G. Smith, Trans. Charles Scribner's Sons.

Bugental, J. F. T. (1965). *The search for authenticity*. Holt, Rinehart and Winston.

Collaborative for Academic, Social, and Emotional Learning. (2020, April 5). What is SEL? Casel.org. https://casel.org/what-is-sel/.

Cozolino, L. (2014). *The neuroscience of human relationships: Attachment and the developing social brain* (2nd ed.). W. W. Norton & Company.

Cozolino, L. (2020). *The pocket guide to neuroscience for clinicians*. W. W. Norton & Company.

Damasio, A. (2018). *The strange order of things: Life, feeling, and the making of cultures*. Pantheon Books.

de Waal, F. (2009). *The age of empathy: Nature's lessons for a kinder society*. Three Rivers Press.

Domitrovich, C. E., Durlak, J. A., Staley, K. C., & Weissberg, R. P. (2017). Social-emotional competence: An essential factor for promoting positive adjustment and reducing risk in school children. *Child Development*, 88(2), 408–416. doi:10.1111/cdev.12739.

Eklund, K., Kilpatrick, K. D., Kilgus, S. P., Haider, A., & Eckert, T. (2018). A systematic review of state-level social-emotional learning standards: Implications for practice and research. *School Psychology Review*, 47(3), 316–326. https://doi.org/10.17105/SPR-2017.0116.V47-3.

Frankl, V. E., (2006). *Man's search for meaning*. Beacon Press.

Garner, P. W., Bender, S. L., & Fedor, M. (2018). Mindfulness-based SEL programming to increase preservice teachers' mindfulness and emotional competence. *Psychology in the Schools*, 55(4), 1–390. https://doi.org/10.1002/pits.22114.

Gresham, F. M., Elliott, S. N., Metallo, S., Byrd, S., Wilson, E., & Cassidy, K. (2018). Cross-informant agreement of children's social-emotional skills: An investigation of ratings by teachers, parents, and students from a nationally representative sample. *Psychology in the Schools*, 55(2), 208–223. https://doi.org/10.1002/pits.22101.

Harari, Y. N. (2015). *Sapiens: A brief history of humankind*. HarperCollins.

Haymovitz, E., Houseal-Allport, P., Lee, R. S., & Svistova, J. (2018). Exploring the perceived benefits and limitations of a school-based social-emotional learning program: A concept map evaluation. *Children & Schools*, 40(1), 45–54. https://doi.org/10.1093/cs/cdx029.

Jackman, K., Kreuze, E. J., Caceres, B. A., & Schnall, R. (2020). Bullying and peer victimization of minority youth: Intersections of sexual identity and race/ethnicity. *Journal of School Health*, 90(5), 368–377. https://doi.org/10.1111/josh.12883

Kazanjian, C. J. (2021). *Empowering children: A multicultural humanistic approach*. Routledge.

Lemberger, T. M. E., Carbonneau, K. J., Atencio, D. J., Zieher, A. K., & Palacios, A. F. (2018). Self-regulatory growth effects for young children participating in a combined social and emotional learning and mindfulness-based intervention. *Journal of Counseling & Development*, 96(3), 289–302. https://doi.org/10.1002/jcad.12203.

Mikulincer, M., Florian, V., & Hirschberger, G. (2004). The terror of death and the quest for love: An existential perspective on close relationships. In J. Greenberg, S. L. Koole, & T. Pyszczynski (Eds.), *Handbook of experimental existential psychology* (pp. 287–304). Guilford Press.

Moon, K. A., & Rice, B. (2012). The nondirective attitude in client-centered practice: A few questions. *Person-Centered & Experiential Psychotherapies*, 11(4), 289–303. doi:10.1080/14779757.2012.740322.

Moustakas, C. E. (1972). *Loneliness and love*. Prentice Hall.

Moustakas, C. E. (1994). *Phenomenological research methods*. Sage.

Moustakas, C. E. (1995). *Being-In, being-for, being-with*. Jason Aronson.

Murphy, D., & Cramer, D. (2014). Mutuality of Rogers's therapeutic conditions and treatment progress in the first three psychotherapy sessions. *Psychotherapy Research*, 24(6), 651–661. doi:10.1080/10503307.2013.874051.

Presti, D. E. (2016). *Foundational concepts in neuroscience: A brain-mind odyssey*. W. W. Norton & Company.

Rilke, R. M. (1930). *The journal of my other self*. John Linton, Trans. W. W. Norton.

Rilke, R. M. (1995). *Ahead of all parting: The selected poetry and prose of Rainer Maria Rilke*. S. Mitchell, Trans. & Ed. The Modern Library.

Rogers, C. R. (1939). *The clinical treatment of the problem child*. L. Carmichael , Ed. Houghton Mifflin Company.

Rogers, C. R. (1969). *Freedom to learn: A view of what education might become*. C. E. Merrill Pub. Co.

Rogers, C. R. (1970). *Carl Rogers on encounter groups*. Harper & Row.

Rogers, C. R. (1977). *Carl Rogers on personal power*. Delacorte Press.

Rogers, C. R. (1980). *A way of being*. Houghton Mifflin.

Rogers, C. R. (1989). *On becoming a person: A therapist's view of psychotherapy*. Houghton Mifflin. Rowe, H. L., & Trickett, E. J. (2018). Student diversity representation and reporting in universal school-based social and emotional learning programs: Implications for generalizability. *Educational Psychology Review*, 30(2), 559–583. https://doi.org/10.1007/s10648-017-9425-3.

Sapolsky, R. (2017). *Behave: The biology of humans at our best and worst*. Penguin Press.

Thomson, R., & Carlson, J. (2017). A pilot study of a self-administered parent training intervention for building preschoolers' social-emotional competence. *Early Childhood Education Journal*, 45(3), 419–426. doi:10.1007/s10643-016-0798-6.

Valosek, L., Nidich, S., Wendt, S., Grant, J., & Nidich, R. (2019). Effect of meditation on social-emotional learning in middle school students. *Education*, 139(3), 111–119.

van Deurzen, E. (2019). Facing an uncertain future: The next 30 years of existential therapy. *Existential Analysis: Journal of the Society for Existential Analysis*, 30(1), 4–17.

Vidic, Z., & Cherup, N. (2019). Mindfulness in classroom: Effect of a mindfulness-based relaxation class on college students' stress, resilience, self-efficacy and perfectionism. *College Student Journal*, 53(1), 130–142.

5

THE BOLD COMPANIONSHIP OF DEFEAT

Creating meaning in growth-promoting relationships can be challenging for young adults, because the pandemic has altered the greater psychosocial atmosphere of their communities. Re-engaging social spheres may not be immediately possible for some individuals, as they may need more time to heal and acclimatize to the new sense of normal. The lockdowns, quarantines, death anxieties, and extreme loneliness may have developed social anxieties. The virtual interactions during the pandemic could not replace the social dynamics of real-world encounters. These interactions are important for promoting the growth of socio-emotional intelligences. Virtual worlds are important in modern times, but young adults generally wish to utilize them as supplementary to augment real-world interactions and dynamics.

As young adults learn about themselves and others through social encounters, it is natural to experience failures (e.g., disagreements, inability to establish a relationship, challenges with communication). Encounters in real time have a unique dynamic that involve empathy, decision-making, emotional attunement, sensations, body language, and facial expressions. The circumstances and personal abilities in which a relationship can succeed or fail are diverse. Relational failures can either provide opportunities for growth and enlightenment or become motivators to retreat into familiar virtual worlds. Although the experience of relational failures may not be pleasant, young adults must come to appreciate them as important sources of meaning.

Relationships with peers and caring adults are bound to have rifts during when communication fails. As Moustakas (1995) explained, "The problem, which begins with a breakdown in communication and the failure of being listened to and heard, soon grows into serious distortions of who one is and who one wants to be" (p. 149). When communication fails, young adults become dispirited for

DOI: 10.4324/9781003251651-7

expressing themselves authentically and directly, as the needs to be recognized and understood are deeply motivating forces. The duration, frequency, and intensity of relational rifts will determine how interested and willing the person will be for forming new, diverse, and authentic relationships. However, most young adults have an enthusiasm to try again and are willing to explore encounters with new ways of communicating and relating.

Human beings are by nature community-seeking creatures (Harari, 2015). During young adulthood, these innate tendencies blossom as youth seek complex and intimate relationships and a sense of meaning through belonging. The processes of creating meaning within relationships is an education about the self and abilities, while also offering phenomenological lessons in emotion. Cohesion amongst a group of friends entails support, acceptance, risk-taking, and helping, in ways that build self-esteem (Yalom, 1985). Self-expansion happens when conditions are favorable within the group to where a person can realize a potential just beyond their current ability. The dynamic of a young adult's close social circle can provide meaningful and honest feedback. The responsibility of friendship is not a duty, but mutually beneficial and rewarding interactions. However, expressions from developing wills can result in confrontation, disagreement, or fall-outs.

Unfortunately, failures in young adult relationships can be influenced by trauma, abuse, or victimization. A study by Rey Anacona and Martínez Gómez (2021) investigated the distinctions found within psychopathological variables for biological sexes (male or female) that experienced dating violence during young adulthood. As an operational definition, "dating violence refers to all conduct which causes harm or discomfort at a physical, psychological or sexual level, in unmarried couples or couples who do not cohabit, generally adolescents or young adults" (Rey Anacona & Martínez Gómez, 2021, p. 2). Of the 757 young adults surveyed in Columbia (12 to 19 years old, enrolled in secondary educational institutions), a significant percentage of males reported a history of victimization for interpersonal and physical violence. Consequently, these males were shown to have had issues with maladaptation to school settings, whereas victimized females reported significantly greater instances for psychopathological symptomology, maladjustment, and negative relationships with peers and family members. This supports previous research that females most often have greater complications from victimization, such as suffering from a mixture of anxiety, depression, somatization disorder, and/or loneliness. These effects can be magnified or reduced depending on cultural resources and support available. Rey Anacona and Martínez Gómez (2021) concluded that interpersonal conflicts and violence, such as bullying and dating violence, intensify during the years of young adulthood. This study is important for educators, mental health professionals, and community leaders seeking preventative measures and interventions for the physical and psychological well-being and safety of individuals during young adulthood.

Rifts within relationships not only take place between peers and romantic partners, but with parents or guardians as well. In Taizhou, China, Wang et al.

(2021) studied the mental well-being of young adults during a period of school lockdown during the pandemic (April 16 to May 14, 2020) and the mediating effects of parent–child relationships. In an online survey of 6,435 young adults enrolled in middle and high schools, the researchers investigated three categories of challenges: dissatisfaction with online learning, problematic recreational use of screen-time, and challenges with home study. Of the entire sample population, 17.7% reported for depressive symptomology, which negatively affect studying time for school. Positive parent–child relationships were moderating factors that lessened the severity of depression. Those that had poor relationships with parents had stronger symptomology. Wang et al. (2021) concluded that the pandemic revealed many challenges for young adults and that the quality of relationships with parents or guardians is an important moderator in mental well-being and academic success.

The interpersonal challenges that young adults face with adults can become influential for understanding the self and ways to relate to others. According to Moustakas (1995), young adults suffer from the

continual experience of not being listened to, not being recognized, not being understood. Repeated failures in attempting to communicate one's own feelings, preferences, desires, and thoughts inevitably leads to painful and frustrating doubts about one's own competency and value as a person.

(p. 148)

The result is a significantly diminished concept of self. Misunderstandings carry the same detriment, as the young adult's self-confidence wanes with each relational failure to gain recognition or value. Typically, they find other ways to attain significance in the adult world, where "recognition is sought through forms of withdrawal or aggressive tactics. Often a battle ensues rooted in the determination and will to retain one's power and authority as a self" (Moustakas, 1995, p. 148). These methods for gaining attention do not resonate with the person's inner-core values, interests, abilities, insights, or curiosities. Instead, the young adult finds ways of expression that reflect their anguish, distrust, anger, or despair.

Inauthentic communication has ill effects for relationship development in young adulthood. Adults and peers that display an incongruence between what is truly felt inside and their outer expressions appear as performers. When young adults sense performers, they recognize the absence of honesty in encounters. Only visible are people talking at each other with empty words, filling a relationship with absolutely nothing. As Moustakas (1972) described,

When I am with such persons I experience deep feelings of loneliness, and I want to break through the empty words and come into touch with the feelings; I want to go beyond the icebergs on top, and into what is actually happening deep down.

(p. 130)

102   Part I

Young adults tend to avoid these lonely encounters. When given the opportunity they will most often express themselves with honesty and sincerity. Offering this sense of authenticity to the world seeks to establish connections that affirm identity and experience. Although the manner in which young adults express themselves may not always be as sophisticated as they would like, their honesty seeks to build, know, and explore.

Peers and adults that deny or fail to provide the same honesty in an encounter will remove motivations for self-expression. Many times, young adults will be made to feel shame or guilt for how they express or what is expressed. There are natural senses of guilt or shame that are organic to childhood and young adulthood. They can be guides to help evaluate one's own behavior and develop impulse control in future circumstances. Natural feelings of guilt and shame can provide meaningful directions to develop empathy and conscience. These elements help build confidence in the processes of relationship formation. However, there is also an unnatural experience known as core shame, as Cozolino (2014) explained:

> Core shame develops earlier in childhood as a function of overwhelmingly negative attachment experiences. The emotions of core shame are distinguishable from healthy shame in that they are not related to behavior but to the experience of the self. Children and adults with core shame come to experience themselves as fundamentally defective, worthless, and unlovable: the polar opposite of self-esteem.
>
> *(p. 282)*

In this way, core shame can cause lifelong challenges for the young adult. Relationship failures are believed to be due to problems or deficiencies of the self. Many young adults that experience core shame will avoid opportunities to establish meaningful relationships. They feel that they are not worthy or will disappoint others, ultimately leading to future relationship failures and reinforcing core shame. In some instances, young adults with core shame may seek out toxic relationships that support their distorted beliefs about the self—that they do not deserve better or justify poor treatment. In these instances, professional therapy is needed to bring about healing and understanding, removing barriers to growth, so that the person can once again value the self.

"My Deathless Courage"

The opportunities for failures in either establishing or within existing relationships are plenty during young adulthood. These have the ability to generate a sense of core shame, loneliness, low self-esteem, and create future challenges for socioemotional development. The emotions associated to failure and loneliness are intense during young adulthood because experiences are new, motivations are high, and there is not a lifetime of experiences behind one to use as points of reference. Defeat, in all phases of young adulthood can be felt, completely. However, the process of relationship building will inevitably involve defeat. It is not how many, nor the depth of defeats one engages, but rather how one chooses to derive meaning from them. The meaning will determine stagnation, growth-promotion, or destruction. Cultivating resilience (i.e., the ability to emotionally recover from setbacks) is important for ensuring that defeat is always a companion and not a foe.

The poem "Defeat" by the Lebanese American writer Kahlil Gibran (1883–1931) offered a perceptual shift for appreciating failures, because within the experiences of defeat are the extraordinary opportunities to realize profound meanings. One's relationship with Defeat actualizes inner potentials, as the poem stated:

> Defeat, my Defeat, my bold companion,
> You shall hear my songs and my cries and my silences,
> And none but you shall speak to me of the beating of wings,
> And urging of seas,
> And of mountains that burn in the night,
> And you alone shall climb my steep and rocky soul.
> Defeat, my Defeat, my deathless courage,
> You and I shall laugh together with the storm,
> And together we shall dig graves for all that die in us,
> And we shall stand in the sun with a will,
> And we shall be dangerous.
> *(Gibran, 2021, paras. 4–5)*

Young adults that experience the emotional depths of defeat in relationship failures have the opportunities to courageously face realities with strength, compassion, and curiosity. Defeat is a faithful companion through existentialism. It develops an awareness for how valuable life challenges are for creating meaning.

Defeat may bring people to the depths of confusing, uncomfortable, and painful emotions. Young adults must come to appreciate that all emotions are ubiquitous and necessary for personal growth. Emotions are an evolutionary marvel which have been observed as "a complex interaction between genes and environment, between innately programmed mechanisms and learned associations" (Adolphs & Anderson, 2018, p. 167). The organism's capacity or abilities for emotional experience came into being as persistent challenges with the external world required adaption for survival. According to de Waal (2019) emotions are,

> bodily and mental states—from anger and fear to sexual desire and affection and seeking the upper hand—that drive behavior. Triggered by certain stimuli and accompanied by behavioral changes, emotions are detectable on the

104 Part I

outside in facial expression, skin color, vocal timbre, gestures, odor, and so on. Only when the person experiencing these changes becomes aware of them do they becomes feelings, which are conscious experiences. We show our emotions, but we talk about our feelings.

(p. 4)

Organisms that began to experience and paid attention to emotional states as adaptive responses were able to be just good enough to pass on their genes. Emotions are an evolutionary advantage. The term *organism* is appropriate here because emotions are not just found in humans, but are experienced by many other forms of life including primates, mammals, fish, and corvids (de Waal, 2019). Our limited means of research instrumentation and perceptual limits separate us from knowing the emotional experiences of other organisms.

Our understanding of emotions is still in its infancy—categories and languages are naturally limited for capturing the full phenomenon of experience. Each culture and language has its own vocabulary to describe an emotional experience, which is why a multicultural dialogue is imperative to build collective under-standings. Although emotions are ubiquitous, languages cannot represent their infinity of nuance and quality. For example, the word sadness has many experi-ences. The sadness experienced during defeat is different than the sadness of losing a loved one—the subjective experience is always more than what words define. The interconnected nature of emotions, body, and environment make it challenging for young adults to discern which exact word could define an emo-tional state and the specific external triggers that are associated. They may also experience a state of emotional hybridity, such as angry disappointment or a fearful disgust. Emotions are an infinitely complex phenomenon.

Memories of relationship failures are emotionally charged and are often quite easy to remember. This is because the brain has a bias toward negative emotional experiences. The amygdala plays an essential role alongside the hippocampus to facilitate the memory storage and retrieval of negative emotional experiences. These are easily recalled as data references, so that the person can anticipate, foresee consequences, or consider meanings of future experiences. Negative emotional memories are distributed and interconnected throughout long-term memory networks. They are highly myelinated so that neurons fire at faster speeds along stronger connections to produce the appropriate response for certain environmental triggers. However, young adults must appreciate that negative emotional experiences in relationships are not determinants for the quality or meanings of future relationships, but are resources from which to learn, grow, and expand understandings (Cozolino, 2014; Damasio, 2018; Goodlad, 2004). Defeat holds a considerable amount of valuable data that can inform improve-ment. However, failures of the past are not to be dwelled on. They are useful to reflect upon and learn from, but all life, as Kierkegaard (1959) affirmed, "must be lived forwards" (p. 89).

The emotional power of defeat in relationships is essential for growth, not only for personal success but also for young adults' academic and career achievements (Salmon et al., 2018; Thomson & Carlson, 2017). Socio-emotional intelligence (SEI) represents high levels of ability for cognitive, behavioral, and socio-emotional awareness, regulation, and communication. SEI contributes to their self-reflective capacities, emotional management, decision-making abilities, and lifelong habit formation. Managing and understanding emotions at school is vitally important for academic success and high level of life satisfaction—from navigating peer relationships during recess time or between college classes, to resolving test-anxiety, forming study habits, and collaborating with diverse peers in projects. There are bound to be rifts and misunderstandings, in which SEI is essential for learning and growing from what may appear as negative experiences (Jones & Khan, 2017).

Research has shown that a young adult's SEI is a significant predictor for lifelong academic and social success (Bierman et al., 2017). Those that were able to develop diverse relationships with empathy, manage negative emotions and resilience, and use failures to enhance problem-solving skills, had greater rates for higher-education degree completion and lower chances for emotional disturbances (Dorman, 2015; Jones & Khan, 2017; Yang et al., 2018; Zeng et al., 2016). This makes SEI an essential curricular component so that schools can offer equitable opportunities for academic and developmental growth for minority and marginalized populations. SEI acts as a preventative measure for coping and overcoming the risks and circumstances in financial challenges, victimization, home conflicts, and other negative stressors caused by inequity (Gray et al., 2018).

Developing a critical consciousness for social relationships helps transcend awareness into multicultural realms of meaning and communicating (Au, 2012). Young adults need safe spaces in which cross-cultural interactions can take place in order to develop cultural humility. Within relational process, they will come to know that failures are necessary parts for building relationships. The differences found in cultural paradigms offer opportunities to affirm diversities, resolve challenges collaboratively, and strengthen bonds (Nathan et al., 2015). Instances of words being lost in translation, conflict, and misunderstandings are common. Young adults will realize that most communication is non-verbal and will find creative ways in which to build a relationship.

To learn from defeat, one needs opportunities for self-reflection to expand awareness through empathic dialogue. Within empathic conversations, the inequities, ill treatment, misperceptions, and marginalization that culturally diverse peers experience become real to their peers (Markowitz & Puchner, 2014). Diverse relationships open perceptual avenues to recognize the economic, social, and political realities of other people. When young adults become mindful of their emotions, especially when rifts are present, it can provide opportunities to transcend current meanings in order to find partnerships for social change.

106 Part I

Mindful Defeat

Developing a mindful awareness of defeat in relationships can be difficult as most young adults wish to avoid the unpleasant emotions of sadness, anger, despair, and feelings of pain, disregard, and loneliness. When relationship fractures come in the form of violence and victimization, negative emotions are amplified tenfold and inner destruction ensues. Young adults in these hostile situations must remove themselves, seek help, or find those who can help them to safety.

For growth-promoting relationships, becoming mindful of negative emotions develops socio-emotional intelligences. Mindfulness has become a mainstay of contemporary United States pop culture, as new smartphone applications provide instruction, Internet videos can play meditative ambience, and many public schools have implemented it as part of their social and emotional learning curriculum.

The history of mindfulness dates back to roughly 2,500 years ago. It is an ancient tradition that originated in Asian countries to promote spirituality, Zen, holistic health, and mental well-being. Mainstream U.S. culture became introduced to these practices and philosophies from scholars like D. T. Suzuki and Alan Watts around the mid-twentieth century. However, mindfulness has only become a recent pop-cultural phenomenon in Western societies because its secularized version has been marketed for self-development and validated with empirical research studies (Harpin et al., 2016; Harley, 2018; Larrivee & Echarte, 2018; Williams et al., 2018). In the U.S., mindfulness may have its own philosophical variations or even distortions, but it has offered avenues in which promote equanimity, holistic well-being, healing, and spirituality.

Mindfulness is a compassionate, holistic, perceptual, and nonjudgmental awareness that focuses on interoceptive experience or external circumstances themselves. Finding clarity amongst the emotions and feelings, one hones in on the current state of being to understand reality in the here-and-now (Pivarunas et al., 2015; Tsur et al., 2016). Attuning to the holistic process of experience helps one become more knowledgeable of emotional phenomenon. Mindful diligence may be new to young adults, but through practice their skills will develop. Popular forms of mindfulness include focused breathing techniques or verbal statements exploring sensations in the body. However, mindfulness is a diligent practice of many sorts which also includes walking, eating, seeing, touching, or hearing.

Mindful meditation does not have to be a static or quiet activity, but can involve movement and vociferous expression. There are other senses for knowing things other than reflective thoughts. Mindfulness does not always have to be within cognitive focus, but practiced in a way that lets the body attune to experience. Becoming appreciative for all the senses as ways of knowing existence broadens young adults' abilities for mindfulness awareness. Hugging a loved one and allowing that tactile and emotional experience to take over is mindfulness.

Throughout life, young adults can seek opportunities to be mindful, such as sitting amongst trees practicing a deep forest bathing, dancing to allow the limbs to explore the space about oneself to know the experience or vibe, or even feeling the digestion of delicious food where the body is mindful of the nutrients.

Meditation is most effective when it does not involve a goal or purpose for self-development. The cognitive reflective-type of mindfulness entails explicitly knowing an experience through descriptive inner-vocabulary/dialogue—which in many ways can remove one from the actual event. Young adults need be able to differentiate between *being in* the moment and *reflecting on* the moment. For example, playing a game with peers may bring great joy, and if the person is continuously reflecting, *I am having fun*, then they are only thinking it and not actually within the phenomenon of the moment.

Although the brain has a predilection for remembering and focusing on negative experiences, the practice of mindfulness supports young adults to manage emotional states by appreciating their impermanence (Brody et al., 2018). Realizing that everything is in constant change or flow, whether it be with the experience of time, thoughts, or emotions—one can neither hold anything in the past, nor grasp what is in the future. The eternal flow of *now* is a realization that brings young adults to value defeat and failure in relationships. According to Nhat Hanh (1998):

> We need to learn to appreciate the value of impermanence. If we are in good health and are aware of impermanence, we will take good care of ourselves. When we know that the person we love is impermanent, we will cherish our beloved all the more. Impermanence teaches us to respect and value every moment and all the precious things around us and inside of us. When we practice mindfulness of impermanence, we become fresher and more loving.
>
> *(p. 123)*

Impermanence helps young adults live by inner-core values, tending to the things and beings they care for most, while not allowing negative experiences to cause damage or distraction. Self-compassion is important for letting negative emotions pass. Offering presence means embracing the negative emotion as a loved one in order to promote healing. Nhat Hanh (2007) continued:

> With mindfulness we do not have to regret the way we have lived. Mindfulness helps us see and be in touch with our loved ones. It is the energy that allows us to come back to ourselves, to be alive and truly happy.
>
> *(p. 23)*

The profundity of impermanence and mindfulness is realized in Zen Buddhism (Watts, 2001). Many speak of attaining a state of Zen that is designated by no-

108 Part I

thing-ness, where there is no focus or reflection, but rather just everything all at once. There are no things to be separate from, just everything to be connected to. In the no-thing-ness state of Zen, people get with whatever is happening. They *dig it,* so to speak. The word *tathātā* is the appropriate Mahayana Buddhist term in Zen that means suchness or essence of Being. For a young adult to experience tathātā, it means noticing that whatever is being noticed just *is.* This sense of Being is profound. Watching peers at the lunch table talking, teachers walking around the halls, a professor distributing syllabi, customers coming and going at work, or watching the dog stroll down the street is just as the birds sing, the leaves rustle, flowers turn colors and float away. Our actions are as natural as the rest of the universe because we are an expression of it, not an alien entity thrown into it. Tathātā is important for young adults as they begin to realize the nature of impermanence and experience Zen.

When a young adult can come into a state of Being in which nothing is to be pursued or gained, Zen is experienced (Watts, 1985). The illusion of the self is not in pursuit of betterment, more skills, or knowledge; rather the self is dissolved into the stream of eternity (Epstein, 1999; Watts, 2003). The Zen experience is not meant as a source for ideas, data, pleasure, or avoidance of pain. Zen is only meant to be experienced (Nhat Hanh, 1998). As Watts (2001) described:

> The heart of Zen is not an idea but an experience, and when that experience happens (and "happens" is just the right word) you are set free from ideas altogether. Certainly, you can still use them, but you no longer take them seriously. Picture yourself, then as a person very earnestly concerned with making sense of life, of a world involving intense pleasure and appalling pain, and trying to understand how and why there is this weird sensation called "myself" will have been turned upside down and inside out.
>
> *(p. 340)*

Zen brings one to realize that the self is inter-connected and inter-dependent with the universe. Young adults experiencing defeat may feel a sense of loneliness, low self-esteem, or worthlessness. In a state of Zen, they realize the illusion of the self, and that they are as valuable and phenomenal as the world around them. This aligns with what Krishnamurti (1973) declared, "the world is me and I am the world" (p. 108). The negative emotional experiences that one feels are not to dissociate or estrange the young adult from the world, but rather bring them closer. Mindful Zen diligence can be realized in moments such as riding a bus, watching the clouds, sweeping the floor, or even in the presence of another—it is an effortless practice because Zen is a natural state (tathātā).

Mindful practices encourage young adults to constructively explore culturally relative meanings within their experiences of solitude. To identify the feelings of emptiness, anxiety, and despair within circumstances is an ability that fosters agency during loneliness. Yet, learning to let go of some relationships can be

The Bold Companionship of Defeat   **109**

distressing for those that experience loneliness anxiety. They tend to cling on or salvage the failed relationship at all costs. The intent is not motivated for repair, learning, or growth, but out of fear that without this individual the emptiness and void of loneliness would be consuming. A relationship of this sort is devoid of encounter, empathy, or growth because the other person is used as an abstract thing to complete an incomplete illusion. As Moustakas (1972) described,

> The truth is not learned by reinforcement and habit; it is learned by being in touch with one's own self and by being present to the other, by letting the inner reality contact the outer reality without filtering or censoring perception and awareness.
>
> *(p. 68)*

Mindfulness is preventative against loneliness anxiety because it aligns young adults with an inner reality that resonates with outer circumstances. Although the pain of relationship loss may be intense, the person finds inner sources for the courage to let it go or to rebuild.

In the mid-late twentieth century, humanist psychologists Clark Moustakas and Cereta Perry conducted workshops at a school that had major challenges with student behavior, academic achievement, parent engagement, and building relationships with the community. Moustakas and Perry (1973) gathered parents/guardians, students, teachers, and school administrators to lead them in hands-on group sessions to the build relationships through self-exploration and discovery. One of the sessions was focused on mindful awareness, which may have been the first time some of the participants were exposed to the practice. In a large room, the group was directed to spread out and find their own space. They were then guided to move their bodies in ways that brought about awareness—linking mind and body into a state of Zen. After, the two researchers led the group through a mindfulness practice as they asked the group to reflect:

> What am I feeling at this moment? What is happening within me right now? What is my mood? Do I feel tensions in my body? If I listen carefully, can I actively be in touch with the source of my discontent? What do I want? What do I prefer? How many different levels of awareness can I reach when I am alone? Can I describe each feeling? What thoughts and feelings stand out?
>
> *(Moustakas & Perry, 1973, p. 3)*

Moustakas and Perry (1973) guided the group through memories of school, emotional experiences, and the sensations in the here-and-now. They had extraordinary results; not only did parents/guardians, teachers, and administrators develop a greater sense of community, they also became more attuned to their role in the child's life, and invested in the children's schooling and personal

110 Part I

development. The students were able to appreciate the guided mindfulness sessions as well. At the end of the program students did better with emotional regulation, had less behavioral issues, and improved in academic performance. Moustakas and Perry (1973) reflected:

We have observed, with excitement, parents and teachers relaxing together and learning to be free with one another. At times the climate amidst the adults was heavy and the knots became more and more pronounced, but as the struggles continued, frustration and failure shifted, and "grownups" dropped their defenses, their stiff sense of pride, and their role expectations. They learned to laugh and cry together. They learned to work together on joint projects. They created a better world, one they could believe in and care about. We experienced a new world opening up in a school setting where voices of people rang out in freedom, in joy, in love.

(p. 168)

The researchers helped participants develop a compassionate appreciation of the self and others that was sensitive and nonjudgmental. Such compassion helped them to develop higher-quality growth-promoting relationships. Years later, Moustakas (1995) affirmed that, "We must continue to reserve a place for ourselves, to make time and space for knowing the essence of who we are as individuals, the deep and abiding core, that is now, that is growing, that is forever" (p. 19).

Mindful diligence is important for young adults to stay centered as they explore new and complex relationships with the world. According to Sun et al. (2021), "In the midst of great uncertainty, anxiety, and despair during the COVID-19 pandemic, dispositional attentiveness to the present moment may protect young adults from excessive worries, rumination, and fear" (p. 11). Or as Moustakas and Perry (1973) described:

Once children learn to focus, concentrate, and notice, once they are open and aware of their feelings, learning becomes exciting and unique; it becomes a personal adventure. With the child is fully present as an individual, and with awareness of the immediate situation, there is also freedom from within to explore real interests and to use appropriate resources and talents.

(p. 3)

Learning from Defeat in Relationships

The negative emotions that arise during relationship rifts and failures can be overwhelming for young adults. True learning can only happen in the here-and-now; where emotions bring significance to experience (DeRobertis & Bland, 2020). Mindful diligence is an enlightening and healing process. Nhat Hanh

The Bold Companionship of Defeat   111

(1998) developed a five-step process to help people develop mindful awareness to grow and heal from what may appear as negative experiences.

In the first phase of mindfulness, Nhat Hanh (1998) recommends that young adults begin the practice of *recognition*. Within recognition, the person is able to explicitly identify what is happening within the body. Early in a relationship there may be instances of conflict. Mindful recognition seeks to ascertain what is happening within the person during the event. The young adult may state to their self or the other person, "I am aware of a deep frustration within me…" This provides a sense of clarity to explore reasons why the person is frustrated. Expressing oneself in an honest manner allows other individuals an empathic perceptual avenue to build understanding. However, the process of recognition during the early phases of young adulthood may bring about frustrations in itself, as the person may struggle to find the vocabulary to elaborate on the emotions or specify certain feelings. Failure at discovering the specific words to describe an awareness or misidentifying an emotion is common at all stages of life. However, practice surely makes better. When others share their process of recognition, young adults will explore their own perceptual self-awareness abilities. An emotional experience may be more than what it appears. A young adult may have experienced anger toward a family member and, by exploring that emotion, they might discover greater feelings of disappointment.

In the second phase of the mindful awareness process, the young adult seeks a nonjudgmental *acceptance* of their current state. There is no denial or distraction, but greeting the emotional state as it is. For instance, a person may experience sadness for losing a relationship. Peers and caring adults may tell the person to *get over it*, not to focus on it, or even to distract oneself from the emotion. This not only minimizes the person's experience but also trivializes deep inner workings. Validating an emotional experience is vitally important for learning and growth. To create meaning within defeat, the young adult needs to recognize and accept realities. Within this acceptance are gateways into existential concerns and themes.

Acceptance then leads to the third step of the mindfulness process, *compassion*. Once negative emotions are identified and accepted, they need to be given compassion—a loving care that seeks to bring about healing. Young adults learn to develop compassion toward negative emotional states by perceiving them as meaningful phenomena in need of attention. Compassion promotes self-acceptance and awareness in that these unpleasant experiences are not meant to harm the individual, but teach something significant about life. For example, to accept the sadness in loss with compassion will cultivate a deeper appreciation for the privilege of relationships.

The importance of failures within relationships is explored in the fourth step, *looking deeply*. Exploring the phenomenon of a negative emotion can offer enlightened insights for developing one's personal existentialism. This is where defeat is realized as a bold companion that opens up new perceptual avenues. The person looks deeply within defeat, in a nonjudgmental way, to see how a negative emotion originated.

112   Part I

Looking deeply brings one into the fifth phase of Nhat Hanh's (1998) mindful awareness practice, *insight*. Within insight, the person explores existential meanings in which to reveal connections with the universe. The failures in relationships provide perspicacity into realities. To illustrate, the loss of a relationship reflects the impermanence of life, an existential theme in which young adults can recognize in their everyday encounters. Or that relationships are not found, but created upon the meanings that people determine. The educational value comes from learning from emotional experiences and being able to navigate future challenges with wisdom.

Nhat Hanh's (1998) five steps for mindful awareness is vitally important for creating meaning in young adulthood. Mindful awareness fosters acceptance of reality and the self in the here-and-now. The five-step process is not meant to focus on how unfair the universe is or how all life is suffering; nor it is a way to draw negative conclusions or reductions on existential givens. Rather, it helps one appreciate that all parts of existence, especially negative ones, are essential. As Nhat Hanh (2007) described:

> Mindfulness is the capacity to recognize things as they are. When you are mindful, you recognize what is going on, what is happening in the here and now. When you recognize something positive, you can enjoy it; you can nourish and heal yourself just by recognizing these positive elements. And when something is negative, mindfulness helps you embrace it, soothe it, and get some relief.
>
> *(p. 22)*

Young adults can learn that mindfulness is not just an acceptance of realities, but a process where one has the power to greet all elements of Being with love and compassion. Mindfulness promotes equanimity, especially during existential crisis (Brody et al., 2018; Sanger et al., 2018). Defeat in relationships is not something outside the self, happening to it; rather, it is a bold companion within that is willing to explore the most challenging areas of life in order to help young adults create meaning.

One must be careful of the mindfulness strategies that are sold as quick remedies to rid negative emotions, or even as a culturally exclusive practice that can make one more unique. Mindfulness cannot be achieved if motivations are driven by self-development, materialism, or narcissism. Leaving behind the illusory game of self-development widens one's perceptions to the infinite relationships that exist in life. Mindfulness becomes a practice,

> about protecting the lives of human beings, animals, vegetables, and minerals. To protect other beings is to protect ourselves. The second is to prevent the exploitation by humans of other living beings and of nature. It is also the practice of generosity. The third is to protect children and adults from sexual abuse, to preserve the happiness of individuals and families.
>
> *(Nhat Hanh, 1998, p. 184)*

Knowing Relationships within the Darkness

Coming to know relationships within the shadows of existential realities may be complex and frightening processes for young adults. Emotions can appear to be immense and indefinable, which cause disorientation during relational rifts. When one gives up the illusion that emotions can be resisted or battled, the person discovers sources of profound meaning. Negative emotions are as equally wise as positive ones.

Emotions are natural occurrences, just as clouds form and pass in a blue sky. Neither passivity nor proactivity that can deny them. To realize that one is the world, just as much the world is the person, affirms that

> inside the skull and the skin as well as outside, there is simply the stream flowing along of itself. The bones flow too, and their inner texture has the same patterns as moving liquid. In nature, there are neither masters nor slaves.
>
> *(Watts, 2001, p. 154)*

Mindfulness is the art of achieving clarity, compassion, equanimity, non-judgmental awareness, and insight into how inner experiences are the gateway for discovering relationships with others (Fuochi et al., 2018; Pivarunas et al., 2015).

Regardless if emotions are positive or negative, they are signs of intelligence—as an organism resonates with the world (de Waal, 2019; Watts, 2003). To develop socio-emotional intelligences, it is important for young adults to learn how to listen to emotions with curiosity and compassion. Many times, social and emotional learning curriculum will teach young adults strategies to master their emotions. It may be comforting to believe emotions can be controlled, especially when one is in a positive emotional state. When negative emotions develop, they reveal the reality that emotions are too powerful to be controlled—as they can be depthless, disorienting, overwhelming, all encompassing, and much more pervasive than the preconceived abstraction. Young adults may wonder how to manage emotions so that positive and negative states can provide insight.

Emotions cannot be mastered, but one can develop mastery in abilities to regulate and learn from states. Regulation through mindfulness is not about control, but rather a caring attention to heal, learn, and expand awareness.

Empirical Explorations of Mindfulness

Mindful diligence demands less brain resources and energies than compared to other therapies that have a sole cognitive focus (Williams et al., 2018). Studies have found that the prefrontal cortices of the brain are stimulated during mindful mediation. This excitation leads to enhanced neural white brain matter (neural connections)—where more efficiency means less power is needed to accomplish tasks (Brody et al., 2018; Morrish et al., 2018). The prefrontal cortices play an important role in emotional regulation, impulse control, and response. When young adults practice mindfulness it promotes successful emotional regulation. These achievements result in a higher sense of self-esteem and motivation to engage new relationships (Gray et al., 2018; Vidic & Cherup, 2019).

For youth that need assistance learning to regulate emotions and have challenges with home financial situations, travel, or accessibility, virtual online mindfulness sessions can be an effective avenue. However, Antonson et al. (2018) found that in a study of 95 adolescents enrolled in an online mindfulness self-help program, only 15 participants logged on to complete the program trial. Many of the adolescents that did not participate reported challenges with time or lack of interest. Online participation was even lower when youth had greater levels of stress from school. This is why young adult engagement and retention strategies for online mental well-being programs are in need of development.

Furthermore, in an eight-week study by Xu et al. (2019), the researchers surveyed how mindfulness affected adolescents that had been clinically diagnosed with mild depression. The participants were asked to complete a daily focused breathing practice for three to six minutes a day, along with keeping a mindfulness journal. The log documented personal reflections during the meditation and provided useful qualitative data. The researchers found that participants that completed the tasks scored higher on post-tests for emotional balance, meaning in life, and lower in levels of depression when compared to the control group. Xu et al. (2019) concluded that mindfulness breathing is a highly effective method for young adults to regulate light to moderate mental disturbances. Mindful breathing can be practiced without formal training, costs nothing, and can be done anywhere.

Mindfulness practices have holistic effects to the person to increase physical well-being (Brockman et al., 2017). For example, learning to mindfully breathe and focus on inner states of the body

> enable[s] the brain to shape its anatomy and physiology to accommodate experiential input, including subcellular and molecular alterations, microcircuit modifications, and network restructuring that generate localized as well as global changes in brain issue over short and prolonged time scales.
>
> *(Larrivee & Echarte, 2018, p. 961)*

In this way, when pain or negative emotions arise, mindful awareness lessens the degree of mental and physical suffering, while also reducing severity in future instances (Singh et al., 2017).

With the increasing rates of emotional disturbances, substance abuse, suicides, and somatization disorders for young adults, the World Health Organization advocated for schools to help students develop mindful awareness practices to mitigate the stressors and challenges of a rapidly changing world (Sanger et al.,

2018). Mindfulness helps filter cognitive processes so that there are reduced opportunities for misperceptions, negative meanings, and destructive behaviors. Micromanagement of symptoms or thoughts rarely provide positive long-term results; instead, the holistic approach that mindfulness brings allows for a broader definition of well-being (Brody et al., 2018). The existential concerns of young adults may not be addressed at home, amongst peers, or in the classroom. The unhealthy ways of distraction, such as problematic cellphone use or social media disorder are just symptoms to a greater disturbance. According to Sanger et al. (2018), "Mindfulness encourages openness to both positive and negative experience whilst minimizing reactivity or rumination. It can promote activation, and neural connectivity in regions associated with social understanding, bodily awareness, and empathy— the insular cortex" (p. 2).

Mindfulness not only produces recognition of the complex and nebulous states when existential concerns intensify, but also supports young adults to appreciate their inner states as valuable forms of knowledge. Practicing mindfulness can take just five minutes a day. With practice one can increase focusing abilities to 20 minutes or more per day. Data on school implementation have shown that daily mindfulness practice lessened the symptomology of mental disturbances and decreased time spent on classroom management (Morrish et al., 2018). Nhat Hanh (1998) supported, "Schools are not just places for transmitting technical know-how. They must also be places where children can learn to be happy, loving, and understanding, where teachers nourish their students with their own insights and happiness" (p. 235).

The momentum of mindfulness practices in Western culture has made significant changes for many elementary and secondary public schools. Mindfulness diligence in the classroom increases abilities and duration of focused attention as well as a somatic awareness that helps navigate complex interpersonal encounters (Halland et al., 2015; Tan et al., 2016; Tsur et al., 2016). Furthermore, Valosek et al. (2019) found that mindfulness meditation decreased levels of antisocial behaviors, high school dropout rates, and promoted degree completion and long-term academic performance.

Still, there is an absence of mindfulness practices across higher education curriculum. When surveyed, a majority of young adults, regardless of cultural orientation, expressed a desire to develop spirituality or mindful connections to the universe (Cobb et al., 2015). Institutions of higher education can cultivate spirituality by facilitating mindfulness awareness practices. Brody et al., (2018), found that while mindfulness has extraordinary benefits for young adults, the challenge appears to be in developing it as a long-term habit. Once young adults graduated secondary school most stopped their mindfulness practice. The goal then, is to help young adults continue mindfulness as a lifelong diligence by continuing its curricular implementation in higher education.

Young adults may need time and opportunities to understand the unfolding processes within their selves in social contexts. Mindfulness is a vital practice that generates socio-emotional awareness to regulate impulses, hone interoception, and increase cognitive focus (Cobb et al., 2015; Lemberger et al., 2018). Each of these factors are crucial when forming diverse relationships. There may be superficial relational rifts or defeats early in a relationship, but through empathic encounter, young adults can find each other within deeper cultural archetypes. Meeting others in the foundations of culture creates opportunities to create multicultural meanings together.

References

Adolphs, R., & Anderson, D. J. (2018). *The neuroscience of emotion: A new synthesis.* Princeton University Press.

Antonson, C., Thorsén, F., Sundquist, J., & Sundquist, K. (2018). Upper secondary school students' compliance with two Internet-based self-help programmes: a randomised controlled trial. *European Child & Adolescent Psychiatry*, 27(2), 191–200. https://doi.org/10.1007/s00787-017-1035-6.

Au, W. (2012). *Critical curriculum studies: Education, consciousness, and the politics of knowing.* Routledge.

Bierman, K. L., Heinrichs, B. S., Welsh, J. A., Nix, R. L., & Gest, S. D. (2017). Enriching preschool classrooms and home visits with evidence-based programming: Sustained benefits for low-income children. *Journal of Child Psychology & Psychiatry*, 58(2), 129–137. doi:10.1111/jcpp.12618.

Brockman, R., Ciarrochi, J., Parker, P., & Kashdan, T. (2017). Emotion regulation strategies in daily life: mindfulness, cognitive reappraisal and emotion suppression. *Cognitive Behaviour Therapy*, 46(2), 91–113. https://doi.org/10.1080/16506073.2016.1218926.

Brody, J. L., Scherer, D. G., Turner, C. W., Annett, R. D., & Dalen, J. (2018). A conceptual model and clinical framework for integrating mindfulness into family therapy with adolescents. *Family Process*, 57(2), 510–524. https://doi.org/10.1111/famp.12298.

Cobb, E., Kor, A., & Miller, L. (2015). Support for adolescent spirituality: Contributions of religious practice and trait mindfulness. *Journal of Religion & Health*, 54(3), 862–870. https://doi.org/10.1007/s10943-015-0046-1.

Cozolino, L. (2014). *The neuroscience of human relationships: Attachment and the developing social brain* (2nd ed.). W. W. Norton & Company.

Damasio, A. (2018). *The strange order of things: Life, feeling, and the making of cultures.* Pantheon Books.

de Waal, F. (2019). *Mama's last hug: Animal emotions and what they tell us about ourselves.* W. W. Norton & Company.

DeRobertis, E. M., & Bland, A. M. (2020). From personal threat to cross-cultural learning: An eidetic investigation. *Journal of Phenomenological Psychology*, 51, 1–15. https://doi:10.1163/15691624-12341368.

Dorman, E. (2015). Building teachers' social-emotional competence through mindfulness practices. *Curriculum & Teaching Dialogue*, 17(1/2), 103–120.

Epstein, M. (1999). *Going to pieces without falling apart: A Buddhist perspective on wholeness.* Broadway Books.

Fuochi, G., Veneziani, C. A., & Voci, A. (2018). Exploring the social side of self-compassion: Relations with empathy and outgroup attitudes. *European Journal of Social Psychology*, 48(6), 769–783. https://doi.org/10.1002/ejsp.2378.

Gibran, K. (2021, May 29). Defeat. Poetry Foundation. https://www.poetryfoundation.org/poems/58713/defeat-56d23d566b4c3.

Goodlad, J. (2004). *A place called school* (2nd ed.). McGraw Hill.

Gray, L., Font, S., Unrau, Y., & Dawson, A. (2018). The effectiveness of a brief mindfulness-based intervention for college freshmen who have aged out of foster care. *Innovative Higher Education*, 43(5), 339–352. https://doi.org/10.1007/s10755-018-9433-3.

Halland, E., Vibe, M. D., Solhaug, I., Friborg, O., Rosenvinge, J. H., Tyssen, R., ... Bjørndal, A. (2015). Mindfulness training improves problem-focused coping in psychology and medical students: Results from a randomized controlled trial. *College Student Journal*, 49(3), 387–398.

Harari, Y. N. (2015). *Sapiens: A brief history of humankind*. HarperCollins.

Harley, J. (2018). The role of attention in therapy for children and adolescents who stutter: Cognitive behavioral therapy and mindfulness-based interventions. *American Journal of Speech-Language Pathology*, 27(4), 1139–1151. https://doi.org/10.1044/2018_AJSLP-ODC11-17-0196.

Harpin, S., Rossi, A., Kim, A. K., & Swanson, L. M. (2016). Behavioral impacts of a mindfulness pilot intervention for elementary school students. *Education*, 137(2), 149–156.

Jones, S. M., & Khan, J. (2017). The evidence base for how we learn: Supporting social, emotional, and academic development. *National Commission on Social, Emotional, and Academic Development*. The Aspen Institute.

Kierkegaard, S. (1959). *The journals of Kierkegaard*. A. Dru, Trans. Harper & Row.

Krishnamurti, J. (1973). *The awakening of intelligence*. HarperCollins.

Larrivee, D., & Echarte, L. (2018). Contemplative meditation and neuroscience: Prospects for mental health. *Journal of Religion & Health*, 57(3), 960–978. https://doi.org/10.1007/s10943-017-0475-0.

Lemberger, T. M. E., Carbonneau, K. J., Atencio, D. J., Zieher, A. K., & Palacios, A. F. (2018). Self-regulatory growth effects for young children participating in a combined social and emotional learning and mindfulness-based intervention. *Journal of Counseling & Development*, 96(3), 289–302. https://doi.org/10.1002/jcad.12203.

Markowitz, L., & Puchner, L. (2014). Racial diversity in the schools: A necessary evil? *Multicultural Perspectives*, 16(2), 72–78. doi:10.1080/15210960.2014.889568.

Morrish, L., Rickard, N., Chin, T. C., & Vella-Brodrick, D. A. (2018). Emotion regulation in adolescent well-being and positive education. *Journal of Happiness Studies*, 19(5), 1543–1564. https://doi.org/10.1007/s10902-017-9881-y.

Moustakas, C. E. (1972). *Loneliness and love*. Prentice Hall.

Moustakas, C. E. (1995). *Being-In, being-for, being-with*. Jason Aronson.

Moustakas, C. E. & Perry, C. (1973). *Learning to be free*. Prentice Hall.

Nathan, D., Trimble, D., & Fuxman, S. (2015). Building partnerships between Israeli and Palestinian youth: An integrative approach. *Israel Affairs*, 21(1), 148–164. doi:10.1080/13537121.2014.984436.

Nhat Hanh, T. (1998). *The heart of the Buddha's teachings: Transforming suffering into peace, joy, & liberation*. Parallax Press.

Nhat Hanh, T. (2007). *The art of power*. HarperOne.

Pivarunas, B., Kelly, N. R., Pickworth, C. K., Cassidy, O., Radin, R. M., Shank, L. M., ... Shomaker, L. B. (2015). Mindfulness and eating behavior in adolescent girls at risk for Type 2 Diabetes. *International Journal of Eating Disorders*, 48(6), 563–569. https://doi.org/10.1002/eat.22435.

Rey Anacona, C. A., & Martínez Gómez, J. A. (2021). Differences between sexes in psychopathological variables among adolescent victims of dating violence. *Psicología Desde El Caribe*, 38 (2), 1–23.

Salmon, A. K., Gangotena, M. V., & Melliou, K. (2018). Becoming globally competent citizens: A learning journey of two classrooms in an interconnected world. *Early Childhood Education Journal*, 46(3), 301–312. doi:10.1007/s10643-017-0860-z.

Sanger, K. L., Thierry, G., & Dorjee, D. (2018). Effects of school-based mindfulness training on emotion processing and well-being in adolescents: evidence from event-related potentials. *Developmental Science*, 21(5), 1. https://doi.org/10.1111/desc.12646.

Singh, N. N., Lancioni, G. E., Myers, R. E., Karazsia, B. T., Courtney, T. M., & Nugent, K. (2017). A mindfulness-based intervention for self-management of verbal and physical aggression by adolescents with Prader–Willi syndrome. *Developmental Neurorehabilitation*, 20(5), 253–260. https://doi.org/10.3109/17518423.2016.1141436.

Sun, S., Goldberg, S. B., Lin, D., Qiao, S., & Operario, D. (2021). Psychiatric symptoms, risk, and protective factors among university students in quarantine during the COVID-19 pandemic in China. *Globalization & Health*, 17(1), 1–14. https://doi.org/10.1186/s12992-021-00663-x.

Tan, J., Yang, W., Ma, H., & Yu, Y. (2016). Adolescents' core self-evaluations as mediators of the effect of mindfulness on life satisfaction. *Social Behavior & Personality: An International Journal*, 44(7), 1115–1122. https://doi.org/10.2224/sbp.2016.44.7.1115.

Thomson, R., & Carlson, J. (2017). A pilot study of a self-administered parent training intervention for building preschoolers' social-emotional competence. *Early Childhood Education Journal*, 45(3), 419–426. doi:10.1007/s10643-016-0798-6.

Tsur, N., Berkovitz, N., & Ginzburg, K. (2016). Body awareness, emotional clarity, and authentic behavior: The moderating role of mindfulness. *Journal of Happiness Studies*, 17 (4), 1451–1472. https://doi.org/10.1007/s10902-015-9652-6.

Valosek, L., Nidich, S., Wendt, S., Grant, J., & Nidich, R. (2019). Effect of meditation on social-emotional learning in middle school students. *Education*, 139(3), 111–119.

Vidic, Z., & Cherup, N. (2019). Mindfulness in classroom: Effect of a mindfulness-based relaxation class on college students' stress, resilience, self-efficacy and perfectionism. *College Student Journal*, 53(1), 130–142.

Wang, H., Lin, H., Richards, M., Yang, S., Liang, H., Chen, X., & Fu, C. (2021). Study problems and depressive symptoms in adolescents during the COVID-19 outbreak: Poor parent–child relationship as a vulnerability. *Globalization & Health*, 17(1). https://doi.org/10.1186/s12992-021-00693-5. Watts, A. (1985). *The way of Zen*. Vintage Books.

Watts, A. (2001). *In my own way: An autobiography 1915–1965*. New World Library.

Watts, A. (2003). *Become what you are*. Shambhala Publications.

Williams, C., Meeten, F., & Whiting, S. (2018). 'I had a sort of epiphany!' An exploratory study of group mindfulness-based cognitive therapy for older people with depression. *Aging & Mental Health*, 22(2), 208–217. https://doi.org/10.1080/13607863.2016.1247415.

Xu, L., Chen, G., & Li, B. (2019). Sadness empathy facilitates prosocial lying. *Social Behavior and Personality: An international journal*, 47(9), e8371.

Yalom, I. D. (1985). *The theory and practice of group psychotherapy* (3rd ed.). Basic Books.

Yang, C., Bear, G. G., & May, H. (2018). Multilevel associations between school-wide social-emotional learning approach and student engagement across elementary, middle, and high Schools. *School Psychology Review*, 47(1), 45–61. doi:10.17105/SPR-2017-0003.V47-1.

Zeng, S., Benner, G. J., & Silva, R. M. (2016). Effects of a summer learning program for students at risk for emotional and behavioral disorders. *Education & Treatment of Children*, 39(4), 593–615.

6

HEALING, GROWTH, AND ENLIGHTENMENT

The effects of technological advancements and COVID-19 are changing the world at disorienting speeds. This may overwhelm the cultural coping mechanisms and exceed the inner-resources of young adults, causing mental distress and existential anxieties (Watters, 2010). When seeking resources to heal or cope, young adults are at the mercy of dominant Western mental health paradigms. Indigenous and diverse cultural paradigms for healing, existential meanings, and well-being have been marginalized, if not destroyed. This was the case in 1879 at the Carlisle Indian Industrial School, which was a boarding school founded by Captain Richard Henry Pratt for children of the Cherokee Nation. The school was located off the reservation and for the curriculum:

> All of the academic subjects were tightly integrated with the view that learning such a curriculum would undo the "savagery" of Tribal Nations' cultures by cutting against all aspects of their worldviews. Physical geography challenged Indigenous knowledge systems entirely. It contradicted lessons about the cosmos and creation stories passed along by tribal elders, and it diminished the geographic and spiritual significance of major aspects of the Indian physical world. However, the cultural contradictions did not end with physical geography, and we would argue that these subjects represented an explicit curriculum of cultural genocide while also carrying with it a Western worldview that left no room for other worldviews.
>
> *(Au et al., 2016, p. 32)*

Destruction to the Cherokee children's cultural paradigm created trauma by shattering systems of existential meaning, healing, dignity, and holistic well-being. The historically exclusive and sometimes violent nature of Western medicine and psychology have limited its ability to support human flourishing.

DOI: 10.4324/9781003251651-8

Holistic well-being in young adulthood has become precarious, even though global economies progress, technologies advance, and quality of life increases (Hariharan & Kapoor, 2020). Rapidly developing urban societies have seen more computer jobs, with young professionals sitting in front of screens inside of offices. Although many technological advancements have made aspects of work and social life more convenient, less physical activity and exercise have translated into a decline for physical and mental well-being. Balancing the pressures and stressors of online worlds, career and economic demands, and social expectations have created challenges for well-being. Many young adults have become estranged from their cultural communities, relationships with families, friends, nature, and animals.

In the U.S., the nuclear families of the modern century have both parents/caregivers working without the familial support systems (relatives) that the older generations experienced. Children and adolescents have been alone after school hours, sometimes even weekends, as the proverbial latchkey kids. The stress of life without caring adult guidance is coupled with the pressures to achieve academic and social success. Research has shown that youth in these situations are more prone to develop emotional disturbances (i.e., anxiety, depression), maladaptive behaviors (e.g., substance abuse, problematic Internet use), and lack constructive stress management strategies (Radhika et al., 2020). It was found that half of all adult psychological disturbances and issues with behavior were developed during young adulthood.

In 2021, social restrictions were slowly lifted and young adults ventured out into the world once more. However, the existential trauma that COVID-19 created followed them. For some, returning to the social world became an even more lonely experience than quarantine. The young adults that did not have effective coping strategies or resources for the existential terror during the pandemic may experience a sense of estrangement from peers, adults, social situations, and even connections with the natural world. Without spirituality, young adults are vulnerable to the mental disturbances and physical malaise that are endogenous to loneliness anxiety in existential terrors.

This chapter will understand spirituality in a multicultural humanistic psychological paradigm by utilizing the ideas of philosopher Alan Watts (1915–1973) to explore how spiritual practices promote well-being and equanimity for young adults in existential turmoil. Watts' philosophical work was seminal for emerging a multicultural spiritual paradigm by connecting ancient philosophies and contemporary circumstances, Eastern and Western cultural paradigms, and culture with the natural world (especially animals).

Although this chapter discusses the necessity of spirituality for realizing the goals of multicultural humanistic psychology, it does not purposely delve into the field of transpersonal psychology—a school of psychology which holds that spirituality is important for the transcendence of consciousness in order to achieve human potentials. Although ideas from prominent figures in humanistic psychology, such as Abraham Maslow, contributed to the development of this field, transpersonal psychology has seen opposition from other members such as Rollo May. Transpersonal psychology may stray too far from the person, seeking to find something beyond itself, without appreciating the subjective experiences and meanings within existential concerns. Furthermore, the discourse does not have a strong empirical and theoretical foundation, which existentialism and humanistic psychology have. Therefore, this discussion on spirituality is situated within a multicultural humanistic psychology paradigm.

The nature of all existence is relationships (Watts, 2017). Spirituality is a being's relationships to all forms of existence and phenomena. For human beings, spirituality means accessing cognitive and physical capacities in order to find and establish connections with the universe (Hariharan & Kapoor, 2020). Human spirituality is a secular form of practice and belief that focuses on the autonomy of the person. There is an encouragement to explore personal freedom and to develop relationships with the natural world. One can be spiritual without ascribing to a religious order. Spirituality cultivates a "high life satisfaction, meaning or life purpose, and to put it simply it [is] the ability to feel well across without any stress or duress in any aspect of life" (Hariharan & Kapoor, 2020, p. 253). In addition, spirituality has been observed as an integral human characteristic, as people seek transcendence in the form of connections or meanings with others, the environment, animals, and the universe (Shahina & Parveen, 2020; Testoni et al., 2021). Artefact creation, rituals, symbols, value formation, dance, prayer, song, and meditation are just a few ways in which human beings explore or express spiritual connections.

Developing spirituality during young adulthood means expressing and exploring intrinsic motivations to establish meanings or purposes in life through relationships with world domains (Hariharan & Kapoor, 2020; Vazifeh doust et al., 2020). Spirituality is a protective factor against mental disturbances, especially during difficult times. Young adults learn to build resilience for future life challenges by having spiritual support/meanings. The cultural paradigm is a guide for how existential concerns can be explored through spirituality, such as seeking support from family members, community, or nature. Each supportive resource provides teachings, empathy, presence, practices, experiences, and advice for how to achieve equanimity and connections with the world.

Cultures are renewed when they mix with the complex diversities of other paradigms—offering a triangulated positionality that offers a multifaceted perspective of reality. Young adults are able to view existential concerns and spiritual meanings from other perspectives, while the distance from their own paradigm helps recognize unnoticed phenomena (Watts, 1979). Cultural paradigms frame how youth should develop relationships with the world and which tools can construct meaning. As Watts (2017) explained, in Western culture,

> Children ask their parents, "How was I made?" or "Who made me?" But these aren't questions asked by Chinese or Indian (specifically Hindu)

Healing, Growth, and Enlightenment **123**

children. Now, a Chinese child might ask her mother, "How did I grow?" but *growing* and *making* are entirely different procedures. You see, when you *make* something, you put it together—you arrange its parts, you work from the *outside* to the *in*.

(p. 4)

In Eastern cultural paradigms, growth indicates an inner expansion, a realization of potentials, and a blossoming of everything all at once, much like a flower or a fetus in a womb. Existence of the universe blossomed in the same manner. We are as much the force and stuff of the Big Bang as the current contents of the universe; there is a primordial energy that is us, not to be separated with titles, names, or dates (Watts, 2017). From within the existential bedrock of cultural paradigms, youth seek to know their existence through relationships.

Developing relationships with the world brings vibrancy to existential meanings. The young adult then recognizes the absurdity of illusions that were firmly held: the self, value of material possessions, social titles and status (Watts, 2003). Faith through spirituality is a detachment from worldly things and in return is the discovery of an isolated existential self that is interconnected with everything all at once. It is important not to misunderstand what spiritual detachment entails. According to Watts (2003):

Detachment means to have neither regrets for the past nor fears for the future; to let life take its course without attempting to interfere with its movement and change, neither trying to prolong the stay of things pleasant nor to hasten the departure of things unpleasant.

(p. 10)

Faith enlightens youth to live harmoniously with the world around them, detached from the illusory past and future in favor of living in the here-and-now. Watts (2003) explored the spiritual nature of Buddhism to find that it

perceives the beauty of change, for life is like music in this: if any note or phrase is held for longer than its appointed time, the melody is lost. Thus Buddhism may be summed up in two phrases: "Let go!" and "Walk on!"

(p. 60)

Embracing impermanence means letting go of the desire for a reified self, in order to begin living with the flowing nature of existence. Spirituality includes a process of mind, where emotions and thoughts can be reflected upon in encounters with the world, such as with the stars, nature, streams, animals, bugs, trees, cactus flowers, all of which are beatific (Watts, 2003). The spirituality of the mind achieves salvation or transcendence when it has become attuned to the beat of the life.

Young adults often become downhearted from influential adults' reductionist conclusions on life. For example, some scholars/authorities feel that the universe is an unintelligent game of chance, reducing it to atoms and molecules, which is an insult to all life (Watts, 2017). Reductionist views seek to gain power over phenomena. This power struggle estranges people from reality and they become angry towards life. For reductionists and fatalists, life is mechanical or stupid processes of which happened to them accidently. Adults that educate young adults in this resentment and reductionism lessen opportunities to discover their own relationships with the world, ultimately limiting spiritual potentials.

Furthermore, spirituality is not to be mistaken as superstition. To clarify, superstition is a phenomenon observed by unfounded beliefs that certain events/circumstances arise from an unobservable relation to another event or item (Maqsood et al., 2018). Future events can be favorable with a lucky penny or unfavorable, whereby breaking a mirror bestows seven years of bad luck. Superstition has been found to have a negative (or inverse) relationship with rational thinking, and critical analytical abilities. One may suggest that individuals with higher levels of rational thinking have the lowest probability for developing superstitious beliefs. Simply stated, superstition is not spirituality.

There is also an important distinction between religion and spirituality. Religion is a social institution that creates frameworks and guidelines for which bring people together under certain shared beliefs that guide communal and individual behaviors, norms, and values. There are established incentives for following these standards as well as prescribed punishments (Hariharan & Kapoor, 2020). Religion directs people in how to live and provides a basis from which to make decisions. There are communal goals to be achieved and upheld. Religion is similar to spirituality in that it seeks connections or relationships with forces outside of the self by means of virtue. Although some may criticize the practice of religion, it has been shown to have significant benefits for youth.

Spirituality and relationships with God provide compensatory value for relationship insecurities with parents or caregivers. For example, Hiebler-Ragger et al. (2016) studied 481 young adults (18 to 30 years of age) that were raised Roman Catholic in a cross-sectional observational study of attachment styles, spirituality, and mood disorders (such as somatic or emotional disturbances). The researchers stated that "Higher Existential Well-Being—comprised of facets such as hope for a better future, forgiveness and the experience of sense and meaning—seems to have an especially corrective effect on mood pathology, independent of attachment styles" (p. 1). Hiebler-Ragger et al. (2016) found that spirituality was a main factor for emotional well-being and management when other attachments in the person's life were insecure. Religiosity in young adulthood provided an avenue to develop spirituality and experience its benefits. Those that did not have a sense of security in attachments to parents or caregivers typically displayed anger at the missing figure or present figure and the need for closeness. Young adults that had insecure attachments were also susceptible to the negative effects of stress and were typically not successful in seeking help from support circles.

Spirituality is a significant influence for young adults to find their place in an existential paradigm—which supports levels of gratitude and emotional equanimity (Bosacki et al., 2018). Martinez et al. (2020) found that in a six-week happiness study for emerging adults (18 to 25 years), "qualitative journal reflections provided deeper insight into how goals contribute to spirituality. Most participants described enhanced self-actualization, including feeling increased awareness, recognition of self-action, and finding purpose through goals" (p. 256). This study reinforced previous research that found strong correlations of spirituality to well-being and growth. Martinez et al. (2020) argued that young adults need spaces to explore and reflect on spiritual connections.

Spiritual well-being influences the development of socio-emotional abilities and intelligences, such as empathy, responsibility, compassion, and emotional attunement (Fekih-Romdhane et al., 2020). Furthermore, spiritual well-being has been found to have a negative correlation with personality disturbances that cause moral confusion. A sense of moral compass is present in those that embrace their spirituality. Shahina and Parveen (2020) explored how the self-discovery, connectedness, and ecological awareness associated to spirituality factored into the resilience and mental well-being for 60 adolescents (ages 16 to 19 years). The researchers found that levels of spirituality and ecological awareness were positively correlated with levels of resilience and mental well-being (i.e., physically, psychologically, and socially).

Spiritual attunement to the world fosters gratitude for the chance of being alive, encountering things like flowers, and being able to nourish the body with food. Gratitude is an important element of spirituality. Research on gratitude in Ontario, Canada from Bosacki et al. (2018) contributed to a five-year longitudinal study on young adults' social cognition. Gratitude was found to have a strong positive correlation to overall life satisfaction, hope, self-compassion, positive emotions, as well as self-esteem, while being negatively correlated with guilt, depression, anxiety and low self-worth. Participants' perception of well-being, self-value, morals, spirituality, and empathy were all correlated with gratitude. However, some studies found that gratitude can be associated with embarrassment and obligation. Regardless, gratitude within spirituality is a complex phenomenon and cannot be understood in isolation. The subjectivity, cultural worlds, and living contexts of the young adult must be factored in to understand the holistic effects of spirituality.

Exploring Spirituality

The existential trauma of COVID-19 left many youth lost without knowing how to begin coping, find meaning, or heal from traumatic experiences. Opening one's self up to the responsibilities of existentialism can be overwhelming and even frightening. Some young adults may use spirituality to find relationships in which they cling on to for a sense of safety, familiarity, or knowingness. However, to cling is antithetical to spirituality, as it becomes a maladaptive way of coping with reality by precluding one from the deep wisdom that the no-thing-ness holds.

Growth-promoting relationships are not spiritual ways to ward off existential terror. Rather, they support people to face realities with compassion and courage. The connections that come with spirituality offer young adults opportunities to explore the realities of existence in ways that promote open-mindedness. Too great or profound the meaning will be overwhelming, too easy an explanation may not be of interest. Young adults seek spiritual enlightenment that reflects their interests and abilities as unique individuals. Yet, when existential trauma or angst amassed during the pandemic, many young adults without support became lost in despair—where an existential apathy incubated a slow death of the spirit.

In Western culture, stress and trauma are treated as personal responsibilities that young adults need to deal with on their own. They must go off from the community and social spheres to fix themselves or get treatment. The disturbance becomes worse when the *social sphere is the cause of the problem* and the young adult must be cast out, only to learn how to realign with social standards/norms (Watters, 2010). Many young adults return to social spheres with a sense of guilt or core shame. Existential trauma treated as an isolated dysfunction to be fixed by specified Western treatments may end up damaging cultural paradigms that originally brought healing or meaning to suffering. In collectivistic cultures such as Sri Lanka or Mexico, individual healing that is prescribed to be conducted away from one's social sphere causes more problems because the collective is the healing factor. The family and social spheres are resources for vitality, meaning-making, problem solving, and support that cultivate mental well-being. For one to be cast out from the group reinforces the idea that there is a unique and isolated "self" that has a dysfunction.

The dangerous illusion of a self without relationships to the world creates an outward hostility in which one feels it necessary to conquer ecosystems, animals, organisms, and insects, instead of finding harmonious ways of coexisting (Watts, 1966). Creating divisions between self and world also translates to self-misunderstandings. Mind and body distinctions are in languages for referring to her-self, as if the mind was assigned a body structure to inhabit (Watts, 1985). Spirituality helps remove the lines that separate the self and world, as well as the self and body. Young adults can learn to appreciate their lungs as much as the air they breathe (Watts, 1979). The Western cultural focus on an isolated identity apart from the universe creates a schism between the person and reality. Many youth learn to be steadfast in constructing isolated lives and meanings by disregarding their spiritual connections (Watts, 1966).

When the time comes to transition from this life, there is no choice but to let go of one's isolated ego and greet death in spiritual harmony. When given a life-limiting diagnosis, people quickly begin living according to inner values and discard external/socially determined ones. Spirituality promotes the enlightened realization that death is not separate from life and that the person was the universe all along. In the spiritual sense, death is not the cessation of life, but rather an interval that helps one depart this phase of the eternal stream (Watts, 1966). The connections that one develops with the world in the life/death stream are complex. Death encourages people to establish authentic connections with the world in order to create meaning (Nhat Hanh, 2007). These spiritual meanings promote happiness and life satisfaction.

In a post-pandemic world, encouraging young adults to actively forget or ignore that there were extreme threats of death by a quick return to normal will deny opportunities to explore existential concerns. For instance, Testoni et al. (2021) studied how a death education course with the support of palliative doctors and psychologists affected 87 young adults (16 to 20 years of age) that were enrolled in secondary schools. The course meetings were conducted in school and hospices in order to visit with mental health professionals and families of the dying. The mixed methods study included longitudinal surveys of outcomes that were compared to a control group of 76 young adults. Analytic variables included alexithymia, which is a disorder where a person has difficulty or inability to identify and describe emotions for the self and of others. Additional variables included personal values, spirituality, and representations of death.

Contrary to the belief that death education would produce negative effects, the course helped decrease alexithymia and enhanced emotional recognition and expression for participants. Exploring thoughts, emotions, and ideas within safe educational contexts improved students' abilities for understanding and creating meanings of mortality. This course also removed the taboos and denial of death in favor of a critical understanding and acceptance for the ubiquity of death and its irreversible nature. Testoni et al. (2021) found that participants

> reported a change in their death representations from death as total annihilation to death as a passage, suggesting that they had gotten closer to a spiritual and transcendental dimension. For some, spirituality was a positive discovery, while for others, it simply confirmed their faith.
>
> *(p. 9)*

Developing spirituality with existential realities such as death means "to get with it, to let it take over—fear, ghosts, pains, transience, dissolution, and all. And then comes the hitherto unbelievable surprise; you don't die because you were never born. You had just forgotten who you are" (Watts, 1966, p. 40). In the vast ocean of Being, death is not nothingness but a trough to the crest in a never-ending flow of waves (Watts, 1966).

Spiritual Disturbances

Mental disturbances such as anhedonia, depression, psychosis, despair, substance abuse, low impulse control, or neuroticism, coupled with challenging life circumstances, have

128   Part I

the power to distort existential meanings that can lead to self-harm or taking one's own life. Suicide may be categorized in three brackets: ideation, behaviors, and completion (Ibrahim et al., 2019). Most cases of suicide reside in ideation comparably to the completion.

For example, Ibrahim et al. (2019) conducted a cross-sectional study of 176 adolescents in Malaysian urban settings to investigate the correlation amongst social support, spiritual well-being, and suicide ideation. Suicide rates in Malaysia reveal that about 7% of all young adults have had an intent to commit suicide and half of that population have attempted. The Suicide Ideation Scale, Multidimensional Scale of Perceived Social Support, and the Spiritual Wellbeing Scale were used as research instruments to understand the religious, existential, and spiritual well-being of young adult participants. The researchers found that existential and religious well-being had a negative (inverse) relationship with suicide ideation. This correlation indicated that the greater sense of spirituality, the less likely one was to consider suicide. The higher quality of social support from family and friends was also a strong factor in lowering suicidal ideation. Spiritual well-being, participation in a religious community, and social support from loving/caring others "makes the suicidal person feel more belongingness, faithful, accept the truth and feel less burdensome and perhaps, and feeling connected to God and the loved ones are important in working with patients with suicide risks" (Ibrahim et al., 2019, p. 6). Furthermore, Gwin et al. (2020) corroborated this finding by discovering that as religiosity (i.e., communal activities and practices) increases, the young adult's suicide ideation decreases.

The dominance of Western psychiatric medicine has vanquished many cultural knowledges and practices for engaging mental phenomena (Watters, 2010). The indigenous paradigms for healing and cultivating mental well-being have been deteriorating under the rapid forces of globalization, without having a chance to be considered. Many times, Western therapeutic approaches to existential trauma can cause more problems, as Watters (2010) described:

> If you take a group of disoriented and unsettled victims mere hours or days after a life-altering tragedy, put them in a highly charged encounter where they are told to expect certain psychological symptoms, and then they share their experiences, you are creating the perfect setting by which emotions are likely to spread and intensify.
>
> (p. 119)

Psychological definitions and diagnostic criteria for understanding/engaging mental phenomena have traditionally been exported from the U.S. to the world (Watters, 2010). The processes for understanding, categorizing, and determining courses/outcomes for healing mental disturbances are largely culturally relative. However, if Western practitioners do not wish to cause harm to diverse paradigms and wish to gain a greater understanding of mental phenomena, there must be a consilience amongst cultural knowledges and practices. The cultural differences amongst understandings and approaches to mental phenomena must be engaged with cultural humility if clinicians are to develop effective therapeutic interventions.

Therapies for mental disturbances that facilitate spiritual development have shown to contribute to well-being by producing emotions that stimulate holistic health—where body processes (e.g., immune system) function optimally. That is why those that have a strong sense of spirituality recover faster from physical ailments. Warner et al. (2020) explored the effects of childhood and adolescent abuse on telomere length from 3,232 participants and if spirituality could be a protective factor. The quantitative data was based upon relative leukocyte telomere lengths (RTL) from polymerase chain reactions. The researchers found:

> Sexual abuse in childhood or adolescence was associated with a marker of accelerated biological aging, decreased telomere length. The lack of moderation by [religion/spirituality] may be due to inability to capture the appropriate time period for those beliefs and practices.
>
> *(Warner et al., 2020, p. 2)*

Spirituality and religiosity were significant sources for developing resilience during childhood and young adulthood, especially for victims of abuse. This resilience is a protective factor against stress deteriorating telomere length.

However, religiosity and spirituality are not isolated factors as Hariharan and Kapoor (2020) studied the relationships, effects, and differences of spiritual practices to psychological well-being. From a sample of 120 young adults (20 to 30 years of age), data revealed that spiritual practice alone had a low influence on psychological well-being. When considering the effects of stress, how the protective factors (e.g., spirituality, social support, coping strategies) moderate stress is vital for understanding the severity for which risk factors will impact the individual (Mirkovic et al., 2020). Protective and vulnerability factors are engaged in an existential crisis and whichever is dominant can influence the outcome. The effects of spirituality on well-being are complex and interrelated with other life factors.

Spirituality is a leading factor for well-being. Vazifeh doust et al. (2020) found that when spiritual care was given to children and adolescents battling cancer, it decreased levels of anxiety, which "shows that as children have less anxiety, they are more capable of enduring adverse conditions, which brings about psychological well-being. In other words, they experience a higher level of well-being" (p. 2861). Through growth-promoting relationships, spiritual care was able to help foster equanimity and well-being for children and young adults.

In addition, Radhika et al. (2020) discovered that for surveyed adolescent students in India, the higher levels of spirituality meant more effective skills in managing, adapting, and coping with stressful circumstances and challenges.

130   Part I

Overall, the population of adolescent participants demonstrated that spirituality was positively correlated with holistic health. The researchers recommended that during COVID-19 and years after, public school curriculum should cultivate spirituality in students via culture-based religious scriptures such as the Bible, Bhagwat, Vedas, Upanishads, Quran, and Granth Sahib, in order to help students better cope with and overcome existential trauma. Spirituality is a multi-dimensional component to expanding definitions of well-being.

Spirituality for a Personal Existentialism

Spiritual practices, rhythms, and rituals are a significant source for recovery and vitality in young adulthood. They provide support for coping with life challenges, spaces to explore meanings, develop optimism, and attain higher-life satisfaction (Shahina & Parveen, 2020). The protective factors of spiritualism provide buffers to the somatic effects of emotional disturbances. A spiritual experience promotes critical thinking, emotional regulation, exploration of identity, and cognitive development, which are important growth factors in young adulthood. The deep sense of meaning and purpose that are achieved in spirituality emerge positive habits, such as meditation, cognitive reappraisal, or volunteerism.

The global trauma caused by COVID-19 is not likely to be forgotten. Death and loneliness anxieties do not dissipate easily, especially when young adults try to reinvent a new definition of normal. Spirituality does not promote magical ideas in order to deny existential realities. Rather, spirituality supports young adults to venture into the reality of existentialism. The relationships developed within spiritual connections foster compassion, empathy, and emotional management.

Spiritual relationships teach young adults that existential themes are ubiquitous amongst life beings; they must recognize that the path to old age and the ultimate transition is the same for their animal friends. Spirituality promotes acceptance of realities and cultivates agency. When young adults experience negative emotional states, they can choose not to lash out at loved ones or strangers, but develop self-compassion in order to heal their inner angst. They can also decide to find consolation from animals or nature. Through spirituality, young adults learn to live in the here-and-now to cultivate their equanimity—the present moment is the only soil in which seeds can blossom.

The past and future are imaginings. The relationships that young adults establish with the world can only be experienced in the present moment. Within the moment, they can mindfully navigate the challenges of life. The unfortunate reality for young adults is that they are currently under a barrage of measurements and assessments for value and aptitude, where their performance determines worth and ability. Determinisms are plentiful for young adulthood. These measures displace them from the present and when the future actually does arrive, it will always prove unsatisfying. The experience of the journey has been disregarded in favor of the goal. There had been abstract preparation for an illusory

Healing, Growth, and Enlightenment **131**

goal without any real participation in life. The reality is that there can only be an eternal stream *now*, a still movement of inescapability; always here and evanescent when sought to be grasped (Watts, 1985). Spiritual relationships remind young adults not to forget that a wave is made of water and that they exist within an existential ocean of Being.

References

Au, A., Brown, A. L., & Calderòn, D. (2016). *Reclaiming the multicultural roots of U.S. curriculum: Communities of color and official knowledge in education.* Teachers College Press.

Bosacki, S., Sitnik, V., Dutcher, K., & Talwar, V. (2018). Gratitude, social cognition, and well-being in emerging adolescents. *Journal of Genetic Psychology*, 179(5), 256–269. https://doi.org/10.1080/00221325.2018.1499607.

Fekih-Romdhane, F., Ben Hamouda, A., Khemakhem, R., Halayem, S., BelHadj, A., & Cheour, M. (2020). Existential well-being predicts psychopathy traits in Tunisian college students. *Mental Health, Religion & Culture*, 23(7), 639–652. https://doi.org/10.1080/13674676.2020.1786506.

Gwin, S., Branscum, P., Taylor, E. L., Cheney, M., Maness, S. B., Frey, M., & Zhang, Y. (2020). Associations between suicide behaviors and religiosity in young adults. *American Journal of Health Studies*, 35(4), 257–269.

Hariharan, K., & Kapoor, R. (2020). Impact of practicing spirituality on psychological well-being. *Indian Journal of Positive Psychology*, 11(3), 252–257.

Hiebler-Ragger, M., Falthansl-Scheinecker, J., Birnhuber, G., Fink, A., & Unterrainer, H. F. (2016). Facets of spirituality diminish the positive relationship between insecure attachment and mood pathology in young adults. *PLoS ONE*, 11(6), 1–9. https://doi.org/10.1371/journal.pone.0158069.

Ibrahim, N., Che Din, N., Ahmad, M., Amit, N., Ghazali, S. E., Wahab, S., Abdul Kadir, N. B., Halim, F. W., & A Halim, M. R. T. (2019). The role of social support and spiritual wellbeing in predicting suicidal ideation among marginalized adolescents in Malaysia. *BMC Public Health*, 19(1), 1–9. https://doi.org/10.1186/s12889-019-6861-7.

Maqsood, A., Jamil, F., & Khalid, R. (2018). Thinking styles and belief in superstitions: Moderating role of gender in young adults. *Pakistan Journal of Psychological Research*, 33, 335–348.

Martinez, C. T., McGath, N. N., & Williams, K. C. (2020). Pursuit of goals in the search for happiness: A mixed-method multidimensional study of well-being. *Psi Chi Journal of Psychological Research*, 25, 245–259. https://doi.org/10.24839/2325-7342.JN25.3.245.

Mirkovic, B., Cohen, D., Garny de la Rivière, S., Pellerin, H., Guilé, J.-M., Consoli, A., & Gerardin, P. (2020). Repeating a suicide attempt during adolescence: Risk and protective factors 12 months after hospitalization. *European Child & Adolescent Psychiatry*, 29 (12), 1729–1740. https://doi.org/10.1007/s00787-020-01491-x.

Nhat Hanh, T. (2007). *The art of power.* HarperOne.

Radhika, G., Rajendran, R., & Sankar, R. (2020). Systems thinking approach for the promotion of mental health among adolescents: The role of food, sports, music, yoga and spirituality need for a paradigm shift towards a post-COVID-19 India. *Indian Journal of Positive Psychology*, 11(4), 331–337.

Shahina, G., & Parveen, A. (2020). Role of spirituality in building up resilience and mental health among adolescents. *Indian Journal of Positive Psychology*, 11(4), 392–397.

Testoni, I., Palazzo, L., Ronconi, L., Donna, S., Cottone, P. F., & Wieser, M. A. (2021). The hospice as a learning space: a death education intervention with a group of adolescents. *BMC Palliative Care*, 20(1), 1–11. https://doi.org/10.1186/s12904-021-00747-w.

Vazifeh doust, M., Hojjati, H., & Farhangi, H. (2020). Effect of spiritual care based on Ghalbe Salim on anxiety in adolescent with cancer. *Journal of Religion & Health*, 59(6), 2857–2865. https://doi.org/10.1007/s10943-019-00869-9.

Warner, E. T., Zhang, Y., Gu, Y., Taporoski, T. P., Pereira, A., DeVivo, I., Spence, N. D., Cozier, Y., Palmer, J. R., Kanaya, A. M., Kandula, N. R., Cole, S. A., Tworoger, S., & Shields, A. (2020). Physical and sexual abuse in childhood and adolescence and leukocyte telomere length: A pooled analysis of the study on psychosocial stress, spirituality, and health. *PLoS ONE*, 15(10). https://doi.org/10.1371/journal.pone.0241363.

Watters, E. (2010). *Crazy like us: The globalization of the American psyche*. Free Press. Watts, A. (1966). *The Book: On the taboo against knowing who you are*. Vintage Books.

Watts, A. (1979). *The wisdom of insecurity: A message for an age of anxiety*. Vintage Books.

Watts, A. (1985). *The way of Zen*. Vintage Books.

Watts, A. (2003). *Become what you are*. Shambhala Publications.

Watts, A. (2017). *Out of your mind: Tricksters, interdependence, and the cosmic game of hide and seek*. Sounds True.

PART II

7
CREATING MEANING WITH THE NATURAL WORLD

Being an Outsider

Extreme stress has become a leading global concern for the well-being of young adults, as its effects have led to psychological disturbance, cardiovascular malaise, burnout, and immune system dysfunctions (Hassan et al., 2018). These effects have been prominent in urban societies where intense stress is constant and the quality of time to recover and repair is inadequate. A large amount of negative stress comes from worries over environmental destruction. In addition, the exposure to air, light, and noise pollution, global warming, and extreme weather events add stress by affecting sleep and respiratory health (Hariharan & Kapoor, 2020). The consequences are long-term deterioration of well-being. Quality healthcare for many populations of youth may be too expensive, unavailable, or inaccessible. For instance, immigrant youth may not know what healthcare services are available or how to access them in the new host country. Many societies work to treat the symptoms of excessive stress instead of cultivating preventative factors. Well-being during young adulthood now means developing protective management strategies for coping with stress.

Contemporary research suggests that the adverse effects of stress are significantly reduced when people increase their time in contact with natural environments. Research findings corroborate century old-beliefs and practices, such as why outdoorsman Leon Leonwood Bean (1872–1967) began his company L.L. Bean in 1912,

> with the belief that great outdoors has much to teach us—about ourselves and about the world around us. L.L. insisted that time outside in the presence of a snow-capped mountain, a rushing river, or a starry night sky allowed us to forget the stresses of everyday life.
>
> *(L.L. Bean, 2021a, para. 1)*

DOI: 10.4324/9781003251651-10

The famous American outdoor goods company has been helping people enjoy nature for over a century, while offering outdoor educational programs for youth each summer, grants for revitalizing green areas, and year-round community outreach programs. Mr. Bean appreciated that relationships with nature are vital to the well-being and growth of young adults, which ultimately translates to the health of a nation. While the twentieth century experienced mass urbanization and technological advancements (especially for entertainment), L.L. Bean remained, quite literally, an outsider. He worked to help families across the U.S. restore themselves from the nine to five monotony by finding equanimity and excitement in nature.

The experience of nature during youth is without comparison for how it provides aesthetic visual, auditory, and sensory stimuli that enhance well-being, cognition, and emotional development (Hopman et al., 2020). Nature can be understood as an ecosystem that was not artificially created by humans, in which an abundance of diverse organisms and vegetation flourish within. The complexity of nature offers multisensory stimulation that restores cognition, creativity, and biophysiological systems. Nature comprises each biome: tropical forest, grassland, taiga, tundra, freshwater, marine, and savanna. Their restorative powers for humans and mammals alike have been shown to increase positive emotions and moods, while lowering anxiety and rumination (Hopman et al., 2020).

According to White et al. (2019), time spent in natural environments decreases levels/rates of obesity, diabetes, hospitalizations, mental distress, and even mortality. In addition, encounters with nature enhance cognitive development, improve birth outcomes, and increase ratings of subjective well-being (SWB). White et al. (2019) found that people who spent 120 minutes a week in nature had greater levels of life satisfaction and well-being compared to those that were not exposed to nature. Greater than 200 minutes plateaued the effects or even decreased them. The researchers recommended that "120 mins contact with nature per week may reflect a kind of 'threshold', below which there is insufficient contact to produce significant benefits to health and well-being, but above which such benefits become manifest" (White et al., 2019, p. 6). The research study found that it did not matter how the exposure to nature was achieved, whether it be through a public greenspace, walks on neighborhood sidewalks, or visiting a park. Personal preference, accessibility, and circumstances for how nature is experienced can vary and should direct how to achieve exposure to the outdoors.

Furthermore, encounters with nature have been known to alter people's perception of time. This is due to nature's ability to cultivate a *flow state* within the person, where one becomes detached from the perception of time and is lost in the activity (L.L. Bean, 2021b). As Csikszentmihalyi (1975) described of people in the state of flow:

> They concentrate their attention on a limited stimulus field, forget personal problems, lose their sense of time and of themselves, feel competent and in

Creating Meaning with the Natural World **137**

control, and have a sense of harmony and union with their surroundings. To the extent that these elements of experience are present, a person enjoys what he or she is doing and ceases to worry about whether the activity will be productive and whether it will be rewarded.

(p. 182)

The holistic integration during flow achieves intrinsic rewards, but these positive effects are not the goal; rather, they are side effects (Martinez et al., 2020). Nevertheless, the specific contexts and activities are important to produce the flow state.

Flow is similar to what Maslow (1971) described as a self-actualizing moment, where one is fully integrated and realizing potentials of the self in a peak experience. In addition, flow and peak experiences promote forms of potential actualization that are free from external values/goals that reify an illusory ego. Moments of flow and self-actualization foster awareness of existential givens, such as mortality or freedom. Young adults are more likely to experience flow within nature because natural environments have little conflict with personal goals. There is also a sense of harmony that develops with other forms of life.

However, in society, most of a young adult's attention throughout the day is spent on family or school responsibilities and problem-solving tasks. Cognitive focus (i.e., voluntary attention) diminishes the more it is used. This is why decision fatigue is common at the end of the day. The quality of decision lowers with each choice. At the end of a day, one typically chooses the lowest-quality decision because the cognitive resources and brain power have been spent on making well-informed choices, considering possibilities, and making internal trade-offs.

Yet, nature provides an incomparable experience that requires no voluntary attention. Without any effort from the person, nature restores cognitive processes and energies. Decision fatigue is revitalized in natural environments. Moreover, experiencing the visual aesthetics of nature has powerful effects on brain waves that restore focused attention. Hopman et al. (2020) found that nature revitalizes cognitive functioning in voluntary attention by capturing involuntary attention, and that "prolonged environmental exposures uniquely influence neuroelectric power during rest" (p. 8). In other words, nature restores a young adults' decision making power as it shifts the brain activity from the voluntary attention of everyday tasks to the captivating aesthetics of nature. This break in voluntary attention allows it to be restored. Nature supports young adults to cope with life challenges, explore existential concerns, and seek creative solutions.

Shinrin-yoku: *The Restorative Powers of the Forest*

The traditional Japanese practice known as *Shinrin-yoku*, or forest bathing, designates mindfully encountering a forest environment/atmosphere with all one's senses and perceptual abilities (Antonelli et al., 2019; Hassan et al., 2018). *Shinrin-yoku* has

138   Part II

shown to increase relaxation, decrease stress, and cultivate psychological and physical well-being. Its popularity gained momentum in Japan during the 1980s,

> as an essential component of preventive and curative medicine. The popularization of forest bathing in Japan through easy access to the forest environment and governmental recommendations resulted in a reduction of acute psychological disorders due to the time spent in green spaces.
>
> *(Dogaru, 2020, p. 299)*

Today, forest bathing has received attention from scientific communities worldwide in order to understand its natural physical and psychological therapies.

Scientists have studied human biological markers that are altered in the forest atmosphere and are seeking to understand their relationship to the psychological effects. A study done by Lee et al. (2011) compared the psychophysiological responses of forest bathing to urban settings. Young adults in Japan signed up for a three-day, two-night experiment that measured their psychophysiological responses in both natural and urban environments. For participants in the forest bathing group, heart-rate levels indicated a significant increase in parasympathetic nervous system activation (the system responsible for resting and digesting), while also causing a significant decrease in sympathetic nervous system (responsible for the fight, flight, or freeze response when threats are present) activity when compared to those in urban environments. The researchers tested cortisol levels from participants' saliva as well. The forest bathing group exhibited significantly less cortisol levels than the urban participants. In addition, ratings on self-assessment scales reported that forest bathing generated more positive emotions and decreased negative feelings. Lee et al. (2011) concluded that forest bathing produced significant effects for psychological and physiological well-being.

In addition, a meta-analysis done by Antonelli et al. (2019), investigated the biological marker of cortisol levels in saliva to understand the effects of forest bathing on stress levels. From a total of 971 peer-review research articles, both qualitative and quantitative, all save for two of the studies reported that cortisol levels significantly lowered when participants were forest bathing (compared to control urban groups). Therefore, there is strong evidence that forest bathing does provide short-term stress-level reduction. Reduced cortisol levels also have implications for young adults' long-term physical well-being.

How young adults choose to experience the forest does not seem to matter for procuring the positive effects to well-being. Hassan et al. (2018) measured the blood pressures and EEG readings of 60 adult participants (half male, half female) during a 15-minute walk in a bamboo forest (experimental group) and in an urban area (control group). Both groups completed the same walking distance. The results from the questionnaire data revealed that the bamboo forest bathing walks reduced anxiety and improved emotional states. Participants reported that the bamboo forest promoted meditation as well as restoring attention.

Brain activities were assessed through alpha and beta wave analysis in both urban and forest environments. Alpha brain waves are associated with a decrease in focus and increase in relaxation, meditation, and calmness, whereas beta waves are associated with vigilance, focused attention, awareness, and alert. The electroencephalography (EEG) readings showed that the bamboo forest walks increased alpha wave frequency, which indicated a brain state of relaxation. For the urban walk participants, alpha waves were significantly lower, which indicated a sense of brain stress (Hassan et al., 2018). Lower alpha waves have been shown to be associated with emotions such as fear and sadness, where higher alphas are associated with happiness and relaxation. The 15-minute forest bathing walk increased alpha waves, while the urban-setting participants experienced a decrease in alpha waves over the trial period. Hassan et al. (2018) concluded that forest bathing increases alpha wave frequency to promote a high degree of wakefulness, relaxed state, and calmness. The researchers argued that when the brain is in states of calmness and relaxation, there are greater potentials for learning, revitalizing decision-making, creativity, and refreshed attention.

The positive research findings on forest bathing have inspired fields of scientific inquiry to collaborate, where medical sciences, environmental medicines, psychology, and alternative medicines have found consilience. The soothing nature of forest bathing has positive physical and psychological effects, mainly for decreasing cortisol levels. When cortisol levels are consistently within optimal range for the person, it means less the harmful effects of long-term stress system activation. In particular, the restorative effects on the parasympathetic nervous system allow the cardiovascular system to relax and recuperate faster. This reduces the harsh effects that excessive negative stressors have on the body. Forest bathing has been found to have significant positive effects on the "immune system (increase of natural killer cells/cancer prevention); the cardiovascular system (hypertension/coronary artery disease); the respiratory system (allergies and respiratory diseases); depression and anxiety (mood disorders and stress); mental relaxation" (Dogaru, 2020, p. 299). Why are we surprised when research studies that discover how natural habitats promote well-being and vitality, while the artificial human-made living spaces cultivate physical and mental malaise (Kohl, 2020)? Young adults living in a post pandemic world need of wider awareness of what health entails and which environments cultivate well-being.

Although natural environments have the potential to support holistic well-being, there is something unique about encounters with green plant life and trees. Forest bathing exposes one to the natural essential oils that are found in plants, vegetables, woods, and fruits, of which contain phytoncides. Plant life phytoncides are among a wide spectrum of biogenic volatile organic compounds (BVOCs). Phytoncides are used for many functions, such as to ward off insects and germs, protect the plant from herbivores, or attract ones that can eat the herbivores. The forest air is abundant with phytoncides and research has shown that they have a direct correlation for improving immune systems functions of human beings (Livini, 2017). The fresh air of the forest has healing properties.

140 Part II

According to Kim et al. (2020), the two major BVOCs that are given off by forest plant life are known as terpenes and terpenoids. They are biological compounds that not only deter or attract predators, but also have a wide range of effects on human well-being. Kim et al. (2020) analyzed research literature that investigated BVOCs found in Northern Hemisphere forested environments. These areas were known to have 23 major types of BVOCs that had anti-inflammatory effects on humans. Of the 23 types, 12 of the compounds had healing properties for atopic dermatitis, arthritis, respiratory problems, and inflammatory diseases.

Specifically, neuroinflammation takes place within the nervous tissue and is managed by cells known as microglia. The microglia are a type of immune system cell that helps eliminate damaged neurons and destroys general infections that could pose threats to the well-being of the central nervous system. When there is a threatening pathogen, trauma to the body, infection, or stroke, the body responds with neuroinflammation by activating microglia, which are part of the pro-inflammatory response to promote healing and eliminate foreign bodies. The inflammatory response circulates pro-inflammatory cytokines that are produced by the macrophages to protect healthy neurons in the brain. However, this neuroinflammatory response is only beneficial when it is short term. Long-term activation from stress and inflammation is damaging to the brain, and can result in neurodegenerative diseases, where microglia can become overactive and begin to eliminate healthy cells, which results in further inflammation.

Being outside in nature is a healthy habit to promote well-being and acts as a preventative against the harmful effects of long-term stress system activation and neuroinflammation. In regards to forest BVOCs, Kim et al. (2020) found that, "coincident with their anti-inflammatory activity in the peripheral macrophages, some terpenes have been shown to inhibit the activation of microglia under several pro-inflammatory cues in in vitro studies" (p. 21). Pharmaceutical companies are developing concentrated forms of terpenoid-based clinical medications for conditions such as atopic dermatitis. Although topical medicines can provide immediate relief of symptoms, they appear to pose issues with safety and long-term effectiveness. Kim et al. (2020), recommended that forest bathing is a safer avenue than prescription medications in order to experience the positive health effects of BVOCs.

In Awe of It All

Although the biological markers of *Shinrin-yoku* can be recorded, there are also phenomenal effects taking place. Natural environments promote holistic well-being and healing in ways that are both quantifiable and immeasurable. Quantitative research can collect statistical data about an experience, but the meaning of it is in the science of phenomenology. Particularly, nature has been found to increase feelings of *awe*—an emotive state where the person's encounter with a natural environment or phenomenon has powerful effects that promote a transcendental paradigm shift for creating existential meanings. Awe places young adults in a realm where their existence is felt in relation to nature. Just as the outdoorsman L.L. Bean stated, nature is able "teach us to forget the mean and petty things of life" (L.L. Bean, 2021a, para. 5). Within this forgetting is a defocus from the noise of society and irrelevant personal demands.

Awe has restorative powers for young adults that are experiencing existential turmoil. Even when the challenges of developmental phases are exacerbated by death anxiety, loneliness anxiety, isolation, and despair; the forests, sunsets, stars, desert mountains, or ocean shores are there to promote meaning, healing, happiness, reduced stress, and spirituality.

For the biological effects, Keltner (2016) found that awe improves the immune system's cytokine functions. Cytokines are produced by when body tissue is damaged. They act as chemical messengers to elicit the acute inflammatory response in order to eliminate pathogens and stimulate healing. When cytokine responses are long-lasting, the person becomes more vulnerable to other ailments and diseases, ultimately reducing life expectancy. Chronic stress system activation deteriorates the health of cells, causing not only cell death but also shortens telomeres and damages genes.

However, in Keltner's (2016) laboratory, experiences of awe were found to significantly decrease cytokine levels over time. The researchers warranted further research to investigate the relationship between poverty and awe deprivation for understanding underserved populations' barriers to well-being and their reduced life expectancy. There are challenges for many youth living in urban areas to access greenspaces, either because of limited availability or because of transportation/accessibility issues to public parks outside of the home proximity. However, even in the quotidian happenings and encounters in the *beat of life* (in the spirit of Kerouac) there are opportunities where young adults can realize the profound experience of awe (Keltner, 2016). Whether it be from volunteering in a group activity that brings emerging children joy, viewing cloud formations, playing with an animal, or even finding awe in a daily work activity—existential transcendence resides in each moment.

Awe can be experienced everywhere as long as there is a sense of spirituality in the here-and-now. It is most engaging when one's abilities are actively at their peak, even under a challenge (Stone, 2017). The threat of an imminent thunderstorm may bring about awe, or even when a person is performing (or viewing) an extraordinary feat of skill. The contexts are essential but so are the subjective meanings and emotions. Existential-humanistic psychologist Kirk Schneider has studied awe extensively and argued that it brings about humility in the subjective experience of life's mysteries. Awe, according to Schneider (2004) is more than just the razzle dazzle of a spectacle or its paralyzing effect, but more of a transcendental appreciation of one's fragility amidst a powerful universe. Awe has the power to help one create the deepest meanings in life, even if there is no completed vocabulary able to describe their profundity. The exalting elements of awe bring about an existential awakening that dissolve one's ego and social constructions/roles—where the boundaries between person and nature blend (Keltner, 2016). In this blending, the sense of time is disoriented and one can feel peaceful without the past or future, but in an eternal present (L.L. Bean, 2021b).

Time is suspended in nature because it is a concept that implies societal goals and cultural values that require competitive achievements or tasks. Awe and flow experiences are similar in that they cause a transient hypofrontality in the brain; where the prefrontal cortices have shown in neuroimaging studies to power-down during these experiences (Kottler, 2021). Hypofrontality means slower activity in executive functions of the brain for planning, decision making, willpower, and time calculation. Time passes slower in this case. In awe or flow,

> we can no longer separate past from present from future and are instead thrust into 'the deep now'. And the deep now has a big impact on performance. Most of our fears and most of our anxieties don't exist in the present.
> *(Kottler, 2021, p. 225)*

This is known as *time dilation*, where past and future vanish and the immediacy of the moment can feel eternal.

Human beings have been experiencing awe for over seven million years in their evolutionary journey. According to Keltner (2016) awe may have been a socially advantageous component that formed collective bonds and activities amongst hominids which increased the chances for survival. Awe may have generated a greater sense of community and self-sacrifice that motivated humans to share of resources with others. Community activities, rituals, shared beliefs, relationships, and spirituality helped groups of humans travel across lands, endure hardships, and figure out ways to thrive. Keltner (2016) believed there to be a strong link between altruism and awe in which generates humility and compassion toward others.

Cooperation and community building are essential elements for human survival, which means finding a balance between self-interests and welfare, where "brief experiences of awe redefine the self in terms of the collective and orient our actions toward the interests of others" (Keltner, 2016, paras. 10–11). Awe has historical significance, as human beings experienced nature together and redefined purpose, created meanings, all while reflecting on what it meant to experience existential isolation (Stone, 2017). When experiencing awe people tend to redefine their selves within collectivistic parameters or universal categories, such as part of a wider global culture, species, or form of life (Shiota et al., 2007).

Awe is found in extraordinary experiences such as musical performances, encountering reality through auditory capacities (i.e., listening to silence or birds), experiencing art, seeing the views atop Cathedral Rock in Sedona, in Zen meditation, or forest bathing in Baxter State Park. It can also be found in the beat of daily life; walking with a dog, feeling the sun on your skin, experiencing the color of flowers, or marveling at lake effect snow. Awe can support self-actualization processes by attuning people to notice life wonders that have been taken for granted, such as encounters with pets or overcoming a personal challenge (Keltner, 2016). The key is to open one's perception to the phenomena at hand and to find harmony with its vibrations in the beat of life.

Being in natural environments or outdoors can take the form of a walk around the block or a mountaintop view. The flow, awe, and restorative powers that are found within nature are not limited to certain adventures, but rather, "about setting your attention and intention of the restorative power of being outside. And that might be as simple as watching the clouds float across the sky from your back porch" (L.L. Bean, 2021b, para. 6). Encountering natural environments or being outside offers meaningful ways in which to achieve an existential moment—where one transcends current understandings, beliefs, and paradigms. Natural environments are unique in how they affect people, as "the simultaneous experience of vastness and transcended understanding can be transformative, because it encourages individuals to step out of the confines of ego, and re-consider fixed ways of knowing" (Stone, 2017, para. 3). Nature encourages young adults to become open to new experiences as they try out new ways of thinking, behaving, and determining meaning that transcend old ways. With an existential awareness, young adults realize that they are the universe that creates possibilities in which to know itself.

Hyun: For Those I Will Never Meet

Hyun sits at the kitchen table snacking on a bag of Cape Cod Potato Chips in his apartment in Freeport, Maine. There is not much to do today, even though it's a Monday afternoon in late April, 2021. The café that he works at had been temporarily closed last fall due to the high infection rates of COVID-19, but it reopened over the winter. Today, he is enjoying a day off. Hyun stopped watching television over the past year because of the constant breaking news stories that reported death rates, infection rates, and repetitively shown images of overcrowded hospitals. The news caused sleepless nights. He now stares out the window at a tree, while crunching his chips, slowly.

I wonder how Song-yi is doing, he wonders. Hyun's older sister, Song-yi, lives with their parents in Los Angeles and had recently went back to teaching her sixth-grade class in person. He is worried about her well-being and his elderly parents. Hyun is 21 years old and has always dreamed of living near the ocean in the northeastern part of the U.S. He enjoyed Los Angeles but needed an adventure after he graduated high school. Today, Hyun is left alone with himself, questioning if leaving his family was the right choice and if this journey is what he really wanted. There was something deep inside him that called out for excitement and freedom, yet these days he finds solitude in the apartment to be suffocating.

After finishing his crunchy snack, Hyun sips the last of the green tea and decides that some kind of therapy is needed. *The ocean might be the place to find it,* he considers. He puts on his baseball hat, sunglasses, and jacket, grabs the car keys, and leaves the apartment.

Hyun decides to drive to Bailey Island of the Casco Bay. The scenic rocky coastal shores might give him a vantage point in which to gain perspective on life. He used to visit Venice Beach as a teenager when he felt a sense of anxiety or just needed a place to reflect on life's challenges. The ocean has always provided a sense of comfort and meaning. The drive to Bailey Island is short compared to his road trips in southern California.

Hyun finds a private space on the rocky coast to explore. He parks the car. Stepping out he smells the fresh and salty air of the ocean. The sounds of the water call to him a short distance away. Hyun follows a walking path and traverses the large rocks; he wants to stand on them and look at the ocean. There are a few boats floating in the distance. Hyun finds himself immobile and entranced by the sounds of the water on the rocks. He does not want to move. There are no particular thoughts in his head.

The water is pure and washes the coast. Hyun notices the color of the seafoam. The motion of the wave crests and troughs oscillate rhythmically. There are calls from seagulls in the distance, but the sound of the waves crashing on the rocks lulls him into a meditative state. Scattered cumulus clouds float amidst the vast blue sky—Hyun looks up at them from time to time. The clouds look giant, constantly blossoming white and grey flowers. He sits down on the rock, feeling the ancient hardness beneath his body. His body remains still for moments and other times he moves; touching the rocks, looking at the sky. Hyun does not think of moving or staying still, it just happens.

For a moment, he closes his eyes to rest. The sounds of the ocean and the birds intensify. Hyun experiences a harmony between his being and everything around him. The vibrations of the sounds move with the pulsations of his body. His eyes open again to greet the ocean. The colors and movement stimulate his visual senses. There are separate colors, but the more he experiences them, they transform into blending watercolors on a living canvas. His hand drops to feel the cold rock. He feels a connection to the earth through the rock, as if he was as eternal; yet Hyun also feels as impermanent as a wave and as changing as the cloud.

An hour passes without notice. A feeling grows in him that tells him to move on, to get up. *It is time to go.* While driving, Hyun reflects on the encounter with the ocean. He remembers a time when he was 10 years old on Venice Beach and saw the wind blow items from an overfilled trashcan onto the sand. He then remembers watching a disturbing video on YouTube of the turtle with a plastic straw stuck in its nostril. Hyun does not want ocean life to suffer because of human convenience or habit. His recent encounter with the ocean on Bailey Island had been profound, as its cleanliness meant that the ocean could be itself. *When am I most myself,* Hyun wonders?

Hyun returns to the apartment. He washes his hands out of habit, opens the refrigerator, and grabs a bottle of water. He drinks all of the water, crushes the bottle, and throws it in an overflowing bin of plastic bottles. The image of the trashcan on Venice Beach returns in his mind. *I do not want to use plastic bottles anymore*, he realizes. Hyun wishes that his childhood experiences with beaches had been as clean as the ones he had experienced in Maine.

Hyun reflects on his use of plastic; he knows that even if he recycles, the bottle caps will be put in the ocean. Plastic bags from the store, Styrofoam containers, and even straws—he may not have seen his trash affect animals and oceans, but he knows they will. *I didn't like the trash in my childhood, so why should I put my waste in someone else's life?* He thinks about whales, fish, and turtles, who are living by their nature and having the quality of their lives decreased by human convenience. *Who else is out in the ocean? Could there be something out looking at the sky, just as I had looked into the water?* Hyun sits down at the kitchen table and reflects on the emotions streaming through his body—but he is drawn to the emotions that make him feel free. The sense of lightness and freedom begets the question: *how can I help the oceans and beaches be free to be themselves, as they allowed me to be myself when we were together?* Hyun might not know who he was helping by switching to biodegradable products, reusable water containers, and eating less meat; but he knows that it is his decision to live a life that reduces the impact and harm to animals and the natural environments. He feels freedom when he is with the ocean and Hyun knows that it could be free around him too. Perhaps the water reflected more than just his image.

Tala: Finding My Nature

Tala's laptop illuminates her face with its blue glow from within the shadows of the living room. She has been on the computer for about two hours, working on her online undergraduate meteorology class. Her husband Duncan walks in the room where Tala has been stationed on the couch.

"Shouldn't you stand up and move around? You have been there for like 20 hours," he exaggerates.

Tala ignores him in order to keep her flow of thoughts going for her online discussion post.

"Hey, yo! Is anyone there?"

She looks up in annoyance. "I'm busy doing homework. Can you please let me finish this?"

"I haven't seen you all day and you didn't even eat the sandwich that I had made," Duncan replies.

"I am sorry, but this is more important," Tala declares.

"Is it, really?"

The tensions arise as negative streams of emotions begin to flow within Tala and Duncan. They soon exchange words in what might have led to an argument, but the emotional exhaustion caused by the isolation of the pandemic makes them both surrender.

Tala feels anger and also a sense of sadness. She replies, "I have been in lockdown for seven months in this small apartment and it is driving me senseless! You get to go out and do things."

"What? They classified me as an essential worker. I have no choice. Do you even know how scary and dangerous it is out there?"

Just before the couple is about to experience deeper levels of frustration and melancholy, their cat Twinkie walks onto the laptop and sits down. There is a moment of silence as Duncan and Tala try to register what is happening. On the computer screen, various letters are being typed under Twinkie's weight.

Instead of the arguing and feeling downhearted, the couple breaks out in laughter. They are emotionally fatigued from the stress of the pandemic and it feels good to laugh at the situation with Twinkie. Duncan sits down on the couch with a sigh.

"What on earth are we going to do? I feel so bad for people suffering from the virus. We have done well to quarantine and follow all the guidelines, but I feel that this fear is wearing us down. I wish there was something more we could do to help others and find a way to restore ourselves," Duncan states.

Tala takes a moment to register the situation. She carefully places the cat/computer on the cushion between them. With determination she stands up, turns to Duncan, and says: "Get your hiking stuff on, we are going adventuring!"

"What do you mean? Everything is closed!"

"They closed the parks and beaches, but they can't close uninhabited forest terrain," she declares.

"That doesn't sound scary at all," Duncan declares with humor, "Please, explain more."

"We are a newly married couple. I just turned 22 and you are 24. We chose to move up to Central New York to be around trees and nature. So, we are going to go do what we love, together, because *I love you*. We are going to help others by restoring ourselves so that we can stay home more peacefully. I know a place where we can park and get lost in the woods. I don't think anyone has ever explored this wooded area. We cannot give up, we can always be better," Tala proclaims with determination.

"You don't see any danger in *that* plan?" questions Duncan.

"We are not violating any laws, because we aren't going into any parks and there will be no one around."

"I was referring to the getting lost in the woods, or maybe meeting up with the real Bigfoot," he adds lightly.

"Everyone knows that there isn't just one Bigfoot."

Tala leaves the room to start dressing for the adventure and packing supplies. Duncan follows suit. Meanwhile, Twinkie sleeps soundly on the warm laptop.

Creating Meaning with the Natural World   147

The well-prepared couple find their way to the car and set off. Shortly down the road, Tala takes a sharp right down a path between the trees to a hidden spot and parks the car.

Duncan surveys the surroundings. "Isn't this like a make-out spot for teenagers?" he asks playfully.

"Don't get any ideas, hee, hee, hee," she jokes.

The two exit the car and marvel at the verdant forest comprised of trees, shrubs, small flowers, and plant life. They spend a few minutes mindfully breathing the fresh air and letting nature take them over into a sense of awe.

"Whoa, this place is pretty far out, literally and figuratively," Duncan says.

"It is, but before we adventure, let me first calibrate my compass to the map so we can find our way back."

"You never cease to amaze me!"

The couple set off along a subtle path where people once traversed, but was now reclaimed by vegetation. Tala leads the way and notices how good it feels to be back in nature. It has been almost a year since they hiked last and the feeling is strange, yet familiar. Her thoughts quiet under the sounds of their feet navigating the terrain amidst the ambience of bird song, rustling leaves, and the flow of a distance brook. Tala does not feel that she is suppressing her anxieties and thoughts, but that they cannot compete with the power of forest life.

Tala and Duncan have always loved hiking in natural environments, especially together. They had been through deserts, mountains, beaches, and forests. Nature was second to none for helping them find a sense of centeredness, love, and spirituality.

They hike for about 30 minutes across hills and valleys, experiencing the awe of nature. Duncan pulls out his stainless-steel water bottle and offers Tala the first sip of chilled coconut water. Their eyes connect and they feel as if they are dissolving into each other. The couple shares a profound love. As she takes a sip, there is a deafening bang that echoes throughout the woods.

Duncan reacts with a string of profanities, followed by, "What on earth was that?!"

"It sounded like a gun shot," replies Tala.

The couple freeze and strain their ears to listen for further clues.

"Do you think we are being hunted by crazed hillbillies? Or are FBI agents after us? Or maybe Bigfoot is sick of humans trying to find him and he has a—"

Tala cuts him off before he can finish, "First, there is more than just one Bigfoot. Second, it was a tree cracking and falling, babe."

"How do you know that?"

"The tree we passed, just back there, has fallen on our trail. That was the sound of the wood cracking."

"Thank you, Detective Columbo," Duncan says graciously with a bow.

"Oh, just one more thing…" she replies, imitating the detective.

"What?"

"I love you."

Duncan smiles and kisses Tala.

After about more 30 minutes of hiking, Tala and Duncan take another break. They sit upon a large tree stump to take in the opulent green surroundings. Tala feels whole and pure—where nature has lifted her from anxieties, tensions, and facades that separated her from the world and her husband. Tala can breathe in nature. She feels most human here.

Tala takes a long breath and closes her eyes. Her hand finds Duncan's hand. She takes notice of the scents of trees, flowers, and earth. Birds chirp in the background to catch her attention. She hears a breeze rustle the leaves of the surroundings trees—the sound is one of many, an arboreal orchestra. Tala opens her eyes and gazes toward the green treetops. The sun's rays peer through openings, and flicker with the wind. The sun on her face feels warm and nourishing. Her eyes wander through the forest. A mushroom growing from beside the stump catches her eye. Tala then notices the dirt on the path and how the roots of the trees are just beneath the surface. Strong, yet thin, there are so many different sized roots reaching out. Then she looks at Duncan's hand upon hers and notices the veins beneath his skin, and how a warm hand in hers reaches into the heart. She knows that this moment is special, and it will go away as quickly as it came.

The forest has revitalized her with the courage to flow forward in the stream of eternity, knowing that just like the fallen tree there would be decay and regrowth—the same processes were within her. Today, she is blooming. Tala tugs Duncan's hand. Both stand up and follow the wind through the trees.

Companions that Lead Us through the Darkness

Prior to the COVID-19 pandemic, psychological disturbance in the form of major depression affected roughly 30% of all people living in the U.S. over the course of a lifespan; while 42% experienced a major episode of general anxiety (Crossman, 2017). Although longitudinal research is required to learn how the pandemic factors into long-term well-being, one is led to conclude that mental disturbances experienced during the pandemic will have lifelong effects.

When a young adult experiences psychological distress, it means that there are hardships, challenges, and disturbances related to emotions, mood, and cognitive function outside the level of ability to successfully cope. Distress also happens when the available resources are not sufficient enough to manage the state or circumstance. The physical problems associated to psychological distress and disturbances range from heart problems to cancer, susceptibility to catching the common cold, and even increased chances of early death. Physical ailments may be symptoms to greater social, cultural, and economic diseases. There are also limited preventative measures to safeguard against disturbance onset.

For instance, many young adults living in residential care experience psychological challenges in acclimating to school, navigating and forming social relationships, and often have difficult home situations (Muela et al., 2017). Many will experience low self-esteem, insecure attachments, diminished interpersonal skills, risky behaviors, or have a history of ACEs. The conventional psychological interventions are not relevant or appealing, so that attrition is common. These factors place young adults in residential care at higher risks for mental disturbances in adulthood.

Secure attachments are important to mediate life stressors and emotional disturbances because they offer sources of self-esteem, stability, and confidence. Without them, many young adults feel despair as they have no one to root for them or offer relevant knowledge to take on challenges. Without growth-promoting relationships the weight of loneliness anxiety can crush their spirit for living, especially during times of hardship. The psychological interventions available might not be appealing to young adults, as they do not align with their existential concerns, values, cultural paradigms, or offer a sincere form of empathy.

The existential concerns may overwhelm young adults that are emotionally weakened from trauma or long-term stress. How does one seek to create meaning without any support or safety nets? Young adults may wonder where they can find friendships strong enough to endure difficult life challenges and brave enough to explore existential waters.

Who in this life can know what it is like to be them, to meet their eyes, to be able to receive a comforting gesture, and find a form of communication that brings meaning to the word "relationship"? There may be Bodhisattvas in forms other than ourselves; confident companions whose relational encounters courageously guide young adults through life challenges in order to realize existential meanings. Humans and animals have developed meaningful encounters since time immemorial. To have an encounter with animals is to remember *what is*, and most beautifully, decide together *what could be*.

Nevertheless, encounters with animals are often difficult for those who drown out existential angst in with materialistic values and fables of invincibility. These psychological fortifications are meant to provide distancing from reality. Within this delusion, animals are perceived as lower forms of life compared to human beings. This allows the person to believe that they are exempted from reality and will not experience the struggles, suffering, or death as animals do. In reality, people that deny the existential givens in reality are choosing to close their eyes to reflections of the self that animals reveal. The repudiation is a sort of cognitive dissonance, where one seeks to rationalize that they do not want to (or cannot) be in delightful wonder of animals and identify with them. There is a sense of envy of animals, where the person wishes that they could live by inner nature as they do, live in the moment with such authenticity, fall asleep as quickly as them, and can accept reality with equanimity. Rather, the person reasons that one does not want these things because that would mean having to live by the same existential rules. Instead, the person reasons that they are a special form of existence that was assigned to dutifully carry out some kind of social burden, to push forth;

150 Part II

where survival and progress are obligatory to achieve a future vision of happiness or success for the human race.

When the veil of existential denial is removed, young adults can appreciate what Watts (1979) described:

> At times almost all of us envy the animals. They suffer and die, but they do not seem to make a "problem" of it. Their lives seem to have so few complications. They eat when they are hungry and sleep when they are tired, and instinct rather than anxiety seems to govern their few preparations for the future. As far as we can judge, every animal is so busy with what he is doing at the moment that it never enters his head to ask whether life has a meaning or a future. For the animal, happiness consists in enjoying life in the immediate present—not in the assurance that there is a whole future of joys ahead of him.
>
> (p. 29)

Living in the here-and-now is effortless for animals, where people often experience great difficulty. To enjoy life in the present moment requires accepting human nature—as community oriented, empathic, altruistic, and sometimes destructive beings. Those with existential anxieties tend to reject the idea that they are susceptible to old age and death just as animals. In addition, many will reason that animals have inferior intelligence and lower value compared to the human being. However, animal and human intelligences/value cannot be categorized in hierarchies. There is a horizontal plane of value and intelligence for all forms of life. Animals have the privilege of knowing what it is to be in ways human beings never will, and vice versa. Young adults with this enlightened appreciation will encounter the world with dignity and respect.

Although enlisting animals for assistance in psychological interventions that promote healing and therapy has gained popularity in recent years, human–animal interaction (HAI) is a centuries-old practice that has been used to promote mental well-being. According to Sauer and Gill (2020), "Animal-assisted therapy is in its infancy in terms of use in mental health, even though using animals in a therapeutic setting dates back to the 1700s" (p. 375). Human–animal interaction is defined as an encounter between a human being and a nonhuman animal that is typically associated with "animal-assisted interventions (goal-directed programs conducted by trained professionals), animal-assisted activities (informal programs typically conducted by volunteers), interactions between people and their companion animals, and other types of encounters between people and animals" (Crossman, 2017, p. 761). The most commonly reported animals used in HAI are canines, felines, equines, and dolphins (Rhodes, 2020). For example, in dolphin assisted therapy the client is able to encounter dolphins by swimming with them and engaging in verbal target tasks. Practitioners have also sought assistance from farm animals such as rabbits, fish, birds, llamas, and snakes (Seivert et al., 2018).

Equine-assisted therapy is another example where horses are recruited to help cultivate growth-promoting relationships, stimulate creative problem-solving skills, and develop interpersonal communication abilities. Today, the therapeutic and health preventative/promotive effects of HAI are used in schools, nursing homes, airports, courts, institutions of higher education, places of business, corporations, prisons, hospitals, and even after tragedies or disasters. The types of animals employed are diverse and are chosen depending on the appropriate circumstance or availability. HAI has been shown to be beneficial for all demographics.

In controlled research settings with domesticated animals, HAIs became protective factors against negative stress for human beings, especially for those that suffered trauma (Crossman, 2017). In the aftermath of a traumatic event, an individual appraises their abilities to cope, and if the trauma can be overcome or managed, a problem-solving coping strategy is enacted. Contrarily, if the situation is beyond the abilities and available resources, and cannot be changed, then an emotion-focused coping is employed. An encounter with an animal in the aftermath of trauma promotes positive appraisals of the self against negative stressors. This supports self-esteem and self-empowerment.

Animals are associated with positive feelings and emotions which have significant influence in the evaluation of negative stressors. If there is an absence of social support systems in a young adult's life, animal companions help reduce feelings of loneliness and low self-esteem. The unconditional acceptance from the animal companion is important for self-acceptance and believing that one is deserving to receive love. Tactile interaction with animals, either through petting or even a hug, provides meaningful comfort and reduces stress responses (Crossman, 2017). Furthermore, tactile stimulation helps one experience reality and emotional information through different perceptual/sensational avenues. Animals also benefit from being petted, so the relationship is reciprocal in many ways.

Although research has found that HAI reduces stress, not many studies have investigated into why these effects happens—most conclusions stem from an empirical observation to explain a greater theory (Crossman, 2017). For example, the biophilia hypothesis argued that human beings have a preference for animals because humans evolved to use them as sources of food or utility. Similar theories that explain how humans have preferences for animals because they are sources of food, or how they help us survive, do not explain why relationships with animals improve mental well-being. These ideas typically reduce the phenomenon of relationships to be an evolutionary stratagem.

There is also the oxytocin hypothesis, which contended that the relational hormone called oxytocin is elected around animals, which creates a feel-good bond with them (Dravsnik et al., 2018). Oxytocin not only increases bonds between human and animal, but also promotes prosocial behavior. Sapolsky (2017) explained:

Sometime in the last fifty thousand years (i.e., less than 0.1 percent of the time that oxytocin has existed), the brains of humans and domesticates wolves evolved a new response to oxytocin: when a dog and its owner (but not a stranger) interact, they secrete oxytocin. The more of that time is spent gazing at each other, the bigger the rise. Give dogs oxytocin, and they gaze longer at their humans…which raises the humans' oxytocin levels. So a hormone that evolved for mother–infant bonding plays a role in this bizarre, unprecedented form of bonding between species.

(p. 112)

However, there is more to the phenomenon of relationships than just one hormone creating positive associations in our brains. Although the warm and fuzzy feeling of oxytocin produces deeper bonds, it has also been found to increase levels of xenophobia and ethnocentrism by creating a sense of in-group (who has positive associations) against an out-group (negative associations). The bonds that oxytocin forms can become lines of division between us and them. The oxytocin hypothesis is important, but not the final story for what makes bonds strengthen between human and animal, or amongst humans. One must be careful not to reduce the phenomenon of relationships to only neurobiology.

HAI is often associated with improvements in mood, particularly by matching the happiness and vitality of the animals through emotional contagion. The emotional awareness and empathic understandings between humans and animals "suggests that it would theoretically be possible for the kind of facial mimicry and emotional contagion observed between human interaction partners and from humans to animals to occur from animals to humans" (Crossman, 2017, p. 772). One animal species that exhibits strong emotional contagion with humans is dogs. Canines and human beings have been evolving together for over 30,000 years. Humans and dogs have developed an affinity for each other's company. Dogs have an extraordinary ability for attuning to the emotional states of humans and can assist in the emotional regulation processes. In addition, encounters with dogs promote an adaptive disposition to anxious states, because they help young adults return to the here-and-now (e.g., with excessive licks, play, goal-oriented activities, cuddles, or even presence). Young adults are more apt to accept emotional states and existential realities in the presence of a dog. Young adults begin to increase self-care as they care for animal companions (Rhodes, 2020). Self-esteem is promoted as the person feels a sense of worth and value in the animal's life.

For young adults with underdeveloped social skills, many will experience an isolation and loneliness. Animal companions encourage physical activity and facilitate socialization amongst people that would not have interacted otherwise (Crossman, 2017). When animals are present, young adults are more likely to initiate interactions with peers and adults, engage in prosocial activity, and cooperate. Animal companions are conduits for human sociality and well-being. The augmenting and therapeutic effects of animal encounters enhance cognitive, socio-emotional, biological, and even immune system processes. As Rhodes (2020) described, "Interaction with animals can lead to neurological changes and the release of neurotransmitters that suppress anxiety and improve mood. These changes lead to a decrease in depression and increased verbal interaction" (p. 10). Other studies have found that animal companions lower blood pressure, encourage sociality and mobility, as well as eliminate loneliness anxiety.

Therapeutic Animal Encounters

The therapeutic use of human–animal interaction has consistently seen higher success rates for engagement and retention of people experiencing psychological distress than compared to traditional psychological interventions. Animals have an ability to attract people and offer healing in unparalleled ways. As Trujillo et al. (2020) affirmed, "Incorporating animal-assisted therapy into adolescent mental health and substance treatment in a school-based setting may improve treatment access, engagement, retention, and outcomes" (p. 307). In addition, animal-assisted therapy (AAT) in schools has shown to increase levels of empathy for young adults, while reducing problems with behavior. AAT provides structured activities/encounters with animals to achieve a therapeutic alliance that cultivates healing and improved well-being for the client (Muela et al., 2017; Trujillo et al., 2020).

All animals in AAT have undergone training by the Animal Assisted Intervention International Standards to assist therapeutic goals (Rhodes, 2020). In psychotherapeutic settings, practitioners reported that animals create deeper rapport with clients in shorter periods of time. Mental health professionals that utilize AAT must also undergo training.

Having an animal as a companion is a relationship of a different nature than those established in animal intervention programs, because the companion is a long-term relationship that offers consistent interaction/effects. Companion animals may not elicit the intense effects that research studies measure, due to differing triggers that developed or became associated in a long-term relationship. As Crossman (2017) stated, "the time and financial costs associated with companion animal ownership mean that it is not at all guaranteed that the effects observed in the context of time-limited animal-assisted activity/therapy programs will generalize to companion animal ownership" (pp. 765–766). Regardless of the nature of animal interaction, the quality of encounter between the human and animal is critical for any measure of therapeutic effect on well-being (Sauer & Gill, 2020).

More than half the states in the U.S. have HAI programs for people incarcerated in prisons to support mental well-being, decrease disturbance symptomology, and increase positive behaviors and social skills (Holman et al., 2020). Animal assistance in prisons builds relationships based in trust, social responsibility, and emotional intelligence. In a study by Seivert et al. (2018), 138 incarcerated young adults were instructed to either train dogs or to only walk them, twice a week for ten weeks. Each group received a two-hour-per-week educational session on animals and how to interact with them. Self-reports from both groups

154   Part II

revealed an increase in empathy and emotional awareness. The emotional effects on both groups may have stemmed from the encounters with an animal and accompanying didactic instruction.

In a 16-week study of 31 low-income Hispanic young adults (12 to 17 years of age) with mental disturbances and substance abuse comorbidities, Trujillo et al. (2020) found that animal-assisted therapy produced higher success rates for treatment completion, better outcomes of therapeutic effects, more engagement from clients, and a high degree of gratitude when there was the presence of a therapy dog. Trujillo et al. (2020) discovered that the AAT group had generated a higher degree of well-being than compared to the control group. AAT is important for underserved populations living in urban areas for receiving equitable therapeutic encounters and effects, especially for substance abuse engagement and mental well-being interventions.

Adjusting to new social environments can be challenging, especially in school contexts. There has been close to one thousand institutions of higher education in the U.S. that have implemented an HAI program to reduce stress and improve mental well-being for students (Crossman, 2017). Young adults that received animal-assisted psychotherapy (AAP) experienced increases in social and emotional skills, as well as developing positive attitudes toward school and teachers (Muela et al., 2017). Many programs utilize the service of dogs to support young adults in their developmental and academic growth.

Humans' BFFs (Best Friends Forever)

Young adults will most likely find the journey through an institution of higher education to cause higher levels of stress. As Binfet et al. (2018) described:

> Factors contributing to student stress identified over 25 years ago are as relevant today as ever and include transitioning from home to independent living, increased academic expectations, time management challenges, new social and sexual roles and demands and sleep deprivation.
>
> (p. 197)

Reports demonstrate that stress levels have been rising for higher education students since the turn of the millennium.

However, there is positive stress that can come from homework assignments, social dynamics, and deadlines which are most often growth-promoting. Students have the motivation, resources, and skills to overcome these challenges. When there are little to no skills or resources, the stress can be negatively interpreted, detrimental, and marked by emotional disturbances (i.e., depressive or anxiety states), sleep disturbances, unhealthy eating habits, or rumination (Binfet et al., 2018). Educators and administrators must work to eliminate negative stressors on campuses by implementing preventative measures through resource accessibility and socio-emotional development. Otherwise, there will be decreases in enroll-ment, academic performances, and strength of campus community.

Socio-emotional well-being is highly influenced by emotional intelligences, which are fundamental components to students' academic achievement and social success in college (Binfet et al., 2018). Students need to be able to utilize socio-emotional intelligences for regulating emotions, accessing resources and support for coping with stress, exploring diverse relationships, and making positive choi-ces. Those that scored higher on socio-emotional competency evaluations had higher rates of academic achievement than those with lower competency scores. Students that can manage, regulate, and cope with the stressors of being a college student are more likely to establish positive habits of thought and behavior. These skills translate into better grades, degree completion, and deeper learning in the classroom.

To prevent and reduce existing levels of student stress, many institutions of higher education have enlisted the help of dogs to bring relaxation, therapy, and emotional well-being (Binfet et al., 2018). Dogs have a high degree of empathy with humans, which has implications for helping young adults develop socio-emotional intelligences (Seivert et al., 2018). Trained support dogs have given therapy in a diversity of settings. For instance, they have provided comfort and healing to survivors of natural disasters and traumatic events, such as with hurri-canes and mass shootings (Rhodes, 2020). Studies have shown that when a dog is present in a school classroom there are lower levels of aggression and fewer instances of behavioral problems from students. Perhaps there are similar effects for teachers and professors as well. Pre- and post-intervention studies have found that, regardless of demographic, didactic instruction and encounters with dogs increases empathic abilities (Seivert et al., 2018).

There are many students in college that have unresolved or untreated mental disturbances that affect their well-being and academic success. Young adults that experienced ACEs have roughly a 30% chance of developing the debilitating symptoms of post-traumatic stress disorder (PTSD) (Dravsnik et al., 2018). Although there are numerous effective treatment options, many young adult programs experience high attrition rates or disengagement. Dravsnik et al. (2018) sought to understand if the effects of canine-assisted therapy could augment cognitive behavioral therapy (CBT) that is often used to treat PTSD. The results of the study found that regardless of the age that the CBT was administered, the canine-assisted therapy increased engagement, retention, and acceptability of the course of treatment.

A canine therapy program was implemented at the University of British Columbia, known as B.A.R.K., or Building Academic Retention through K9s (barkubc.ca). B.A.R.K. engaged roughly 30% of the student population to decrease stress, homesickness, and adjustment challenges, while increasing first-year students' positive attitudes toward campus and academics. The dogs were available to welcome and provide nonjudgmental interaction to the students in a designated encounter space. Binfet et al. (2018) found that in B.A.R.K., "spending time with therapy canines significantly reduces students' self-reports of stress, contributes to the body of empirical research attesting to the benefits of canine assisted therapy" (p. 200). This knowledge is important for social institutions that serve young adults, not only for the individual well-being but for the community at large.

College examinations provide an abundance of stress for students, in which studies have found that greater levels of exam stress translate into declined academic performance (Barker et al., 2017). The current interventions (e.g., mindful breathing or eye movement desensitization and reprocessing) to reduce student stress may be limited in that these techniques require training by qualified personnel. Also, group-based interventions have had difficulties in generating and retaining participants. To overcome these challenges and increase student engagement and retention, canine-assisted therapy sites have been implemented on campuses so that students may visit dogs prior to exams (Barker et al., 2017). This low-cost intervention requires no training on the part of participants and can draw large crowds of young adults. Students expressed a desire to frequent these college spaces more often if they knew they would be able to interact with dogs. More student traffic means that college counselors can plan to make themselves accessible in these areas to develop rapport with students. Greater rapport with students allows counselors to check in with students' emotional well-being, as well as offer academic guidance.

In a mid-Atlantic university, the University Counseling Services (UCS) initiated an informal canine-assisted therapy to mitigate student stress prior to final exams (Barker et al., 2017). The events were semi-structured, where students could either view the dogs or interact with them as they wished. The average time spent with a dog was about 10 minutes. Popular activities included petting (almost 95% engaged in petting a dog), tricks, and even taking selfies together. Counselors approached students to initiate contact and develop rapport. Barker et al. (2017) surveyed 694 students in a pre- and post-survey of stress, where the majority (60%) stated that they lived with pets at home. Roughly 93% of the participants reported that the interactions with dogs significantly reduced stress. Circumstance of pet ownership, race, or ethnicity were not found to be influential factors. Only 23 students reported negative comments, where the majority felt that there were too few dogs and it was too small of a room for the number of students present. This canine-assisted therapy program was found to attract more students than all of the non-animal programs at UCS.

There is a large body of research on HAI and significant findings that support well-being hypotheses. Conversely, it must also be considered that there are variables that can reduce or increase psychological distress that may or may not be the result of animal interaction, such as a certain environmental trigger, seasonal weather, sleep, hunger, and so on (Crossman, 2017). This is why control groups are important to test if the effects of HAI are the result of the intervention. The

Creating Meaning with the Natural World **157**

peripheral factors that cause therapy or distress must be considered. However, the research findings are sometimes vague or conflicting due to issues with methodology (Crossman, 2017). HAI interventions sometimes include case-specific results, where one researcher's findings may be within unique contexts that cannot be found in another study. Researchers may exclude elements from findings, such as the effects of animal companion relationships.

Regardless of the methodological limitations, empirical evidence should not be the sole criteria to justify the augmented well-being that animal interactions provide young adults. The research is meant to explore, explain, and ultimately improve upon program interventions. The phenomenon of human and animal relationships cannot be fully recorded by data. Our encounters with animals are reflective of the living, flowing moment. To quantify the phenomenon in order to justify or negate it can lead to gross misunderstandings and ignorance. The existential moment that takes place when young adults encounter an animal reawakens them to their life essence. The fact that human beings are motivated to encounter animals is reason enough to develop relationships with them. When human beings have moments of suffering and feel their humanity has been lost, it is magnificent to have it faithfully retrieved by a dog.

Hyun: Two Encounters

On an early Saturday afternoon in April, Hyun is working on a term paper for his undergraduate psychology class. This spring semester, he decided to enroll in a few online classes at the local community college in order to work toward a degree, as well as explore his interests in psychology. His phone vibrates with a text message; it is his friend Darby.

Darby: Hey, man.

Hyun: Hi, Darby, what's up?

Darby: I am having a difficult situation and was wondering if you could help me out.

Hyun: Tell me about what's going on.

Darby: Well, you know that I live with my dad, and he recently got really sick. I need to take him to get tested for COVID and then figure out how to get him better.

Hyun: OMG, I am so sorry to hear this. This must be very scary for both of you.

Darby: It is and, yes, I am worried. But I have a favor to ask.

Hyun: Name it.

Darby: Can you doggy-sit for me? For about a week? I know that you and Floyd get along famously, so you were the first person I thought of and the only person I trust.

At this point, Hyun feels great concern for his friend and his father. When he moved to Maine, Darby was his first friend and helped him get settled and find his way around town.

158   Part II

Hyun had the privilege of having a meaningful relationship with a pet when he was a child. He loved his cat, Marmalade, but never found a way to get over the grief of his passing. To manage the emotions, he chose not to live with any more animals. However, with the intense loneliness he had experienced in lockdown and the elevated threat of infection and death, he thought, *why not?*

Hyun: Of course, Darby. I will watch Floyd for you while you take care of your dad. Just show me what to do and I will take good care of him. Why not bring him over with all of his stuff tomorrow? I am going to go on a socially distanced whale watch today. LOL.

Darby: Thank you, Hyun. Floyd loves you and I am very appreciative that you are my friend. Whales?!

Hyun: Anytime. Call me tomorrow.

Darby: Thanks. L8tr Sk8tr.

Hyun places his phone down on the table and reflects on the adventure that awaits him tomorrow. Perhaps he and Floyd will make good company for each other. Floyd always liked his visits to Darby's house.

Hyun decides that it is time to get ready for the whale watch. He had not been on one since his time in California and wants to meet the whales of the North Atlantic Ocean.

At the docks, Hyun boards the boat and feels a great sense of excitement. The mid-size vessel sets its course. Hyun watches the coast disappear. The ocean waves glisten under a clear blue sky. *This is beautiful,* he thinks. *I hope we get to see a whale up close.* The motors turn off to indicate that they had reached their destination. With the sea quiet, the group was much more apt to encounter a whale.

All of the sudden the boat began to rock side to side, as if something was pushing it from below. The whale watch guide informs the group that the movement was indeed caused by a whale underneath the boat. Hyun grips the side railing and excitedly scans the sea for signs of the whale. The boat stops swaying and the waters return calm. *Perhaps the whale came and left,* he considers. Hyun stares intently at the ocean, hoping for a glimpse of the whale.

Just then, a whale gently surfaces starboard side, just a few feet away from where Hyun is viewing. The enormous whale floats for just a short while as if to say hello to the passengers. Hyun feels an out-of-body experience as this immense being floats closer to greet him. *I am just as curious about you, as you are about me,* he marvels with eyes fixed on the whale. The size of the whale is wonderfully terrifying and beautiful. The whale is so close that Hyun can see her eye. As their eyes connect, Hyun is lost within the deep encounter. He does not reflect on the experience until she descends into the ocean. Hyun thinks about the kindness that he saw from the whale's curiosity. There was a connection that was beyond words or even his understanding. The whale-watching group saw a few more whales splash in the distance but none like Hyun's close encounter.

The next day, Darby and Floyd can be seen from the apartment window as they park their car and walk up to Hyun's door. Floyd is jubilant to see Hyun.

The dog is of a small mix breed that Darby adopted from the local no-kill rescue shelter. Floyd's tail wags and he lets out squeals of excitement. Hyun picks up Floyd and the dog offers incessant licks of affection. After a brief conversation, Darby leaves the apartment to take care of his father. After the door shut Floyd and Hyun look at each other, as if to say, "What do we do now?"

Hyun has to get ready to work the afternoon shift at the café. Although Hyun has to keep his work schedule during the week, he has made sure that in his absence Floyd would be comfortable in his bed, have a large supply of water and food, and be able to enjoy the soothing ambience of a meadow on his laptop. After Hyun left for work, Floyd decides to achieve a little mischief. He walks intently into the bathroom and begins to destroy the toilet paper roll. This provides good exercise and mental stimulation so that Floyd will be able to take a good nap later. When Hyun returns home to find Floyd napping in bed and various things around the apartment destroyed, he decides that he must adapt to his new roommate. Over the course of the week, the two find ways to create a special bond.

Hyun learns that Floyd likes to be chased and then to chase him. There are rhythms and rituals they create that represent their unique situation and relationship. Every day at 4:00pm is Floyd's dinner time and Hyun finds himself happiest when he is successful in preparing a delicious dinner. He knows that it is especially tasty when Floyd finishes, licks the dish, and then licks the crumbs off his placemat. In return, Floyd makes sure there are no short supplies of kisses and cuddles. *What a kind and loving animal; without even talking to me, he accepts me, and knows me.*

Hyun marvels at how close the relationship feels, where no words are needed. On their last afternoon as roommates, Hyun takes Floyd for a walk. "It's a beautiful day for a walk, Floyd! Let's get your harness on and enjoy this weather." Floyd eagerly accepts and waits patiently by the door. Hyun ties his sneakers and then snaps the harness on his friend. The door creaks open and Floyd slips through the opening. It appears that Floyd knows where he wants to go and takes a left on the sidewalk. Hyun watches the dog walk with excitement, bouncing with each step. His little ears flap in the wind as he searches for new smells. At one point, Floyd realizes he is walking much faster than Hyun—he turns to see if he is still behind. Hyun is met with a deep gaze of thought and compassion. Floyd's eyes seemed to say: *Are you still there, my friend? I will wait for you if you need me to, this adventure is ours.* Hyun smiles, picks up the pace and Floyd turns toward the wind—*onward!*

During their last night together, Hyun finds himself deep within a nightmare, where Darby and his father both died of the virus. His anxieties about the pandemic have transferred onto his worries for his friend. Hyun awakens abruptly with shortened breath. He searches the room to shake off the disorientation. Floyd is at the end of the bed and jumps awake after feeling Hyun's sudden movement. The faithful dog stands up ready to defend his friend. Hyun focuses

160   Part II

and regains composure. He pets Floyd and offers reassurance that it was just a nightmare. However, the dog knows that Hyun is having a difficult time. As Hyun lays back down on his side, Floyd walks up to Hyun's chest. *What on earth are you doing*, he wonders. Floyd scratches the covers a bit, circles three or four times and lays down, curling up against his chest. *Is this what they call spooning*, Hyun questions. Hyun can feel the dog's rhythm of breath and warmth against his body; he quickly follows Floyd into sleep.

Tala: The Companionship of Twinkie

Ugh, I don't want to get up, Tala protests, as she lays in bed and checks her cell phone to learn that it is 10:30am on Wednesday. Her partner Duncan has been away for the past week taking care of his parents. They need help grocery shopping and their yard maintenance workers said they could not come for a while, so Duncan is on duty. In his absence, Tala has the week to herself and, with the mandatory social quarantines, this isolation is testing her sanity. She misses hiking, working, volunteering, and going to college classes. Without social interaction, she feels fatigued with a lack of motivation to do anything around the apartment.

Tala grabs her cell phone and decides to scroll through some pictures on Instagram. *Maybe there will be a video of a golden snub-nosed monkey, a meme of a bird, or a cute picture of a sloth.* Unfortunately, the phone application has nothing in which she has not seen already, but she keeps scrolling anyways.

YEEOOOOWW! Tala screams at the top of her lungs. There is an excruciatingly sharp pain in her big toe. She quickly sits up and greets the big yellow eyes of Twinkie the cat. Tala grabbed her right foot compassionately as Twinkie saunters away. Twinkie has a predilection for biting the toes of those in slumber. Tala lays back down as the pain subsides, still clutching her foot. *Why did you do that, cat? Why?*

After a moment, Tala reflects, *Twinkie wants me up, I better get up so she can eat.* As Tala climbs out of bed, she carefully puts her injured toe into a slipper. Twinkie has found a place on top of the refrigerator to spy on her. *She thinks that I can't see her*, Tala notices. Twinkie's eyes are large and kind. She is a small cat with orange and white fur. Tala begins preparing breakfast, and after it is made Twinkie will descend from her perch to eat on her personalized placemat. Twinkie is spoiled, but Tala always told Duncan that Twinkie deserves it, because they have the privilege of sharing a home with a little Buddha.

Tala washes up, dresses, and makes her own elaborate form of brunch: peanut butter on a rice cake, banana, an egg with avocado, and coffee. *I probably would have slept till 2:00pm if I didn't have Twinkie*, she reflects. "Twinkie, I am going to make some coffee, do you want some?" Tala says out loud, jokingly. She also responds in a high-pitched voice for the cat, "No, thank you, Mom."

As the coffee brews in the percolator, Tala lets out a long yawn. In her peripheral vision, Tala sees Twinkie slide across the hardwood floors after her little fish toy. "Oh, you want to play with Mr. Fish?" Tala leaves her chair to grab the fish toy before Twinkie does. She makes the fish move around as if it were real. Twinkie's eyes grow wild with excitement and a wide smile brushes across Tala's face. The two hop, run, leap, and hunt various toys and invent different scenarios in which Mr. Fish must be apprehended. At the end of 45 minutes, Tala is energized and has forgotten about her coffee.

"Okay, Twinkie, enough play time, we need to get to work," Tala declares and responds for Twinkie, "Okay, Mom, I will help!" As she begins to clean the apartment, Twinkie finds vantage points from which to view Tala, watching with curiosity and wonder. *There is no better company*, Tala reflects, as she sweeps the floor with Twinkie watching her from the chair. To further entertain Twinkie and make the moment even more special, Tala puts on some lively pop music and dances with the broom. Twinkie finds this human display fascinating and silly!

When all the daily chores are completed, Tala takes her laptop to her favorite space on the couch to complete her homework assignments. Tala notices that Twinkie has disappeared for the last ten minutes; *maybe she is napping from all of our fun*. Tala has an important final paper due soon, so today she needs to make significant progress in the research. She accesses the university's online library databases for peer-reviewed articles, reads them, and takes some notes. After about 40 minutes of researching she feels ready to write. Tala opens a new Word document and saves it as "Final Essay." She pauses for a second and takes a deep breath to mentally prepare herself to write the essay. Tala prepares her body by stretching her arms high in the air before cracking her knuckles. Her arms rest on her legs and hands slightly touch the keyboard. *I am going to write an amazing essay*, she determines. As she begins to type her name, she feels something furry and soft on her left hand. Twinkie has returned and is now resting her head atop of Tala's hand. The cat appears to have already fallen asleep. Tala gazes at Twinkie's little head and then body. The warmth on her hand is comforting and loving.

"You are going to take a nap on my hand, Twinks?"

"Yes. It is good here," she responds in a high voice for the cat.

"But I have to write a big paper."

"Yes, you do," the cat replies.

"How am I supposed to do this with you on my hand?"

"I am here with you. This is good."

"Yes, this is good," Tala replies, as Twinkie finds her way deeper into sleep. Tala does her best to keep her hand still.

References

Antonelli, M., Barbieri, G., & Donelli, D. (2019). Effects of forest bathing (shinrin-yoku) on levels of cortisol as a stress biomarker: A systematic review and meta-analysis. *International Journal of Biometeorology*, 63(8), 1117–1134. https://doi.org/10.1007/s00484-019-01717-x.

Barker, S. B., Barker, R. T., & Schubert, C. M. (2017). Therapy dogs on campus: A counseling outreach activity for college students preparing for final exams. *Journal of College Counseling*, 20(3), 278–288. https://doi.org/10.1002/jocc.12075.

Binfet, J.-T., Passmore, H.-A., Cebry, A., Struik, K., & McKay, C. (2018). Reducing university students' stress through a drop-in canine-therapy program. *Journal of Mental Health*, 27(3), 197–204. https://doi.org/10.1080/09638237.2017.1417551.

Crossman, M. K. (2017). Effects of interactions with animals on human psychological distress. *Journal of Clinical Psychology*, 73(7), 761–784. https://doi.org/10.1002/jclp.22410.

Csikszentmihalyi, M. (1975). *Beyond boredom and anxiety: The experience of play in work and games*. Jossey-Bass.

Dogaru, G. (2020). Forest bathing in cardiovascular diseases—a narrative review. *Balneo Research Journal*, 11(3), 299–303. https://doi.org/10.12680/balneo.2020.356.

Dravsnik, J., Signal, T., & Canoy, D. (2018). Canine co-therapy: The potential of dogs to improve the acceptability of trauma-focused therapies for children. *Australian Journal of Psychology*, 70(3), 208–216. https://doi.org/10.1111/ajpy.12199.

Hariharan, K., & Kapoor, R. (2020). Impact of practicing spirituality on psychological well-being. *Indian Journal of Positive Psychology*, 11(3), 252–257.

Hassan, A., Tao, J., Li, G., Jiang, M., Aii, L., Zhihui, J., Zongfang, L., & Qibing, C. (2018). Effects of walking in bamboo forest and city environments on brainwave activity in young adults. *Evidence-Based Complementary & Alternative Medicine (ECAM)*, 2018, 1–9. https://doi.org/10.1155/2018/9653857.

Holman, L. F., Ellmo, F., Wilkerson, S., & Johnson, R. (2020). Quasi-experimental single-subject design: Comparing seeking safety and canine-assisted therapy interventions among mentally ill female inmates. *Journal of Addictions & Offender Counseling*, 41(1), 35–51. https://doi.org/10.1002/jaoc.12074.

Hopman, R. J., LoTemplio, S. B., Scott, E. E., McKinney, T. L., & Strayer, D. L. (2020). Resting-state posterior alpha power changes with prolonged exposure in a natural environment. *Cognitive research: principles and implications*, 5(1), 1–13. https://doi.org/10.1186/s41235-020-00247-0.

Keltner, D. (May 11, 2016). Why do we feel awe? Mindful: Taking Time for What Matters. http://www.mindful.org/why-do-we-feel-awe/.

Kim, T., Song, B., Cho, K. S., & Lee, I.-S. (2020). Therapeutic potential of volatile terpenes and terpenoids from forests for inflammatory diseases. *International Journal of Molecular Sciences*, 21(6), 2187. https://doi.org/10.3390/ijms21062187.

Kohl, J. (2020). Heritage interpretation enriches the park experience: How managers deploy thematic interpretation techniques to achieve park goals. *Parks & Recreation*, 55(12), 46–49.

Kottler, S. (2021). *The art of impossible: A peak performance primer*. HarperCollins.

L.L. Bean (2021a, January 4). The restorative power of the outdoors: Finding awe in our everyday. L.L. Bean. https://www.llbean.com/llb/shop/518336?nav=F5t518336-518354.

L.L. Bean (2021b, March 16). How time outdoors can sharpen your perception of time. L.L. Bean. https://www.llbean.com/llb/shop/518354?nav=C12t518354-517561.

Lee, J., Park, B., Tsunetsugu, Y., Ohira, T., Kagawa, T., & Miyazaki, Y. (2011). Effect of forest bathing on physiological and psychological responses in young Japanese male subjects. *Public Health*, 125(2), 93–100. http://dx.doi.org/10.1016/j.puhe.2010.09.005.

Livini, E. (2017, March 23). The Japanese practice of 'forest bathing' is scientifically proven to be good for you. World Economic Forum. https://www.weforum.org/agenda/

2017/03/the-japanese-practice-of-forest-bathing-is-scientifically-proven-to-be-good-for-you?utm_content=buffer1c549&utm_medium=social&utm_source=facebook.com&utm_campaign=buffer&fbclid=IwAR0CtOAnyLIQCVfQBHMcQO9Kw1M8lkt8CFd9i6riQ3WAMiLfwiKPLgjxJuI.

Martinez, C. T., McGath, N. N., & Williams, K. C. (2020). Pursuit of goals in the search for happiness: A mixed-method multidimensional study of well-being. *Psi Chi Journal of Psychological Research*, 25, 245–259. https://doi.org/10.24839/2325-7342.JN25.3.245.

Maslow, A. H. (1971). *The farther reaches of human nature*. The Viking Press.

Muela, A., Balluerka, N., Amiano, N., Caldentey, M. A., & Aliri, J. (2017). Animal-assisted psychotherapy for young people with behavioural problems in residential care. *Clinical Psychology & Psychotherapy*, 24(6), O1485–O1494. https://doi.org/10.1002/cpp.2112.

Rhodes, C. (2020). The healing power of pets. *Healthcare Counselling & Psychotherapy Journal*, 20(4), 8–12.

Sapolsky, R. (2017). *Behave: The biology of humans at our best and worst*. Penguin Press.

Sauer, A. N. K., & Gill, C. S. (2020). Treating disruptive mood dysregulation disorder: An integrated Adlerian and equine therapy approach. *Journal of Individual Psychology*, 76(4), 372–385.

Schneider, K. J. (2004). *Rediscovery of awe: Splendor, mystery and the fluid center of life*. Paragon House.

Seivert, N. P., Cano, A., Casey, R. J., Johnson, A., & May, D. K. (2018). Animal assisted therapy for incarcerated youth: A randomized controlled trial. *Applied Developmental Science*, 22(2), 139–153. https://doi.org/10.1080/10888691.2016.1234935.

Shiota, M. N., Keltner, D., & Mossman, A. (2007). The nature of awe: Elicitors, appraisals, and effects on self-concept. *Cognition and Emotion*, 21(5), 944–963.

Stone, E. (2017, April 27). The emerging science of awe and its benefits. *Psychology Today*. https://www.psychologytoday.com/us/blog/understanding-awe/201704/the-emerging-science-awe-and-its-benefits?nav=F4taE-518336.

Trujillo, K. C., Kuo, G. T., Hull, M. L., Ingram, A. E., & Thurstone, C. C. (2020). Engaging adolescents: Animal assisted therapy for adolescents with psychiatric and substance use disorders. *Journal of Child & Family Studies*, 29(2), 307–314. https://doi.org/10.1007/s10826-019-01590-7.

Watts, A. (1979). *The wisdom of insecurity: A message for an age of anxiety*. Vintage Books.

White, M. P., Alcock, I., Grellier, J., Wheeler, B. W., Hartig, T., Warber, S. L., Bone, A., Depledge, M. H., Fleming, L. E. (2019) Spending at least 120 minutes a week in nature is associated with good health and wellbeing. *Scientific Reports* 9(7730), 1–11. https://doi.org/10.1038/s41598-019-44097-3.

8

PRECIOUS SILENCE OF SOLITUDE

The extreme sense of loneliness caused by the pandemic's quarantines brought many young adults into realms of distress and disturbance (Sun et al., 2021). The naturally occurring therapies for loneliness that are found in cultural paradigms were restricted, and thus the isolation became overwhelming. Cultural paradigms are important for how young adults perceive and experience loneliness. The psychological effects of the paradigm can either be therapeutic or detrimental based on social meanings, norms, and values (Barreto et al., 2020; Franssen et al., 2020). For instance, in Western culture there is a focus on hyper-individualism, which values a preoccupation of the self regardless of contexts, as well as promoting hyper-masculine competition with the self, community, and environment. Personal and professional problems/challenges are internalized to where, if they are not conquered, it is a reflection of person's value, regardless of social, racial, gender, and economic inequalities or barriers. Loneliness is often shamed as if it reflected inadequacies of the person. In this sense, a cultural paradigm can be detrimental to well-being.

Cultural norms and values that alienate youth from the community often promote artificially induced desires that encourage people to feel that they can gain power over the resulting loneliness anxieties by asserting their identities (Bland, 2020). In this case, there are greater feelings of loneliness and decreases in well-being as one creates a self-propaganda machine to wage war on the self. Failing to achieve culturally determined age norms, such as when to enroll in higher education, marry, begin a career, or bear children generates excessive pressures on young adults. These pressures can ostracize young adults from their sense of belonging and self-esteem. Loneliness results when they cannot or do not wish to attain these milestones, meanings, or images as prescribed.

Conversely, the cultural paradigm is also important for how one interprets, copes, suffers, heals, or avoids loneliness. It is a system for collective meaning-

DOI: 10.4324/9781003251651-11

making, where regardless of geographical location, a person's knowledge and experiences find place within a greater schema. The meanings one creates or learns in the paradigm has influence in future experiences of isolation.

The two main classifications of cultural paradigms are collectivistic or individualistic; each have commonalities and differences for the meanings and values of loneliness, independence, and identity. For instance, social responsibility in an individualistic paradigm might mean that a young adult is motivated to focus on self-development or personal achievement in order to be able be meaningful to society. Whereas a collectivistic paradigm may encourage a young adult to focus on the needs of the community first. The person then achieves self-development in order to meet that need. The goal of social contribution may be similar but the motivational focus is different.

Cultural paradigms also influence how one accesses knowledge. For instance, collectivistic cultures place a significant value on the person's ability to be successful as an interdependent part of networks involving social and family spheres. Within family and social units, complex repositories of personal knowledges are available to help young adults navigate the world and make decisions. Loneliness in this realm may designate a removal from the collective sphere and not being able to access the knowledge repository—leading to chronic stress and estrangement. Remedies include group functions that promote harmony, reliance, acceptance, and service that support the unit (Sapolsky, 2017).

Loneliness in a collectivistic culture can also be a time of solitude or existential loneliness, where one reflects on their individual meanings within a group (the focus is on roles and relationships, rather than just the self). The experience of solitude can generate social awareness, authenticity, purpose, and spirituality (Grier & Ajayi, 2019; Johnson & Vallejos, 2019). Loneliness in an individualistic cultural paradigm values a focus on the individual independent of roles in the family or social unit (Sapolsky, 2017). The responsibility to overcome loneliness is up to the person, where resilience and strength are believed to be core traits to be developed. The knowledge repository is up to the individual to discover, within the self or through personal ventures. Individualism promotes self-reliance to succeed and find healing, where there is little to no dependence on others (Barreto et al., 2020). This can generate anxiety for young adults that do not have support and guidance, or it can be growth-promoting in a way that the person develops resilience and perseverance. Although the cultural paradigm has influence in how an experience is valued or its focus, the person is responsible for what meanings are created in order to explore inner-core values and existential concerns.

Cultural blending and diversification are staples of the twenty-first century. Although youth are reared in a culture that has been classified as collectivistic or individualistic; cultural elements are (quickly) blending, becoming hybrid, created together, or being discarded, as young adults gravitate toward cultural paradigms that align with their inner-core values, directions, and global realities. Even

166 Part II

though the two paradigms may blend in certain areas of the world, there are still important distinctions to cultures that can lead to unique dynamics and hybridity of meanings. Cultural paradigms cannot be reduced to generalizations because of their complexities and subcultural evolutions. Young adults explore cultural possibilities in their paradigm, while exploring others through diverse relationships. Testing cultural knowledge against personal experience often takes youth deeper beneath the surface or, perhaps, beyond the orbit of their cultural world.

Young adults gravitate toward experiences and opportunities where they can realize inner/group-potentials. They not only seek challenges and obstacles, but also time in solitude. Regardless of cultural paradigm, existential loneliness is a profound experience that supports culturally relative self-actualization processes. There is precious silence in solitude, which guides young adults through questions such as: *Who am I? Who are we? What do I want to become? How do I feel about life? Where do I (or we) want to go?* Solitude brings one into an isolated space, which if explored deeper contains limitless connections to the world. In existential loneliness, one can realize solitude as a place of strength and vitality (Johnson & Vallejos, 2019).

Within existential loneliness, one faces the organic reality that his/her/their life is a harmony of challenge, pain, stillness, and victory that reveal the solitary nature of self-awareness (Moustakas, 1961). Existential loneliness offers a contrapuntal cultural positionality; where there is a sense of uniqueness but also a deep sense of connection within the paradigm. Being able to transcend cultural barriers within solitude allows one to see the absurdity of many cultural practices and meanings. This critical reflection brings about an open-mindedness to explore other cultural meanings and paradigms, most notably through diverse encounters. These relationships must be explored by way of cultural humility—a continuous critical reflection of one's own meanings, biases, privileges, and absurdities, as a way to learn about other paradigms (Rosen et al., 2017; Soheilian et al., 2014). Loneliness provides the silences and spaces in which to explore the processes of cultural humility. Young adults learn to explore other worlds of meaning with empathy, respect, nonjudgment, and value, while being able to reveal the (mis)perceptions of one's own positionality (Miller, 2017; Morley, 2008).

Seeking out new relationships can be a stressful or overwhelming experience for some young adults (Tsehay et al., 2020). Failures to establish, maintain, or progress relationships may bring about loneliness anxieties. With socio-emotional skills young adults can appreciate that failure contains meaningful lessons that promote growth. Cultural humility in diverse growth-promoting relationships is imperative for loneliness to become a transcendental experience (Atchison et al., 2020; Mead, 2020).

The Mindful Self

The sense of individuality that blossoms in the solitude of young adulthood can be a driving force for exploring, experimenting, and knowing, the realization that the essence of selfhood is uniqueness and that ultimately one can only experience what one's own, from one's own organism, that in each instance the verdict of meaning and relevance must come from the texture and structure of one's own experiencing and a felt bodily sense that speaks to what is actual.

(Moustakas, 1995, p. 17)

The acceptance of one's individuality generates a global awareness to what is important in the immediate reality, which includes the nature of emotions and the meaningfulness of relationships with people, animals, and environment.

Greeting loneliness with courage, compassion, and wonder can be difficult for some young adults, because throughout their lives they were taught that being alone is a painful (or a shameful) experience. Young adulthood is a time of significant personal changes, discoveries, and challenges, in which mindfulness redefines what it means to experience loneliness. Research has found that, when practiced diligently, mindfulness protects the integrity of genes by supporting the stability of telomere length (compound structures at the end of the chromosomes that shorten with age, where associations between shorter the telomere length and malaise or mortality have been found) (Presti, 2016). When young adults experience existential loneliness, mindfulness helps them navigate uncomfortable feelings by identifying unrecognized elements. Clearly identifying that one needs to send or receive a text message in order to provide distraction from anxieties can be in itself therapeutic. Learning the holistic effects of loneliness is important for developing literacies in emotional experiences.

For instance, in China, Zhang et al. (2018) implemented an eight-week mindfulness psychoeducation curriculum to generate self-awareness for college students that experienced significant levels of loneliness. They found that "Mindfulness training enhances the capacities to disengage and de-identify with the perceived social threat, which leads to reduced loneliness" (Zhang et al., 2018, p. 376). Mindfulness re-centers young adults to find equanimity in solitude.

Mindfulness in solitude brings out sources of meaning and opportunities for discovery that align young adults with inner-core values. The emotions and feelings are gateways into knowing what is deeply valued in life. Whether it is through a mindful practice inspired by Buddhist practices or a Christian askesis, the point is not to remove emotions, but develop the compassionate processes of non-judgmental awareness (Halland et al., 2015; Larrivee & Echarte, 2018). Self-awareness is a source of empathy and spiritual connections to others.

Achieving a mindfulness state during lonely episodes can be challenging. Often, the emotions associated with loneliness are perceived as negative and undesirable. This is why the experience of loneliness is often avoided, even though the dread of the event is worse than its actual happening. Young adults may need guidance, modeling, and practice in order to develop their abilities for mindfulness during uncomfortable states of being. Otherwise, "when demands

168 Part II

exceed available resources, the situation is appraised as threatening" (Kalia & Knauft, 2020, p. 3). Anxiety, depression, negative stress, or rumination can threaten equanimity and distort perceptions of the self and world. Mindfulness practices along with cognitive reappraisal strategies help young adults manage disturbances in compassionate and healing ways.

Cognitive reappraisal strategies manage the negative emotions associated with loneliness. Young adults learn to find new perspectives by critically analyzing the initial situation and the circumstances that made it upsetting. This cultivates self-compassion, where young adults no longer hate the experience or fight it. Rather, loneliness becomes a time to reposition oneself with a phenomenological attitude. Self-compassion in cognitive reappraisal means exploring emotions, feelings, and thoughts with a curiosity that does not seek conclusions, but rather an existential awareness. Cognitively reappraisal helps evaluate a threat-response to understand the emotional experience within certain contexts. The development of cognitive appraisal helps young adults manage chronic stress and its adverse effects (Kalia & Knauft, 2020).

Cognitive reappraisal is a growth-promoting way to learn the mindfulness process, such as asking: "Which words describe the emotional and physical experience of loneliness?" "What emotive elements from my relationships with others, either present or imagined, affect my solitude?" "Do I fully know every perspective of this situation?" "What do I want the emotions and physical sensations to mean for my stream of existence?" Questions are important in cognitive reappraisal because they are the basis of critical thinking. They help young adults explore their experiences and contexts in order to create existential meanings. Cognitive reappraisal questions cultivate mindful diligence by their exploratory nature. During states of loneliness, mindfulness teaches young adults to appreciate solitude as precious moments. Without need or want of distraction, young adults find that loneliness is a natural process, where they can embrace the profundity of the stillness and silence.

Monserrat: On My Own

Monserrat is an independent, strong-willed, intelligent, and lively young person of 22 years. For most of her life she had lived with her family that immigrated to the United States from Brazil. Monserrat's immediate family consists of three brothers, three sisters, and her mother. They all share a close-knit bond. The pandemic has been psychologically difficult for them because extended family could not visit, nor could Monserrat or her siblings gather with local friends. However, during the trials of quarantines and curfews, they have stayed strong and resilient because they have each other to lean on. This is the early summer of 2021 and Monserrat just graduated from the local university. She is ready to venture out on her own; a dream she had cultivated during the previous year and a half. We join her now on the day after she settled into her new apartment. It is just after breakfast and she sits down on the couch:

I glance around at the half-empty apartment and suddenly the flow of my life reaches a precipice, for which my momentum takes me over: In these past two years, all I ever wanted was freedom, my own place to come and go as I pleased, being able to do as I wanted without having to ask for permission first; to be on my own. Where did that idea come from? It was so strong at the time. Now, the thrill of getting my own place is not here. This is truly the first time I have ever felt alone as I realize that from this point forth, I am actually on my own.

The silence of the apartment is deafening and suffocating. I dearly miss the non-stop noise from my mom's house. Voices of my family were music by which my soul danced. The talking, people coming in and out, the music or television blasting from the living room, unexpected visitors, and all the things that I had once found to be terribly annoying are now gone. Those aspects of my life at home were like a warm blanket that has been removed, and I now feel the freezing chill of loneliness.

Someone come and watch television with me; talk over coffee; cook with me; I don't care if you are in another room, I just want to know that you are there and that we can face life together. I try to distract myself and think of all the things that I need to get to finalize the apartment: a shower curtain, trashcan, matches, groceries, towels, and the list goes on.

The deeper the loneliness sets in the farther I fall from the comforts of my previous life. This is an alien emotion. It feels like strength with sadness: it tells me to not give up, it tells me that this is reality, that only I can face these dark and scary places. If I am to get out of the freezing cold of loneliness, I will have to find the ways in which to keep warm. No one can do this for me.

I now understand that my actions and my decisions, even the things that I dream and pursue will come with consequences for which I must endure. A deep feeling of regret and fear starts to take over and I know that this is not the person my family wants me to be, nor the person I thought I was. I wanted to be on my own, so now it is my responsibility to make it on my own.

I can only afford five dollars of gas for my car and the dollar menu at the local fast-food restaurant until payday on Friday. If the power goes out, I will need to find a way to light my room. I must find a way to enjoy the freedom of being with myself. To survive means I must learn to budget money, manage emotions, and find places to build a career and people to start my own family. This path alone will teach me to keep immediate desires in check; when to say no, yes, and the insight for determining what I should or should not do versus what I must or must not do, in order to make it.

The silence is still here. The reality is not so terrifying, but remains immense and ever-present. I stand up to make lunch, sit down, and eat alone. The fear subsides. As I fill myself with nourishing food, I realize that my soul was never empty and to be with myself is not scary, but a source of nourishment, energy, and empowerment. I am ready to create my life.

Tala: Compassion for Thyself

A frustrated Tala desperately tries to focus on her environmental science textbook. Her husband Duncan is making a commotion by cooking, while also talking on the phone and watching television at the same time. Even Twinkie the cat is busy running around with her fish toy. Tala feels pressure in her chest, a sense of tightness and heat which means that she is boiling inside. The last thing she would ever want to do is to take her frustrations out on her loved ones, nor would Tala want to bring any harm to the relationships that she holds sacred. She closes her textbook. With determination, Tala puts on her shoes and coat, and walks outside.

A walk will help me, she accepts, *a very long walk*. Thankfully there are pleasant walking paths near the apartment that take her through forested areas. Tala ponders, *I have been in social isolation for two full months, and now that I walk alone I recognize that I feel lonely*. The heat in her chest becomes more intense as she focuses on the loneliness. As she creates distance from the distractions of home, Tala finds herself with the opportunity to recognize that there is a sense of suffering within.

Duncan, Tala, and Twinkie had moved from the deserts of Arizona to live in the greenspaces of the Mohawk Valley in Central New York. The adventure has been exciting, but as Tala journeys alone along a tree-lined path, she realizes that she misses her family. She remembers her great-grandmother and how she is now isolated in an assisted living home. *How lonely she must feel without me there*, Tala reflects. Then, she thinks of her mother and how she always felt strongest and most resilient when they were together. Without them, in this moment of solitude, she feels weak and lost. This is a confusing feeling to Tala because she is married to the love of her life who is always there for her. *How could I feel lonely, with so much love in my life?*

Tala continues walking, even though the clouds grow darker and appear to bring rain soon. The dimming grey of the overcast mutes the vibrancy of green from the grass and trees. Deep within Tala there is a sense of self that speaks to her without words. She does not know what it is explicitly saying, but she feels the urge to be there for herself. *This is where I must find strength. This is where I can find beauty*, she determines. Tala is strong and steadfast for others, but she wonders if she could be such a person for the deepest and loneliest parts of herself. *Compassion for myself*, she repeats twice. As she stops walking, Tala closes her eyes and places a hand over her chest. She feels her own heartbeat and speaks to her inner self: *You can get through this. I can feel the pain, and can learn from it, be better because of it. It is okay. You do not suffer alone. This is okay. I am here for you, as you have always been for me. We are the same and we have always been us. Sometimes we wanted life to be one way and it didn't work out as expected. I love you and will always be there. It is times like these that I recognize you more, and I don't feel so alone when I know you are there.*

Slowly, Tala regains her strength and opens her eyes. She has found an intimate connection with herself in solitude. She saunters meditatively, noticing the trees and clouds as if to experience them anew with her inner self. The colors of the lush woods around her are a deeper green against the darkness of the clouds. As she turns to walk home, she feels a few raindrops. Tala looks down at the paved walkway and sees little wet dots forming faster and faster from the rain. Raising the sleeve of her coat, she exposes her bare skin to the sky. The cool rain touches her. She notices what a privilege it is to feel things. Tala grew up in an environment without much rain, so this experience always had excited her. She walks slowly in the rain. Each drop feels comforting and compassionate in a way that Tala cannot explain, but mindfully appreciates.

References

Atchison, C. G., Butler, J., & Damiano, P. (2020). Adverse childhood experiences: A model for effective 21st-century clinical–community partnerships. *American Journal of Public Health*, 110(4), 450–451. https://doi.org/10.2105/AJPH.2019.305556.

Barreto, M., Victor, C., Hammond, C., Eccles, A., Richins, M. T., & Qualter, P. (2020). Loneliness around the world: Age, gender, and cultural differences in loneliness. *Personality and Individual Differences*, 1–6. https://doi.org/10.1016/j.paid.2020.110066.

Bland, A. M. (2020). Existential givens in the Covid-19 crisis. *Journal of Humanistic Psychology*, 60(5), 710–724. https://doi.org/10.1177/0022167820940186.

Franssen, T., Stijen, M., Hamers, F., & Schneider, F. (2020). Age differences in demographic, social and health-related factors associated with loneliness across the adult life span (19–65 years): A cross-sectional study in the Netherlands. *BMC Public Health*, 20 (1118), 1–12. https://doi.org/10.1186/s12889-020-09208-0.

Grier, R. T., & Ajayi, A. A. (2019). Incorporating humanistic values and techniques in a culturally responsive therapeutic intervention for African American college students. *Journal of Humanistic Counseling*, 58(1), 17–33. https://doi.org/10.1002/johc.12087.

Halland, E., Vibe, M. D., Solhaug, I., Friborg, O., Rosenvinge, J. H., Tyssen, R., ... Bjørndal, A. (2015). Mindfulness training improves problem-focused coping in psychology and medical students: Results from a randomized controlled trial. *College Student Journal*, 49(3), 387–398.

Johnson, Z., & Vallejos, L. (2019). Multicultural competencies in humanistic psychology. In L. Hoffman, H. Cleare-Hoffman, N. Granger Jr., & D. St. John (Eds.), *Humanistic approaches to multiculturalism and diversity: Perspectives on existence and difference* (pp. 63–75). Routledge.

Kalia, V., & Knauft, K. (2020). Emotion regulation strategies modulate the effect of adverse childhood experiences on perceived chronic stress with implications for cognitive flexibility. *PLoS ONE*, 15(6), 1–18. https://doi.org/10.1371/journal.pone.0235412.

Larrivee, D., & Echarte, L. (2018). Contemplative meditation and neuroscience: Prospects for mental health. *Journal of Religion & Health*, 57(3), 960–978. https://doi.org/10.1007/s10943-017-0475-0.

Mead, V. P. (2020). Adverse Babyhood Experiences (ABEs) Increase risk for infant and maternal morbidity and mortality, and chronic illness. *Journal of Prenatal & Perinatal Psychology & Health*, 34(4), 285–317.

Miller, C. (2017). Teachers, leaders, and social justice: A critical reflection on a complicated exchange. *Multicultural Perspectives*, 19(2), 109–113. https://doi.org/10.1080/15210960.2017.1301100.

Morley, C. (2008). Teaching critical practice: Resisting structural domination through critical reflection. *Social Work Education*, 27(4), 407–421. https://doi.org/10.1080/02615470701379925.

Moustakas, C. E. (1961). *Loneliness*. Prentice Hall.

Moustakas, C. E. (1995). *Being-In, being-for, being-with*. Jason Aronson.

Presti, D. E. (2016). *Foundational concepts in neuroscience: A brain-mind odyssey*. W. W. Norton & Company.

Rosen, D., McCall, J., & Goodkind, S. (2017). Teaching critical self-reflection through the lens of cultural humility: An assignment in a social work diversity course. *Social Work Education*, 36(3), 289–298. https://doi.org/10.1080/02615479.2017.1287260.

Sapolsky, R. (2017). *Behave: The biology of humans at our best and worst*. Penguin Press.

Soheilian, S. S., Inman, A. G., Klinger, R. S., Isenberg, D. S., & Kulp, L. E. (2014). Multicultural supervision: supervisees' reflections on culturally competent supervision. *Counselling Psychology Quarterly*, 27(4), 379–392. https://doi.org/10.1080/09515070.2014.961408.

Sun, S., Goldberg, S. B., Lin, D., Qiao, S., & Operario, D. (2021). Psychiatric symptoms, risk, and protective factors among university students in quarantine during the COVID-19 pandemic in China. *Globalization & Health*, 17(1), 1–14. https://doi.org/10.1186/s12992-021-00663-x.

Tsehay, M., Necho, M., & Mekonnen, W. (2020). The role of adverse childhood experience on depression symptom, prevalence, and severity among school going adolescents. *Depression Research & Treatment*, 1–9. https://doi.org/10.1155/2020/5951792.

Zhang, N., Fan, F., Huang, S., & Rodriguez, M. A. (2018). Mindfulness training for loneliness among Chinese college students: A pilot randomized controlled trial. *International Journal of Psychology*, 53(5), 373–378. https://doi.org/10.1002/ijop.12394.

9

VOLUNTEER GROUP ACTIVITY

Young adults that are involved in causes outside of themselves are realizing culturally relative self-actualization potentials. One of the most convenient and effective ways to contribute to a cause that seeks to better the lives of others, the environment, or community is by volunteering. There are many community outreach initiatives across the United States seeking to engage young adults through volunteer opportunities. In some cases, educational institutions (e.g., secondary schools, colleges, universities) along with clinical partnerships (e.g., policy makers, politicians, healthcare institutions) work to achieve an integrated action plan to help young adults develop the skills to better their community and environment (Atchison et al., 2020). Unfortunately, COVID-19 impacted volunteer efforts for most organizations. For over a year, social restrictions limited the spaces and opportunities for young adults to contribute to their community. Although, there were numerous efforts to employ volunteer services through online formats, the overall efforts and effects that were previously known were decreased or at least redefined.

Communities around the world made sacrifices and modifications to their lives, so that they could follow official public health guidelines. Staying home, wearing masks in public, getting tested for infection, and social distancing represented community-oriented efforts to reduce the threat/spread of infection for people across the world (Fegert et al., 2020). The pandemic was not a time of self-centeredness or apathy, despite what a minority of disillusioned sources may promote. The small population of individuals that defied or denied public health guidelines cannot be the basis for generalizations or truths that reflect the human condition. Rather, it was a period of human history that exhibited a global community filled with compassion and empathy. Extraordinary efforts were seen as some ventured out into dangerous conditions to deliver groceries, medical supplies, and educational materials to people

DOI: 10.4324/9781003251651-12

in need. The pandemic limited social interactions, but it did not remove the greater sense of altruism.

Altruism is an innate feature of mammals where one acts with an intention to benefit other beings or environments at cost of the helper (de Waal, 2009; Nye, 2014, 2017). The costs are typically in the form of energy, opportunity, economics, and time. Altruistic behavior rewards people with an intrinsic warm feeling, as it "activates one of the most ancient and essential mammalian brain circuits, helping us care for those close to us while building the cooperative societies on which our survival depends" (de Waal, 2019, p. 105). In addition to neurobiological or genetic observations, altruism remains a unique mammalian phenomenon. Young adults can appreciate the altruistic nature of the human community and recognize it within themselves. Western pop-cultural media that promote human nature as entirely selfish, misanthropic, narcissistic, and apathetic are grossly exaggerating minor features of humanity. These traits can also be seen alongside violence, ignorance, and greed. Although they are ubiquitous qualities observed in humans, they are not the entire story of the human condition. When young adults can critically deconstruct generalizations/exaggerations, they begin to see a world and self that is naturally community oriented, empathic, and altruistic.

When young adults come to value their altruistic nature, they can actualize their potentials by developing a lifelong habit of helping. This not only develops character and a better community or environment, but also supports long-term well-being of the brain. Corrêa et al. (2019) sought to understand how the effects of altruism and volunteerism were associated with increased cognitive performance in 312 healthy adults (mean age of 69.6 years old). Evaluation criteria included demographic data, socioeconomics, self-assessed altruism ratings, days volunteered, cognitive state, as well as elements such as emotional disturbance, religiosity, and social support, all of which are associated to cognitive functioning. The researchers found that altruism was a significant factor in enhancing cognitive performance (e.g., memory, critical thinking, thought regulation) in advanced age, where more altruistic behaviors equated to higher performance. If young adults begin to make their altruistic behaviors a lifelong habit, they can experience the benefits of higher cognitive performance later in life, especially for working memory and critical thinking.

Altruism can be expressed in many forms, especially as volunteer efforts. Volunteers are those that offer their services, talents, or creations without expectation of compensation, but may include tokens of appreciation or small reimbursements. Volunteerism has been reported to increase self-esteem, decease stress from work/school, establish new social contacts, and offer career relevant skills needed for mastery (Wicker & Downward, 2020). Young adults may volunteer through formal organizations or clubs, or informally where groups are spontaneous, seasonal, or noncommittal.

The majority of volunteers have been found to come from rural areas, educated middle socioeconomic levels, and those in young adulthood. Research suggests that volunteerism promotes well-being, especially between the ages of 16 and 24. Lawton et al. (2021) studied the subjective well-being (i.e., self-reported levels of happiness, purpose in life, emotional disturbance, affect, and life satisfaction) and its relation to volunteerism. By controlling for sociodemographic factors, the researchers investigated if volunteering was a causal factor to increase subjective well-being. Previous research in this area posed methodological issues with the causality of well-being being augmented by volunteerism. Many studies have shown that one's sense of life satisfaction increases the more one volunteers. However, those that volunteer may already have a high level of well-being or life satisfaction in which they experience the positive effects. This becomes an upward cycle of virtue and well-being. Due to the fact that studies have failed to explicitly identify the main causal factor in how volunteerism increases well-being, the a priori overestimations have reduced reliability. Conversely, Lawton et al. (2021), found that

> higher frequencies of volunteering are associated with higher wellbeing than lower frequencies. Volunteering at least once a week is approximately twice as beneficial as volunteering several times a year, whereas volunteering once a year or less does not correlate with a significant change in life satisfaction.
>
> *(p. 616)*

The costs of volunteering include time, energy, and even expenses for travel, which can factor into generating negative feelings and stress—this is even more so if young adults have financial challenges. The effects of volunteering must factor in both the positive and negative correlates to well-being. People with challenging life situations must weigh the benefits and costs of volunteering.

In the United Kingdom, almost one-quarter of the adult population reported having engaged in volunteer activity—these efforts contributed as much as 1.3 million full-time employees, generating a £12.2 billion economic impact for the year (Lawton et al., 2021). Volunteering increases the well-being of the community through its economic impact, which translates into a higher quality of life for communities.

Wicker and Downward (2020) conducted an analysis of data taken from 52,957 people from 28 European countries in how subjective well-being was influenced by sports-oriented volunteerism. Concurrent with previous studies' findings, there was a positive correlation between increased subjective well-being and volunteerism. However, the researchers found that the role in the organization or function mattered for how it affected well-being. Administrative roles coupled with sports-related roles generated no positive effects when coupled. The results of the study suggested that in sports-related volunteerism, generalizations cannot be made for the volunteerism and increased well-being phenomenon, because how roles are coupled is an important influence. Wicker and Downward (2020) explained that "happier people are more likely to volunteer in sport-

176   Part II

related and administrative roles, but that performing these roles does not have a causal and positive impact on their personal well-being" (p. 312). The association between increased well-being and volunteerism needs further exploration, so that it does not rest on theoretical deductions, but rather clearly defined empirical data (i.e., qualitative and quantitative) (Lawton et al., 2021).

Expressing Altruism through Volunteer Programs

For most young adults, volunteering must be planned around their school, family, and work schedules. To accommodate these demands, after-school programs have become a fundamental part of many societies, worldwide. After-school programs can take the form of community outreach initiatives, educational, recreational, religious, emotional, or sports-based organizations, to name a few. Programs can focus on specific goals such as for skill development, or may be nondirective where there is time for play and relationship building. Young adults have a keen interest in volunteer programs that align with their core values, as well as personal and professional interests. Prior to the pandemic, there were over 10 million youth participating in an after-school program. Many young adults either facilitated and/or participated in some way. As facilitators, young adults empathize with the children's life situations. Schooling and home life may cause excessive amounts of stress with the demands of standardized testing, less time for sports, play, spirituality, and fun, while emotional and physical violence at home are a reality for many children (de Heer et al., 2011). Young adults seek to bring a higher quality of life to childhood by offering their time and skills to after-school programs. These are safe spaces with optimistic environments for young adults to engage children in influential ways by building growth-promoting relationships (Farrell et al., 2013).

There are also after-school programs directed toward helping teenagers cope with life challenges or offer spaces for personal expression. For instance, middle school can be a time of unique social and emotional challenges. Not only are there greater academic demands, but also new complex social situations. Countless young adults in inner cities have nothing to do after a day at middle school, nor have anyone waiting for them at home. This opens up opportunities to engage in risky behaviors that include experimenting with substances like drugs or alcohol, joining gangs or engaging in violence, developing problematic internet use, dropping out of school, developing emotional disturbances, or having early pregnancies. Instead of experimenting in potentially dangerous behaviors and forming negative habits, after-school programs provide relevant spaces for young adults to explore.

One after-school program called After-School All-Stars has enrolled over 90,000 middle-school-aged young adults in 15 major cities. The program offers sports and recreational activities to build self-esteem, friendships, communication strategies, dignity and self-worth, and, most of all, confidence. Research into

After-School All-Stars has found a strong correlation between the program's operation and a decrease in crime rates for the community. In addition, the program has also shown to increase academic performance for its young adult members.

After-School All-Stars was founded by seven-time Mr. Olympia champion Arnold Schwarzenegger, who knew firsthand that the benefits of sports and team building promotes all areas of development in young adulthood. Sports recreation provides fun/engaging physical activity and educational experiences that teach important life skills, while developing character. Discipline, resilience, relationships, physical activity, and goal setting are just a few of the elements that Schwarzenegger knew were essential to lifelong well-being. After-School All-Stars is both a preventative measure for destructive habits and a growth-promoting force for those with current challenges.

Schwarzenegger immigrated to the U.S. as a young adult from Austria and learned along his journeys that youth with big aspirations like him would need opportunities to develop the characteristics of a champion. Young adults also need spaces to form diverse and supportive friendships. Sports helped Schwarzenegger learn the fundamentals to success—trial, failure, discipline, resilience, strength, and grit. He wished to instill these qualities in youth, so that they could learn to say "I'll be back" after a defeat, and to come back stronger and more resilient. Schwarzenegger also created the weightlifting sector of the Special Olympics, where young adults with intellectual and physical disabilities could actualize the self-empowerment that came with sports. These athletes develop confidence, self-esteem, and skill. Regardless of demographic or life challenges that young adults face, after-school sports recreation has shown to be an engaging avenue for young adults to increase well-being and advance personal development.

After-school programs can range from large to smaller scale, all with different objectives for supporting development and well-being. Many institutions of higher education seek to create partnerships with the community through after-school programs to provide an experience beyond academics. These extra-curricular programs can support socio-emotional development, life exploration, and personal expression (Noam, 2003). These are important initiatives to empower the community youth. These develop relationships with young adults and will encourage them to one day enroll as students (Atchison et al., 2020).

Established in 1946 in the historic and diverse city of Utica, New York is Mohawk Valley Community College (MVCC). The institution was New York State's first-ever community college. MVCC provides Central New York with high-quality higher education and workforce training, as well as community outreach efforts. The college adapts with the needs of the diversifying demographics of the area, so that it can prepare students to meet the demands of an increasingly complex world. One notable MVCC after-school program began in 1983 from the ideas and efforts of James D. Smrtic, professor of psychology. Professor Smrtic had a lifetime of experiences in after-school programs as well as graduate training/education in facilitating humanistic psychological group programs.

Professor Smrtic created Kidz n' Coaches as an after-school program where volunteer college students could plan and facilitate prosocial group activities for emerging children. The group activities were meant to be fun, recreational, and build growth-promoting relationships. A detailed history of Kidz n' Coaches and Mr. Smrtic are found in *Empowering Children: A Multicultural Humanistic Approach* (Kazanjian, 2021). The case study explored how the biography and intellectualism of Professor Smrtic informed the multicultural humanistic psychological methodology of Kidz n' Coaches. *Empowering Children: A Multicultural Humanistic Approach* offered a phenomenological exploration of the growth-promoting relationships that formed within the program. Universal elements of "seeing," "communication," "relationship/encounter," "sincere play," and "freedom to be" were explored. Kidz n' Coaches continues to provide a unique experience for young adults to encounter others in a multicultural humanistic group function by their own design.

Mr. Smrtic was the program director of Kidz n' Coaches, an administrative role that offers guidance and resources to the coaches when needed. The coaches are student volunteers that seek to bring joy and well-being to the lives of children by creating growth-promoting group functions. Coaches are mostly young adults enrolled at MVCC between 18 and 24 years of age that manage family and work responsibilities with college classes. Those that express interest in the program typically major in the fields of psychology, criminal justice, or education. The coaches collaboratively plan innovative recreational games, activities, crafts, local trips, or noncompetitive sports to take place from 4:00pm to 6:00pm on a chosen Wednesday, once per month. The group consists of up 20 children, ages 7 to 12, and up to 15 coaches.

Kidz n' Coaches is a unique multicultural humanistic psychological program in that it supports young adult coaches to develop a positive perception of children in need. The children are known as *emerging children* instead of disadvantaged, at-risk, underserved, or other terms that bring stigmas or entail deficit. *Emerging* is an optimistic term that acknowledges the child as a person, who within unique conditions is seeking growth-promoting activities, environments, and relationships that allows the person to actualize inner potentials (Moustakas & Perry, 1973; Rogers, 1969). Coaches develop interpersonal skills, knowledge on how to work with children, and socio-emotional intelligences by collaborating and facilitating the group activities. They also learn from culturally diverse children in ways that inform the program's methodology. The Rogerian elements of empathy, positive regard, and congruence are at the core of the Kidz n' Coaches experience. The experiential education that young adult coaches receive prepares them for a changing and hyper-connecting world.

Utica is one of the most unique cities in the U.S. because it has one of the highest densities of refugee populations due to the highly active Resource Center for Refugees in the Mohawk Valley (better known as The Center). The Center has worked to settle over 16,500 refugee/immigrant people from around the world (Resource Center for Refugees in the Mohawk Valley, 2021). It continues to work collaboratively with the Utica Municipal Housing Authority to provide housing for incoming people and families. Kidz n' Coaches recruits most of its emerging children from the neighboring Culver Avenue Apartment Complex, which works with the Municipal Housing Authority (that has working relations with The Center). This is why for over 40 years the profile of the emerging child has reflected global conditions.

Many of the coaches are just as culturally diverse as the children. They have come from around the world to settle in Utica and enroll in college at MVCC. Although diversity is a major aspect of Kidz n' Coaches, it is never an explicit focus or goal. This is because the whole of the group function is greater than the sum of its parts. Focusing on one aspect may remove the importance of others. Diversity is always present, valued, and affirmed as an essential component to the methodology. Kidz n' Coaches supports the culturally relative self-actualization processes of coaches and emerging children by engaging them in the here-in-now through group activities that align with the specific group's personal values, identities, curiosities, and abilities. Each event generates vitality through the phenomenal forces of growth-promoting relationships.

Empowering Children: A Multicultural Humanistic Approach (Kazanjian, 2021) also explored how the Kidz n' Coaches methodology was brought to El Paso, Texas to serve emerging children and volunteers coaches recruited from El Paso Community College (EPCC). Kidz n' Coaches-El Paso experienced similar successes as the original program in New York and is a testament to the brilliance of Professor Smrtic for creating an intergenerational multicultural humanistic psychological program. The programs in Utica and El Paso are constantly learning, adapting, and growing with the participation of each coach and emerging child. The program directors are able to establish boundaries, resources, and spaces that promote the growth of the group.

Since his retirement in 2014, Mr. Smrtic became Professor Emeritus and in 2021 was inducted into the MVCC Hall of Fame for embracing the community, empowering students, and creating a significant and lasting contribution to the college. However, in the semester before his retirement, Mr. Smrtic entrusted the program to his MVCC colleagues Richard Kelly and Dina Radeljas, who expressed sincere interest in keeping the program to its original intent and methodology. They wanted to guide the program through the complexities and challenges of the future. Currently, Mr. Kelly and Dr. Radeljas are program directors that exhibit a strong multicultural humanistic psychological spirit that continues to achieve Mr. Smrtic's vision. In a conversation with Dr. Radeljas, she offered me a quote by Mike Satterfield, which stated, "Even if you just change one life, you've changed the world forever." I asked her what this quote meant to her. She responded:

The reason why the Satterfield quote resonates deeply within me is because I was welcomed by Kidz n' Coaches when my family arrived to U.S. in 1995. We relied and cherished all the "little things" a kind stranger would offer...I am thankful and cherish the opportunity to be with Kidz n' Coaches and see the smiles on the kids' faces when our coaches show up to take them to a local arcade or bowling alley. To me, Kidz n' coaches brings joy to this world and puts a smile on the face of every child and young adult.

(D. Radeljas, personal communication, June 10, 2021)

Professors Kelly and Radeljas have taken Kidz n' Coaches to extraordinary levels, empowering young adults with opportunities in which they can actualize inner and group potentials. They have led Kidz n' Coaches through the COVID-19 pandemic, showing the coaches that the children need them most in such times of suffering and uncertainty.

Kidz n' Coaches was no different than every after-school program in the U.S., which had to suspend face-to-face group gatherings due to quarantines and social distancing guidelines. The group complied with every U.S. Center for Disease Control and administrative college guideline to suspended group activities. However, the coaches knew that the children would experience difficult socio-emotional challenges in quarantine, as their routines and peer interactions were removed. The coaches also knew that the emerging children had been looking forward to the club's events for the Fall 2020 semester. In such time of uncertainty, fear, and restrictions, "the club had to innovate—instead of bringing the kids to the pumpkin patch, the club brought the pumpkins to the kids in October. They delivered pies to local families for Thanksgiving" (Mohawk Valley Community College, 2021, para. 3). Furthermore, when the coaches were faced with a cancelled holiday party, Mr. Kelly and Dr. Radeljas collaborated with the coaches to "plan a socially distanced shopping trip. The gifts were then wrapped and delivered, ensuring that 60 kids will get a gift for the holiday" (Mohawk Valley Community College, 2021, para. 5). The program directors and coaches showed altruism in its most organic sense through their volunteerism during the pandemic.

In the Spring 2021 semester, MVCC commended Kidz n' Coaches with a $1,000 Diversity, Equity, and Inclusion Award for their excellence in providing culturally diverse young adults and children equitable opportunities to achieve culturally relative self-actualization. Mr. Kelly, Dr. Radeljas, and the coaches decided to use the award money to buy garden tools and materials (i.e., planting soil, rakes, seeds) for the Culver Apartments where the children live. There is a communal garden at the apartment complex, where residents can plant, tend, and harvest plants, fruits, and vegetables; some of which support their cultural diets and homeland foods. When I asked Dr. Radeljas about the decision to use the award to cultivate the garden, she told me that the pandemic limited their interactions with the children, in which many felt lonely. The seeds they gave the children to plant and help grow would become constant reminders that Kidz n' coaches cares about them. The children will not feel lonely when they tend the garden; because they will become like coaches to the seeds—always providing support and opportunities to grow.

The act of cultivating a garden is one of the finest Buddhist and humanistic psychological metaphors for achieving self-actualization and developing growth-promoting relationships. Carl Rogers (1980) developed this ecological philosophy in his person-centered approach to psychology. For example, Rogers grew up on a farm and once observed some peculiar potatoes:

> I remember that in my boyhood, the bin in which we stored our winter's supply of potatoes was in the basement, several feet below a small window. The conditions were unfavorable, but the potatoes would begin to sprout— pale white sprouts, so unlike the healthy green shoots they sent up when planted in the soil in the spring. But these sad, spindly sprouts would grow 2 or 3 feet in length as they reached toward the distant light of the window. The sprouts were, in their bizarre, futile growth, a sort of desperate expression of the directional tendency I have been describing. They would never become plants, never mature, never fulfill their real potential. But under the most adverse circumstances, they were striving to become. Life would not give up, even if it could not flourish.
>
> *(p. 118)*

Kidz n' Coaches offers children rich soils and resources in which to bloom to full potential.

Community colleges are unique institutions, where young adults can receive high-quality education and skill training while also satisfying family and work responsibilities (Gavin, 2019). Institutions such as MVCC and EPCC provide opportunities for young adults to succeed in their career pathways by utilizing partnerships with the community in after-school programs. In programs such as Kidz n' Coaches, students can realize full potentials by developing growth-promoting relationships with children in the community. EPCC and MVCC community outreach programs experience extraordinary successes because they utilize their students as vital resources. The college programs reflect student interests, career goals, and personal needs. When institutional goals reflect the diversities and realities of the community, young adults are drawn to these spaces in order to learn, explore, and become.

Institutions of higher education offer young adults opportunities to express their altruism through volunteer programs. All programs have learning curves, challenges, and even failures. However, Kidz n' Coaches is unique in that it *learns with* the community. Each person contributes to the culture and methodology of the program. This has kept it evolving and emerging for over 40 years in Utica, and for over five in El Paso. The multicultural humanistic psychological methods

182   Part II

that helped build the program have kept it relevant to students' needs and goals. Kidz n' Coaches reflects a global reality where growth-promoting relationships offer more than just an academic, diversity, or skill-based experience. The program is a multicultural humanistic education that provides opportunities to explore existential meanings in the here-and-now. Even amidst a pandemic, amongst the fear and isolation, young adult coaches found ways to reach out to emerging children so that they could find ways to create meanings, together.

Monserrat: Open Eyes, Open Heart

There are signs of spring in early March, as Monserrat sits in her apartment starring out her window at the buds on the tree. She is reflecting on the meaningful relationship she had with her grandfather, Avô. He was a powerful influence in her life because he helped raise her like his own daughter. Avô gave Monserrat advice, care, and guidance when her parents were busy trying to survive in a new country and provide for the family. Whatever Avô told her was the way; the whole family had the greatest respect for him.

Although her grandfather's passing was a few years back, Monserrat feels that she will never fully emotionally recover. She wondered what Avô did in his free time before he came to live with them in the last few years of his life. As she reflects, Monserrat feels a deep motivation to reach out to people of advanced age in the community and help increase the quality of their lives. With such care that Avô had given her, she wants to give that back to others.

Monserrat searches the Internet for the contact information of a nursing home nearby. She calls the main office number and asks about volunteer opportunities. Thankfully the home has vaccinated all of their residents and Monserrat is happy to provide documentation for hers. Over the next few days, she follows through with the protocols for volunteering. The home tells her she will start the following weekend.

Throughout the week, in much anticipation, Monserrat has visions of groups of people in advanced age playing games, having lively discussions, enjoying meals together, and taking walks. When the day for volunteering finally arrives, she finds herself excitedly entering the building. However, it is as if a blindfold had been suddenly removed. There are no happy images that she had previously imagined. Instead she finds that most of the people are sitting or lying down in their rooms all alone. Her heart feels heavy. Monserrat volunteers the full weekend and the ones to follow, each time coming to learn the stories of the residents.

After a month of volunteering, she once again sits in her kitchen and views the flowers on a once budded tree. Monserrat pulls out her journal from the backpack seated beside her. She needs to reflect on what she had experienced in order to understand or maybe just find a greater meaning,

At the home, I was able to make the acquaintance of a sweet and lovely woman named Agnes. She had the whitest hair that I have ever seen. I used to notice things about her that

revealed her age, such as wrinkles on her face and hands, deteriorating eyesight, or even how she walked. But over our time together, I learned to look into her eyes—to greet a person not so different than me. Many people would tell me, including her, how beautiful she once was. I found myself able to see beyond the aging body. She has and continues to be beautiful. Age just happens in the subtlest and hastily of ways, and I know that I too will one day look at my own wrinkled hands upon a worn face. Time and age are nothing compared to the power and beauty of a soul.

Every day Agnes would tell me that her son was coming to visit her after work. The light in her eyes brightened and glistened as she spoke of her son. At the end of every shift, I thought of how happy Agnes would be when her son stops by after work and spends time with her. However, one day I asked a fellow volunteer that worked evenings, what her son was like and how the visits were. He told me that her son had never came to visit her; not even once. I tried not to judge him, because I knew there were reasons beyond my current understanding. Maybe he got out of work late, maybe he had difficult home or work situations, but I'll never forget the sadness I felt for her as I thought of how heartbroken she must have felt every evening while she waited for him. I made it a special point during my shift to sit with her and just be there with her. Even if she talked excitedly about her son, I shared her excitement. We found things to do that brought us together. During our games, walks, or stories, she focused on the moment, and we didn't talk much about her son.

Thankfully, many of the other residents were visited by their family members. Visitors were the hope and lifeblood of the residents. Fridays were always happy days as they told me who was coming to visit them and what they were going to do. Mondays were a little more gloom as the residents knew that they had a lonely week ahead, with the desperate hope that their loved ones would return and not forget them.

In this volunteer experience, Monserrat realized the power of relationships, and how volunteering just a little of her time could make a world of difference for another person. She thinks of Avô each day and how elderly people like him helped raise others, only to ask for their company in the end. The times she spent with Avô watching telenovelas, drinking coffee and eating sweet bread, making food for the holidays, and even the simple act of cleaning the beans before she put them to cook, are sacred to her. Monserrat realizes he must have felt the same.

Monserrat decides to continue volunteering over the summer. She has learned that the here-and-now is powerful in developing a relationship. That was how she lived with Avô. Throughout the month of April, Monserrat learns to develop her patience and presence, as she cultivates her relationships with the residents through craft building, taking walks, watching television, and even just sitting outside and enjoying the sun and birdsongs. No matter how much love she gives, she knows that even more is received. She always feels warm around the residents. *No matter how old or young,* she thinks, *we can create loving memories together.* She thinks of Avô every day, and with each act of helping others finds him.

184 Part II

Tala: Helping Others, Faith Restored

"Didn't your pre-workout kick in yet?" Duncan questions, as he speeds ahead of Tala on the running/walking trail.

"You mean *my coffee?*" she replies. Tala is something of a naturalist when it comes to diet.

"Yes, yes! Coffee! You love your coffee!" Duncan replies jokingly as he tires from the run.

The couple is out for an afternoon run together because the spring weather in Central New York has decided to be accommodating today. The air is fresh and cool. Mostly cloudy skies let the sun peak through every once in a while. The trees will soon bud.

Tala and Duncan always run for about five miles on Saturdays, weather permitting. They like to have small conversation about what they see: nature, animals, historic buildings, passersby. On today's run, Tala notices a small pizza box that had been tossed at the side of the trail.

"What on earth is that!" she exclaims as the couple slows to a walk.

"Why, that looks like an average pizza box."

"How terrible, people throw their trash out anywhere, with such disregard for the environment," she admonishes.

"It really is. I mean, who even does that on a trail? Are they eating a whole tomato pie while on a bike or run, and then just throw the box in the grass?"

"Well, it's not right. This is someone's home, and you don't trash others' homes."

"Is this one of those save the world moments?" asks Duncan.

"Heck yeah, it is!" Tala exclaims.

Tala runs over to the pizza box and picks it up.

"I'm going to pick up all the trash we see and carry it to the next garbage can. See if you can keep up!"

Tala does just that and Duncan joins in. They make the cleaning activity into a type of game; anytime the couple sees a piece of trash, they run to pick it up and carry it to one of the trail's waste bins. Duncan finds a disposable face mask and with his Swiss Army keychain's little scissors he cuts off the ear loops. He recently saw some unsettling pictures of wild animals caught in the ear loops of disposed masks. The couple does not focus on how disrespectful people can be to the environment; rather, they choose to focus on how beautiful the trail looks with their help. There was no doubt that Tala has a unique relationship with nature, and Duncan feels warm as he develops his own connection. When the couple returns home, they both reflect on the experience.

"I think we ran ten miles, babe. I am tired!" Duncan says with a loud sigh.

"I know! But it didn't feel like it when we were running and cleaning up. We were so lost in the little game that we made, of who could run to the trash first and throw away the most pieces," Tala responds.

"I liked our little game. I was thinking we could do it again, or maybe find a place to volunteer where we can clean up the environment. I feel so spiritually invigorated after our run."

After they wash up, the couple decides to explore the Internet to see what local volunteer opportunities are available. One option peaks their interest. It is with the Central New York Conservancy, who offers volunteer opportunities to clean up and tend (i.e., planting trees and flowers, raking, picking weeds, and other environmental grooming activities) to the parks and green areas.

"This looks fantastic," Tala proclaims. "We could even ask to volunteer at Proctor Park, which is not too far away."

"Let's call them up tomorrow and see what they say," Duncan suggests.

The couple has success in setting up a time when they can help clean and tend to Proctor Park and Memorial Parkway in Utica. They enjoy every aspect of tending to nature and the fact that it was a volunteer activity. They feel good to be volunteers; that they are there by choice, and that their labors are driven by love and not necessity. Tala and Duncan are able to make new friends as well. Learning the stories of others and the reasons for why they volunteer inspire the couple because these people are also driven by altruism. Tala thinks it wonderful that she and her husband can be part of a group of helpers that improve life for nature. Her faith in humanity restores itself. There is such a pure sense of community amongst the volunteers that Tala and Duncan both agree that volunteering does not just help the environment flourish, but also blossoms core elements of who they are, in a spiritual sense.

After the day's work, Tala and Duncan want to volunteer their efforts in other ways and for different communities. The couple reaches out to elderly people in need that are deeply affected by the pandemic. Tala bakes her famous cranberry nut bread and delivers it to those who live alone. Meanwhile, Duncan calls elderly neighbors to offer his technical savvy to help them register for a COVID-19 vaccination. Tala and Duncan realize that volunteering is not a hobby or just something they do to build their résumé; but, rather, it is an expression of who they are as individuals and as a couple.

References

Atchison, C. G., Butler, J., & Damiano, P. (2020). Adverse childhood experiences: A model for effective 21st-century clinical–community partnerships. *American Journal of Public Health*, 110(4), 450–451. https://doi.org/10.2105/AJPH.2019.305556.

Corrêa, J. C., Ávila, M. P. W., Lucchetti, A. L. G., & Lucchetti, G. (2019). Altruistic behaviour, but not volunteering, has been associated with cognitive performance in community-dwelling older persons. *Psychogeriatrics*, 19(2), 117–125. https://doi.org/10.1111/psyg.12372.

de Heer, H. D., Koehly, L., Pederson, R., & Morera, O. (2011). Effectiveness and spillover of an after-school health promotion program for Hispanic elementary school children. *American Journal of Public Health*, 101(10), 1907–1913. https://doi.org/10.2105/AJPH.2011.300177.

de Waal, F. (2009). *The age of empathy: Nature's lessons for a kinder society*. Three Rivers Press.

de Waal, F. (2019). *Mama's last hug: Animal emotions and what they tell us about ourselves*. W. W. Norton & Company.

Farrell, A.F., Collier-Meek, M.A., & Pons, S.R. (2013). Embedding positive behavioral interventions and supports in afterschool programs. *Beyond Behavior*, 23(1), 38–45. https://doi.org/10.1177/107429561302300106.

Fegert, J. M., Vitiello, B., Plener, P. L., & Clemens, V. (2020). Challenges and burden of the Coronavirus 2019 (COVID-19) pandemic for child and adolescent mental health: A narrative review to highlight clinical and research needs in the acute phase and the long return to normality. *Child & Adolescent Psychiatry & Mental Health*, 14(1), 1–11. https://doi.org/10.1186/s13034-020-00329-3.

Gavin, V. J. (2019). Moving on creatively: Creative existential therapy for children, adolescents and adults. *Existential Analysis: Journal of the Society for Existential Analysis*, 30(1), 45–58.

Kazanjian, C. J. (2021). *Empowering children: A multicultural humanistic approach*. Routledge.

Lawton, R. N., Gramatki, I., Watt, W., & Fujiwara, D. (2021). Does volunteering make us happier, or are happier people more likely to volunteer? Addressing the problem of reverse causality when estimating the wellbeing impacts of volunteering. *Journal of Happiness Studies*, 22(2), 599–624. https://doi.org/10.1007/s10902-020-00242-8.

Mohawk Valley Community College. (2021, March 9). Kidz n' Coaches delivers joy this holiday season. MVCC.edu. https://www.mvcc.edu/news/2020-12-14-kidz-n-coaches-delivers-joy-this-holiday-season.php.

Moustakas, C. E. & Perry, C. (1973). *Learning to be free*. Prentice Hall.

Noam, G. G. (2003). Learning with excitement: Bridging school and after-school worlds and project-based learning. *New Directions for Youth Development*, 2003(97), 121–138. https://doi.org/10.1002/yd.39.

Nye, B. (2014). *Undeniable: Evolution and the science of creation*. C. S. Powell, Ed. St. Martin's Press.

Nye, B. (2017). *Everything all at once*. C. S. Powell, Ed. Rodale Books.

Rogers, C. R. (1969). *Freedom to learn: A view of what education might become*. C. E. Merrill Pub. Co.

Rogers, C. R. (1980). *A way of being*. Houghton Mifflin.

Wicker, P., & Downward, P. (2020). The causal effect of voluntary roles in sport on subjective well-being in European countries. *Journal of Sport Management*, 34(4), 303–315. https://doi.org/10.1123/jsm.2019-0159

10

THE NATURE OF GROWTH-PROMOTING RELATIONSHIPS

To reiterate Rogers' (1989) operational definition, growth-promoting relationships are those "in which one of the participants intends that there should come about, in one or both parties, more appreciation of, more expression of, more functional use of the latent inner resources of the individual" (p. 40). These participants, as we have discussed, can be found throughout a young adult's life journey—from friends, family members, and teachers, to dogs, birds, nature, streams, clouds, or snow. Positionality is a key factor for making a growth-promoting relationship become inclusive of other forms of life, not just with other humans. Growth-promoting relationships are fundamental for young adults to create meaning amidst existential concerns.

In *Empowering Children: A Humanistic Multicultural Approach* (Kazanjian, 2021), there were five invariant qualities identified in the phenomenon of growth-promoting relationships. These elements were revealed in the growth-promoting relationships developed by the after-school program Kidz n' Coaches. The first invariant quality was a sense of *seeing*, where the phenomenological study's participants developed a mindful awareness of the presence of other people and their surroundings (i.e., the brilliance of colors and flow of movement). The second was *communication* in the growth-promoting relationship, where there was a sincere and honest expression of one's inner world in ways that transcended words. The third invariant quality, *relationship/encounter*, designated a connection between two or more people in the here-and-now of the unique moment that they created.

Sincere play was the fourth invariant element of the relationship. This discovery corroborated the phenomenological research findings from Moustakas (1995), who also found that during play the person was able to let go of the facades, thoughts, feelings, and roles that acted as limitations. Instead, there was a holistic integration and a sincere immersion of the self in a creative journey as it became

DOI: 10.4324/9781003251651-13

188 Part II

new at every moment. Within the moment, "energy, life, spirit, surprise, fusion, awakening, and renewal are possibilities of play, openings and expandings for exploring self-interests and for developing the self" (Moustakas, 1995, p. 152). Children and young adults need opportunities for nondirective play. Free expressions and creations are fundamental sources of their life forces. When immersed in sincere play children and young adults are able to give energy to the healing processes that help them cope and overcome life challenges. It is through play that one develops the resilience and strength to re-enter reality and fare the existential sea.

The fifth invariant quality of the phenomenon of growth-promoting relationships was the *freedom to be*. The freedom of being in a relationship encourages people to open themselves to the existential no-thing-ness, which are spaces of possibility. The opportunities are ever present to listen, express, take another perspective, and to live with openness and presence so that the being may disclose its nature. There is no judgment or criticism. Everything is accepted and valued for its honesty. Relationships encourage others to exist in their own way, unfolding and revealing at each moment (Moustakas, 1995).

In growth-promoting relationships, young adults find ways to establish rituals in order to create unique bonds that reflect a shared private reality. Rituals generate hope, imagination, desire, and purpose. As Moustakas (1995) illustrated:

> Rituals can continue to hold a particular meaning into adulthood and old age, adding zest, enthusiasm, spirit, and life, to meetings with significant others. Some activities in which rituals may be created and sustained throughout life are storytelling, reading poetry, painting together, listening to music, lying quietly side-by-side, taking a walk, dancing creatively, preparing and sharing special foods, setting aside a regular time to be together, writing special messages, and creating unique names for each other.
>
> *(p. 77)*

In the rituals and rhythms of a growth-promoting relationship, both parties disclose their unique phenomenological essences.

Social Support and Relationship Challenges

Growth-promoting relationships are integral for socio-emotional development, as they provide opportunities and spaces for personal and interpersonal exploration. As Ang (2020) described, young adults "need to gain more clarity and confidence in their own ideas, values, and feelings, as well as need to develop new skills and understanding related to all areas of life to build a sense of self-worth that comes from accomplishments" (p. 1888). With this clarity, relationships become significant sources of meaning. As young adults explore their abilities to create meanings with others they find that empathic engagements offer existential perspectives. Perspective taking is an important skill in which can enhance communication and understanding during disagreements or conflicts (Jensen et al., 2019). Accuracy of others' perceptions can be difficult. In order to achieve empathic awareness, both parties may need to create opportunities to understand the each other.

When conflicts, rifts, and disagreements arise in growth-promoting relationships, many young adults will seek additional sources for guidance. This is why relationships with caring adults need to be consistent, trustworthy, and long term (Katz & Geiger, 2019). Young adults know that they can depend on these adults during difficult or troubling times. Caring adults can be found through professional services (e.g., teachers, counselors, psychologists) or informal encounters (e.g., friends, neighbors, volunteers, social circles, parents). The adults serve as sources of knowledge for relationship skill development. They may also become role models for how to engage future rifts and challenges.

Role models are important for a young adult's socio-emotional development. These individuals represent values, lifestyles, characteristics, goals, and meanings that many wish to emulate or achieve. Young adults watch them carefully and learn how to navigate life challenges, how to treat people, and even their fashion choices. Most often, they are people, but there are admirable characteristics in animals as well. Role models can help young adults create their own stories in order to become role models for the next generation. Unfortunately, the role models that Western pop culture promotes through its media machines are typically not the most enlightened individuals. Distorted illusions of happiness, love, and success are promoted through the images of these individuals because,

> Our culture conspires to reinforce this image and to disguise the reality: how few media stars out of the innumerable aspirants actually succeed and how few of those who succeed lead happy and contented lives. Teenagers build shrines in their bedrooms to movie stars and singers in the hope that they too will become rich and famous; few surround themselves with the likeness of successful engineers or accountants.
>
> *(Csikszentmihalyi & Schneider, 2000, p. 15)*

Role models are also guiding factors for determining what type of relationships are desirable and how to manage them. Some young adults look up to antisocial or arrogant celebrities or seek guidance in songs for how to manage and achieve romantic partnerships. Young adults need to develop a greater appreciation for the diverse community in which they live, where people are achieving success that is relevant to their values, circumstances, and conditions. They can find that community elders, adults, peers, and pets that may appear ordinary have actually done extraordinary things in their lives. Some people in the community may have immigrated from other countries and have had epic adventures across the world. While others display characteristics of heroism in their profession, such as nurses, teachers, and crossing guards.

Within the study of relationships, a popular theoretical model is self-determination theory (SDT), which focuses on the person's psychological need fulfillment for relation, competence, and autonomy (Ang, 2020). SDT believes that one can only satisfy these psychological needs within social contexts due to the evolutionary nature of humans as social creatures. This is an important theory when understanding relationships in young adulthood. However, this book utilizes a multicultural humanistic psychological framework to explore the creation of existential meanings within growth-promoting relationships. When young adults establish these relationships, they have limitless opportunities in which to understand death, meaninglessness, isolation, and freedom. When relationships are culturally diverse, young adults are able to achieve transcendental existential meanings that place existential concerns beyond a paradigm's position. This is why multicultural encounters are an essential component to well-being and development—they provide perspectives in which to create inclusive meanings. Widening one's perspective to relational encounters also means incorporating animals, nature, fish, weather, and plants.

Friends and peer circles have significant influences on a young adult, especially for how they engage challenges or goals with school, romance, careers, and existential concerns (Katz & Geiger, 2019). When young adults seek support, friendships are reliable and safe sources. Peer circles can change over the years as they develop and explore new interests and encounters. The friendships developed in middle school may not be the same as in community college, but the flexible nature of peer relationships during this developmental phase means that there does not have to be rifts or conflicts to leave a peer circle.

Regardless of a period's intensity or absence in a certain peer circle, long-term relationships are decisive factors for long-term socio-emotional growth. Stable friendships offer optimism, self-validation, and esteem, as well as motivation/ encouragement. Instability in relationships causes long-term challenges in self-perception and goal attainment, because sources for self-esteem are not secure. With the advent of the Internet and creation of social media, young adults have sought and established online relationships (Ang, 2020). Virtual relationships have the benefits of security and abundance of options for meeting people. There are also limitations, from the dangers of cyber-predators to the lack of physical connection. High-quality and successful in-person peer relationships are matchless for supporting socio-emotional development.

The quality and diversity of relationships in young adulthood are greatly affected by domestic violence and ACEs. Exposure to violence or victimization at home can cause maladaptive adjustment issues that ultimately disturb interpersonal relationships with peers, adults, and potential romantic partners. Young adults that are victims of bullying "report poorer social competence, are more passive or less assertive, more anxious, insecure, and have lower self-esteem" (Hlavaty & Haselschwerdt, 2019, p. 763). Moreover, coercive control from relationships at home places young adults in a constant anxiety and fear. Hlavaty and

Haselschwerdt (2019) found that a greater amount of exposure to coercive control at home meant a higher quality of friendships for young adults. This positive association may be due to the fact that friendships are a source of peer support, which young adults utilize during difficult times and traumatic events.

In young adulthood, the seeking, formation, and progression of romantic partnerships are important for socio-emotional growth (Jensen et al., 2019). These types of relationships often hold great disappointments and conflicts, for which young adults need to learn to manage; either for knowing which partnerships are not desirable or how to develop effective communication skills in order to express needs in an empowering manner. Conflict management is often influenced by cultural norms for gender socialization. Within a paradigm there are knowledge stores for how to navigate difficult situations or determine certain meanings. Sometimes, the gender norms within a paradigm are absurd and even detrimental; for example, shaming males for not exhibiting the masculine characteristics associated with "manly," so that they are not allowed to express emotions in ways that are considered "feminine."

Peers can be helpful in exploring the absurdities of cultural meanings. They may be more aligned to the changingness of a global youth culture than adults that have become stagnant in their personal development. Emotional support from friends is often sought to help manage the anxiety and stress of relationship rifts and conflicts (Jensen et al., 2019). Friendships influence how one works on a romantic partnership; they are influential factors if a romantic partnership is to continue or be terminated (Jensen et al., 2019). For example, social networks that approve of the romantic partnership encourage the young adult to work harder at maintaining the relationship. In addition, friends offer different perspectives when considering how to work on a relationship.

Goal-setting is different for young adults in the twenty-first century. Romance, happiness, career stability, and relationship longevity are no longer certainties or entitlements. No longer can young adults rest assured that their schooling and training will remain relevant or desirable in a volatile global job market (Csikszentmihalyi & Schneider, 2000). Katz and Geiger (2019) found that, for young adults, self-reliance is an important twenty-first-century skill/characteristic that helps develop security, esteem, and pride. This is one of the many reasons why young adults seek to have their voices heard and desire greater responsibilities. When in leadership roles or given the space to make decisions, young adults draw upon their self-reliance as a source of strength and ability. Preparation for the future means being able function in a world of rapid change. Although self-reliance espouses many important life skills, it may also inhibit the depth and quality of relationships or willingness to seek help. Self-reliance is as fundamental as the willingness to reach out to others for help, assistance, or collaboration. This is true for all spheres of young adulthood: family life, romantic partnerships, schooling, career pathways, friends, and community.

Although academic curriculum may interest young adults, most will find an education in relationships more relevant, captivating, and motivating. Young

192   Part II

adults seek to explore potentials in relationships to learn about others as well as themselves. Relationships are an existential avenue in which to realize the innate will to create meaning.

Tala: Climbing Mountains of Emotions, Together

Duncan had left the apartment around 7:00pm to work the night shift. Tala opens her eyes to see the digital clock on the face of her phone read 12:02am. The dark room is only lit by the ambient glow of the bathroom nightlight and the soft yellow light of the street lamp filtered through the curtain sheers. Everything is just so still, especially the shadows. There is a powerful sense of nothingness in this night—no time or events. It feels stuffy, frozen, like being trapped within a memory in which she cannot remember what happens next. Tala finds herself fascinated by the glow of the street lamp right outside her window. She is unsure why she is up, but is certain that the return to sleep is a way off. *Maybe I have a lot on my mind*, she considers. To help her mind relax, she pulls out her journal:

Duncan is at work and Twinkie is hiding, waiting until I fall back asleep so that she can bite my toes again. I feel thankful for Duncan at this moment. I know that he is not here right now, but I appreciate all the things he does, and that I am lucky to be with him. This pandemic has been tough on us, especially since we moved to New York. There has been a lot of loving together-time, but we have also navigated some rough waters. Through it all, we survive together, like a team. What is most meaningful to me is how we are both willing to constantly evolve ourselves in a way that creates a sense of harmony. We choose to grow together. No matter how different we become as individuals, there is always that sense of connection that we both deeply care for.

I think about the past year and how we lived and survived in fear of the virus, for ourselves, and for our loved ones. I think about all the little mountains that we had to climb together. Often, I would meditate to center myself. Duncan expressed interest in learning how to meditate. So, I taught him. He sat by me during my most difficult times. He meditated, just as I taught him. At least I hope he was, he might have been resting his eyes, but it felt so sincere. We found ways to communicate more clearly, and we encouraged each other when it was difficult to find the words or expressions. It was the effort and support that mattered. Things were not always happy. We had some of our darkest moments as a couple this past year. At times, these mountains of emotions seemed insurmountable, but we always saw them through, just like when we go hiking!

As I saw Duncan trying to be better, it motivated me to do the same, for him. As of late, we can handle more as a couple. These days are good for us...and we are getting better at working through things.

I am also thinking about a few months back, during the thick of the pandemic, when Mom experienced a life-changing car accident. I remember how she needed my help, and I took the risk and drove to across a few states to see her. Thankfully she moved from Arizona to be a little closer to New York. I felt so bad because her own father, my grandfather, wouldn't take her in or help her. I feel that no matter how cruel family can be, we have to take care of each other in times of need. Duncan was gracious enough to tend to Twinkie and made sure that I didn't worry about them. It bothers me that people can be so caustic to one another, even within a family. Thankfully Mom's friend Lewie came over and gave her such sincere and thoughtful care. Lewie is an elderly man. A retired detective from the 1960s! He told me that he would help her in every way possible, and that I needed to get home because it was much too dangerous to travel and be out. Lewie also said that his sister, Jane, also a good friend of Mom, would help her with any personal or private nursing activities. I am thankful they were there and how sincerely interested they were for her recovery. It was so genuine and compassionate.

I am dozing off now. Thank you, Journal, for letting me reflect. I think supportive relationships like the ones with Lewie and Jane, and the loving one I have with Duncan are so meaningful and powerful. When we can encourage each other to grow, support one another, and even help each other heal, it makes life feel so much more vibrant and loving. Well, Twinkie is staring at me from atop the dresser now. I better go to sleep so she can bite my toes. Hope I don't wake up the neighbors again when I yell. Yes, even Twinkie supports me, and lets me know she loves me, even if it's in her own toe-biting way.

Monserrat: Celebrating Kovacs

Monserrat's Journal: December, 2020

I have always been so close to my sister, Alessandra. I don't know what I would do without her. Even during the quarantine, we find ways to virtually connect with each other. We both follow all of the city and CDC guidelines for staying safe. However, it has almost been a year and we are having a difficult time now. I think it is so hard because before the pandemic we had been used to large family gatherings, every weekend! Grandparents, uncles, aunts, cousins, and siblings all gathered to celebrate a special occasion or sometimes just gathered because it was Sunday. This is how we grew up.

We never really needed a reason to get together, spending time together was the only justification necessary. The nonstop coming and going, the laughter, the sharing of stories, and listening to the elders reminisce about the "olden days," was my normal. When COVID-19 devastated our community, family gatherings became a thing of the past. Sharing meals and stories were suddenly put on hold. Although for some people, having to stop seeing extended family may be welcomed. For someone like me, I consider all extended family as close family and not spending time together is extremely difficult.

I feel disconnected from loved ones, but we try to make the best out of our video calls. Instead of in-person gatherings, we gather around our computers with food and drink and recreate our beloved tradition. My uncles wait patiently by their cell phones for the once a week call that brings us all together. Although we are unable to gather in person, we still keep sharing our stories and building memories, which brings me to Kovacs.

Last night on FaceTime, I spent most of the time watching Kovacs, that's Alessandra's dog. I love my dog-nephew. He is funny, sweet, and kind. As a Chihuahua, Kovacs is tiny and he wears a sweater most of the year because he is always cold. Alessandra loves to baby him and I have come to know him as an essential part of the family. I never thought I would care for him as equally as my other family members, but I have come to do so. Thanks to Kovacs, I have understood my sister more and relate to her even deeper.

Yesterday was Kovacs' ninth birthday. Alessandra was sad that we could not have a big party with the whole family, like we had in previous years. So, I wanted to surprise her. I was going to invite her and Kovacs over for a surprise birthday party. I figured that we would be safe because it would just be us two, and we have both followed all of the CDC guidelines.

I decorated the apartment with colorful balloons and ribbons. I even had a mini-dog party hat that I ordered online, ready at the head of the kitchen table. When Alessandra came over she was almost as surprised and ecstatic as Kovacs. My sister hugged me and cried for a while. She was appreciative for my efforts. We also missed each other. I had baked a small dog-friendly cake from a recipe that I had found on Pinterest. I also made a human-friendly cake too.

As I looked around the room and saw the colorful balloons, the twinkling of the candles, and my closest loved ones, all the feelings of separation slowly started to drift away. I knew that the love for my family (both human and canine) was deeply rooted within me, and it is moments like those that blossom beautiful and lovely things. Sitting beside me were my anchors, the person and dog that held me together and grounded me to this earth in a time of great fear and uncertainty. As we sang happy birthday, happiness grew inside of me and it felt more powerful than ever. Kovacs gave me a look, as if he knew what this was all about. He felt appreciated and loved, and loved us even more deeply. This was my family. Even during the pandemic and social distancing, the love felt between us was stronger than ever. After cake and gifts, we had a dance party. Kovacs knows how to salsa.

References

Ang, C.-S. (2020). Attitude toward online relationship formation and psychological need satisfaction: The moderating role of loneliness. *Psychological Reports*, 123(5), 1887–1903. https://doi.org/10.1177/0033294119877820.

Csikszentmihalyi, M. & Schneider, B. (2000). The evolving nature of work. In M. Csikszentmihalyi & B. Schneider (Eds.), *Becoming an adult: How teenagers prepare for the world of work* (pp. 3–19). Basic Books.

Hlavaty, K., & Haselschwerdt, M. L. (2019). Domestic violence exposure and peer relationships: Exploring the role of coercive control exposure. *Journal of Family Violence*, 34 (8), 757–767. https://doi.org/10.1007/s10896-019-00044-4.

Jensen, J., Fish, M., Dinkins, Q., Rappleyea, D., & Didericksen, K. W. (2019). Relationship work among young adult couples: Romantic, social, and physiological considerations. *Personal Relationships*, 26(2), 366–382. https://doi.org/10.1111/pere.12279.

Katz, C. C., & Geiger, J. M. (2019). 'We need that person that doesn't give up on us': The role of social support in the pursuit of post-secondary education for youth with foster care experience who are transition-aged. *Child Welfare*, 97(6), 145–164.

Kazanjian, C. J. (2021). *Empowering children: A multicultural humanistic approach*. Routledge.

Moustakas, C. E. (1995). *Being-In, being-for, being-with*. Jason Aronson.

Rogers, C. R. (1989). *On becoming a person: A therapist's view of psychotherapy*. Houghton Mifflin.

CONCLUSION

Through a multicultural humanistic psychology lens, we explored the existential concerns (i.e., death, isolation, meaninglessness, freedom) of young adults and the self-actualizing power of their relationships. Within these relationships, the processes of creating meaning were integral for enduring existential trauma and critical for healing and growth thereafter.

In the U.S., the breakthrough discoveries in virology have battled COVID-19 so that hospitalizations and death rates decreased significantly. This has been an epochal achievement for humanity—a history that reveals a global human community working together to eradicate the virus, reduce suffering, and increase the quality of life. As infection rates dropped and social restrictions were lifted, many young adults were relieved to return to personal and professional goals. However, the existential trauma caused by COVID-19 shook the very foundations of every major cultural paradigm on the planet. Death and isolation were prevailing existential concerns. Everywhere that young people turned were distressing images, death tallies, medical warnings, and stories of loved ones suffering and passing away. The extreme threats to mortality coupled with intense isolation from the social quarantines left people to explore these existential anxieties or deny them.

Young adults searched for ways to cope and create meaning during the pandemic. Some were more successful than others, while situations and circumstances were critically influential to well-being and developmental outcomes. Young adults that experienced ACEs, such as victimization at home, economic hardships for the family unit, and even the death of loved ones, had significant challenges to holistic well-being. As previous chapters discussed, the harmful effects of anxieties were prominent for communities of color, in which the pandemic revealed greater systems of inequality, racism, discrimination, and violence. As we explored the foundations of multicultural humanistic psychology, we saw

DOI: 10.4324/9781003251651-14

196 Conclusion

that most young adults would not stand for social injustices and were altruistically motivated to do their part in creating a society based on equality and compassion.

During the pandemic, young adults reached out to the world to establish relationships, whether in real life or virtually. Many were met by psychologists, teachers, educational professionals, and counselors who extended their services to offer guidance, support, and resources to support well-being and development. However, the return to social normalcy could not calm the existential currents flowing with immense forces within. Young adults need growth-promoting relationships more than ever to help them create meanings that bring about healing, growth, and enlightenment.

Through the case studies with young adults Hyun, Tala, and Monserrat, we explored the self-actualizing power of relationships with nature, animals, solitude, volunteerism, and meaningful others during the COVID-19 pandemic. Each of their stories exemplify the multicultural humanistic psychological tenets in which people are by nature empathic, optimistic, community-oriented, and have existential concerns in which they seek to explore in solitude and within relationships. Their diverse relationships cultivated self-actualization experiences, where they found empowerment to increase the quality of life for others and the environment.

Growth-promoting relationships are the keys to cultivating a multicultural global community. The different cultural paradigms and ways in which young adults create meanings in their relationships help affirm, blend, innovate, or change ways of Being. Young adults are the harbingers of an inclusive community in which all forms of life and their environments can actualize potentials.

The realities of death, isolation, absence of inherent meaning, and freedom are not alien conditions in which human beings were thrown into. Instead, they are organic elements of life that bring forth our unique essences. Young adults may appreciate that existential realities are primordial soils in which they grow. The impending transition from this life is a precious reminder to live diligently and to tend to sacred and spiritual relationships. Within these relationships young adults find the courage to explore the existential night and to light the darkness with their own constellations of meaning.

INDEX

After-School All Stars 176–7
altruism 49, 142, 174, 176, 180–1, 185
animal assisted psychotherapy 154
animal assisted therapy 150, 153–154
animal-assisted interventions 150
anxiety 15–18, 21–23, 28, 52, 70, 100, 105, 108, 110, 121, 125, 129, 136, 138–9, 144, 148, 150, 153–4, 165, 168, 190, 191
awe 140–143

Bean, L. L. 135–6
behaviorism 28–9, 78
biogenic volatile organic compounds 139–40
Buddhism 31, 54, 107, 123

canine assisted therapy 155–6
canine: see *dogs*
civil rights 29, 32,
cognitive reappraisal 130, 168
congruence 39, 78–9, 94, 101, 178,
cortisol 21, 138–139
COVID-19 1–2, 4, 11–14, 16–23, 41, 46–7, 49, 56, 58, 61, 69, 76, 110, 121, 125, 130, 143, 148, 174, 180, 185, 195, 196
cultural humility 43, 80, 83, 95, 105, 129, 166
cultural paradigm 1, 5, 31, 36–38, 40, 42–3, 46, 48–9, 52, 54, 63, 65, 67, 69, 84–5, 90, 95, 105, 120–123, 126, 149, 164–166, 196

culturally relative self-actualization 35–39, 54, 83–4, 166, 173, 179, 180
cytokine 140–1

death anxiety 12, 22, 28, 48, 56–58, 62, 141
depression 15–6, 18, 21–2, 33, 63–65, 67, 85, 100–1, 114, 121, 125, 127, 139, 148, 153, 168
determinisms 3, 29, 34, 130
dogs 32, 96, 152–156, 187

egocentrism 46–7
El Paso Community College 179
emotional contagion 87, 152
emotions 3, 6, 14, 16, 29, 35, 40, 47, 55, 58, 70–1, 79, 84, 86, 88–91, 94, 102–107, 110–114, 123, 125, 127–129, 136, 138–9, 141, 145, 148 151, 155, 158, 167–169, 191
empathy 17, 32–3, 39, 40, 41–43, 50, 57, 62, 66, 68, 76, 78–79, 82–84, 85–88, 91,102, 105, 109, 115, 122, 125, 130, 149, 153–155, 166, 167, 173, 178
encounter 15, 32, 37, 39–41, 76–83, 87, 90–1, 94, 99, 102, 190; with nature 62, 125, 136–7, 139–140, 142–143, 187; with animals 93, 149–157
enlightenment 5, 24, 28, 31, 40, 42, 58, 61, 71, 89, 95, 99, 126, 196
existential concerns 3–6, 11, 22, 24, 28, 30, 36, 40–1, 49, 52, 54–5, 57, 61, 81, 89,

93–95, 111, 115, 122, 127, 137, 149, 165, 187, 190, 195–6

existential trauma 1–2, 19, 21, 23–4, 37, 71, 126, 128, 195

existentialism 5, 22, 24, 47, 49, 50–56, 71, 76, 78, 81, 103, 111, 122, 125, 130

flow 136–7, 142–3

forest bathing (Shinrin-yoku) 107, 137–140, 142

Gibran, K. 103

growth-promoting relationships 1, 5, 15, 19, 28, 31–2, 36, 39, 41–2, 47, 49, 53–4, 60, 64, 70, 76–84, 87, 89, 90, 93, 95, 99, 106, 110, 126, 129, 151, 166, 176, 178–9, 181–2, 187–190, 196

Hebbian network 92

human-animal interaction 150, 153

humanistic psychology 29–35, 37, 53, 78, 122

impermanence 40, 49, 52, 107–8, 112, 123

institutions of higher education 115, 151, 154–5, 177, 181

Kidz n' Coaches 178–182

loneliness 18, 22, 56; existential loneliness 11, 58–9, 61; loneliness anxiety 47, 61–64, 6–71

Maslow, A. 37, 122,

microglia 140

mindfulness 82, 106–7, 109–115, 167–8

mirror neurons 33, 80, 87,

Mohawk Valley Community College 170, 177, 179

Moustakas, C. 109–10

multicultural humanistic psychology 5, 24, 28, 35–39, 41, 43, 49–50, 54, 84, 121–2, 195

nature: natural environments, 56, 62, 84, 95–96, 130, 136–7, 139, 140–142, 143, 145

Nhat Hanh, T. 107, 110–112, 115,

oxytocin 93, 151–2

Perry, C. 109–10

phytoncides 139–140

post-traumatic stress disorder (PTSD) 16, 155

presence 60, 65, 81–2, 107–8, 122, 152, 183, 187–8

problematic Internet use (PIU) 43, 68, 121, 176

psychoanalysis 28–9, 78

Rogers, C. 32, 78, 181, 187; Rogerian method 78, 79–80, 81, 85, 93, 178

shame 53, 61, 92, 94, 102, 126, 164, 167

social and emotional learning 87, 88, 106, 113,

social media disorder (SMD) 43, 68, 115

socio-emotional intelligence 24, 32, 39, 67, 70, 87, 89–92, 105–6, 113, 125, 178

solitude 71, 89, 108, 164–168, 196

spirituality 31, 106, 115, 121–129, 130, 141, 142

subjective well-being 5, 14, 136, 175

suicide 12, 21, 60–1, 63–66, 128

tathātā 108

terror management theory 48,

transcendental 82, 90, 127, 140–1, 166, 190

transpersonal psychology 31, 121–2

unconditional positive regard 78–80

volunteer 3, 130, 141, 150, 173–176, 178–181, 196

Watts, A. 106, 121

Zen 31, 54, 82, 106–109